And the Crooked Places Made Straight

The American Moment   Stanley I. Kutler, Series Editor

And the Crooked Places Made Straight

The Struggle for Social Change in the 1960s

David Chalmers

The Johns Hopkins University Press : Baltimore and London

The Johns Hopkins University Press
701 West 40th Street
Baltimore, Maryland 21211

The paper used in this book meets the minimum requirements of
American National Standard for Information Sciences—Permanence
of Paper for Printed Library Materials, ANSI Z39.48-1984.

Library of Congress Cataloging-in-Publication Data

Chalmers, David Mark.
And the crooked places made straight : the struggle for social change
in the 1960s / David Chalmers.
    p.   cm. — (The American moment)
Includes bibliographical references and index.
ISBN 0-8018-4173-9. — ISBN 0-8018-4174-7 (pbk.)
1. United States—History—1961–1969. 2. United States—Social
conditions—1960–1980. 3. Social change—United States—History—
20th century. I. Title. II. Series.
E841.C46   1991
973—dc20   91-11021

For Jean

I will go before thee, and make the crooked places straight: I will break into pieces the gates of brass, and cut into sunder the bars of iron.
— Isaiah 45:2

I have a dream that one day every valley shall be exalted, every hill and mountain shall be made low, the rough places will be made plains and the crooked places will be made straight and the glory of the Lord shall be revealed and all flesh shall see it together.
— Martin Luther King, Jr.
Washington, D.C., August 28, 1963,
transcribed by David Chalmers

Contents

Editor's Foreword

Proximity to the past tends to fragment time. Inevitably, it seems, we calibrate our recent history by decades. We speak of the forties, the fifties, the eighties, and so on. Such splintering provides convenient boundaries for some simple level of understanding. Historical processes, unfortunately, are not so orderly and do not dramatically alter with the passing and beginning of a decade. But occasionally, a particular time frame provides a convenient shorthand for describing a unique series of events that had important ramifications beyond the immediate time segment.

The 1960s witnessed profound changes in American life, certainly ones that sharply differentiated the society from what it had been a decade earlier. David Chalmers has given us a thoughtful, incisive account of those momentous events—the civil rights movement, the assault on poverty, the student rebellions, the development of a counterculture, a new wave of feminism, and, pervading so much of all this, the veritable civil war at home over the Vietnam War abroad. Chalmers's graceful narrative is sharpened with his sensitive, informed portraits of both famous and lesser-known persons who left an indelible imprint on the times.

A generation and more later, the meaning of the sixties remains contested ground. Was it a moment of idealism, springing from the spontaneous enthusiasm and energy of people struggling to gain control of their lives? Or was it a veritable lark of self-indulgence by comfortable elites? Undoubtedly, the times had elements of both. The legacy, too, is ambivalent. "Much from the decade remained," as Chalmers writes; yet much was forgotten and even angrily repudiated. For some, much of the next two decades can be read as a conscious repudiation of the excesses; yet, who can deny the existence of a new national consciousness on issues of war and peace, race, gender, and class?

Without doubt, the powerful, convulsive political and social movements of the time commanded exceptional national and international attention. Succeeding generations must measure and evaluate those events for themselves. Perhaps the moral and ethical concerns of the period have faltered and waned over time. But any fair evaluation, of course, obligates us to consider the events in their context and on their own terms. David Chalmers has done exactly that in an account that is at once compassionate and involved, yet sustained with a critical historian's perspective.

Stanley I. Kutler
THE UNIVERSITY OF WISCONSIN

Acknowledgments

I greatly appreciate the help given me by Judith Benninger Brown, Jean Chalmers, Jack Chatfield and the Trinity College Conference on SNCC (Hartford, Connecticut), David Colburn, Louise Cooke and the Martin Luther King, Jr., Center for Non-violent Change Library and Archive (Atlanta, Georgia), Arthur Dudden, James Forman, Shirley Gibson, Andrew Gordon, Kermit Hall, Samuel Hill, Mary Elizabeth King, Mildred Hill-Lubin, Robert McMahon, Barbara Oberlander, Mario Savio, Irene Thompson, Margaret Thompson, Eldon Turner, Dolores Jenkins and the staff of the University of Florida Libraries, the staff of the Department of History at the University of Florida, particularly Ann McDaniel, Joyce Phillips, Addie Elder, and Patti Fabré, and the students in my classes on the 1960s. For guidance and encouragement I am also greatly indebted to the editor of this series, Stanley I. Kutler of the Department of History of the University of Wisconsin–Madison, and to Henry Y. K. Tom, executive editor of the Johns Hopkins University Press.

Portions of the account of the life of Martin Luther King Jr. in chapter 2 are based on my review in *Southern Changes* (August 1987).

Introduction

The history of the 1960s is to be found in the names of places: Montgomery, Greensboro, Birmingham, Selma, Oxford and Philadelphia (Mississippi), Memphis, Dallas, Port Huron and Berkeley, Haight-Ashbury and Woodstock, the Bay of Pigs, Saigon, Khe Sanh and My Lai, Watts and Detroit, Chicago, Kent State and Jackson State. The social agendas of the sixties were not set in New York and Washington, but worked their way up from distant places and from the streets of the cities across America.

The dominant Western versions of social change are incorporated in Marxism and Christianity. In the 1960s they were embodied in the concepts of "structure" and "consciousness," whose clash and commingling ran through the politics and turmoil of the decade. For Karl Marx, the material conditions of life defined the arena of social existence. In his *Critique of Political Economy* (1859) he wrote the classic lines, "the mode of production in material life determines the general character of the social, political and spiritual processes of life. It is not the consciousness of men that determines their existence, but on the contrary, their social existence determines their consciousness." Although there is room for growth and diversity of social institutions and ideas, basic needs and economic conditions shape their acceptance and use. Social change would come with the construction of new institutions that adjusted behavior and beliefs to the realities of the productive system. Attitudes would respond. Structure would command consciousness. The classical alternative is the primacy of consciousness: only when people's values are recast can their basic behavior be changed. "Except a man be born again," Jesus taught, "he can not see the kingdom of God." To be free externally, you must be free internally. The conversion experience is the change in consciousness. The "New Jerusalem" is the product not of a new technology or a new building code, but of a new way of seeing the world.

At the beginning of the 1960s, the Prohibition experience of the 1920s was frequently introduced into discussions of race. The nation went dry, but people remained wet. The way the argument went was that laws could not change people's beliefs and prejudices—and, therefore, their behavior. President Eisenhower often commented privately that the school desegregation decision Brown v. Board of Education (1954) was a mistake that would set back progress in the South at least fifteen years. "I don't believe you can change the hearts of men with laws or decisions," he said. Martin Luther King Jr. responded to such arguments when he offered testimony to the Massachusetts legislature on the power of laws. "It may be," he told them, "that you can not legislate morality, but behavior can be regulated. It may be true that the law can not make a man love me, but it can restrict him from lynching me, and I think that is pretty important also."

Particularly for King, however, the attack on American racism sought to change people's ways of thinking and feeling. The combination of nonviolent confrontation and Christian love was aimed at black pride and white guilt. The willingness to accept punishment for refusing to obey unjust laws was a psychological weapon to bolster the self-image of blacks and to put pressure on whites to face the evils of a system of racial dominance and subordination. Out of an awakened sense of injustice would come the institutional changes that would sweep away segregation and open up equal opportunity for all. That restructuring of society would in turn change behavior. If people were judged by the quality of their character rather than the color of their skin, racial prejudice itself would disappear.

Basically, the civil rights movement sought to reach through conscience to consciousness, through consciousness to institutional change, through institutional change to behavioral change, and through behavior to consciousness. The 1960s was particularly marked by the extent to which this strategy emerged as the chosen path. King led his people through the streets of Montgomery, Albany, Birmingham, Selma, and Chicago to appeal to the consciousness, first of the South and then of Washington, D.C., and the nation. The neatly dressed students who "sat in" at the lunch counters of Greensboro and other Southern cities had only the power of making a statement. Subsequently organized as the Student Nonviolent Coordinating Committee (SNCC), they came to believe that the white consciousness in the deep South was a killer. SNCC undertook to build both a new consciousness and an independent institutional base within the black communities of Georgia, Mississippi, and Alabama. When the strain became too great, SNCC gave up its organizational effort among the Black-Belt poor and lost its way in a search for Black Power consciousness in the urban ghettos.

Broadly speaking, the campaign against poverty also meant a major shift in consciousness. During the 1930s, society had faced the problems of economic depression, but the idea that the government should—or, indeed, could—undertake the eradication of poverty was new. In *A Thousand Days* (1965), his memorial history of John F. Kennedy's presidency, Arthur Schlesinger Jr. indicated the psychological underpinnings of the undertaking. Giving credit to two widely read contemporary social critiques, he wrote that John K. Galbraith's *The Affluent Society* (1958) had "brought poverty into the national consciousness" and that Michael Harrington's *The Other America* (1962) had "placed it on the national conscience."

The manifesto-writing members of Students for a Democratic Society (SDS) and the anti–Vietnam War demonstrators chanting "Hey, hey, LBJ, how many kids did you kill today?" were reaching for the same consciousness levers of change that the army did when it spoke, unconvinced and unconvincingly, of winning "the hearts and minds" of the Vietnamese people. The mantras and acids of the counterculture were seeking a consciousness breakthrough, and the counterculture itself was a cumulation of shifts in personal and social values. In consciousness-raising groups across the country, women were concluding that all aspects of their lives were defined by their gender, that the personal was political.

Never before in American history had there been so much conscious talk of raising and changing consciousness. Writing at the end of the sixties, the Yale law professor Charles Reich and the hard-nosed New York City political scientist Andrew Hacker deduced conflicting American futures from the changing social values. In *The End of the American Era* (1970), Hacker lamented the changed consciousness of a people who were no longer willing to sacrifice and accept class discipline. In contrast, Reich's best selling *The Greening of America* (1970) celebrated that refusal. A liberating, new "Consciousness III" was changing America from a controlled, uptight, production-oriented society into a relaxed, anything-goes, counterculture world, which was emerging "out of the wasteland of the Corporate State, like flowers pushing up through the concrete pavement."

The sixties was a decade in which group consciousness emerged among blacks, the poor, the young, students, women, gays, Hispanics, and Native Americans. There was a civil rights revolution, an assault on poverty, campus unrest, an antiwar movement that sometimes threatened to become an insurrection, and an apparent cultural disaffiliation of the young that seemed to challenge the moral values of American society. The spreading contagion of social dissent placed great strain on American institutions. What was going on in the streets of the nation raised doubt about the assumption of American liberalism that an unseen hand would guide the diverse efforts of a pluralistic society toward a greater social unity. However challenging the new ways of looking at the world might be, their long-run effect would be determined largely by the ways in which they were translated into both national and local organizations and institutions that would shape governmental and social behavior.

Behind the headline events of the 1960s, there was both a replacement of local standards and ways of doing things with more open, national ones; and a search for grass-roots participation and community, a dialectical interaction of changing consciousness and institutions, and the explosion of classic social questions into politics and into the streets of the Republic.

At the beginning, there was no question about what was important. In an afternoon meeting the day after Rosa Parks had been found guilty of not getting up to give her seat on a bus to a white man, Martin Luther King Jr. was picked to head the hastily formed Montgomery Improvement Association. Only a few minutes later, the young minister addressed the several thousand people crowded into the Holt Street Baptist Church and massed around the loudspeakers outside:

If you will protest courageously, and yet with dignity and Christian love, when the history books are written in future generations, the historians will have to pause and say, "There lived a great people—a black people—who injected new meaning and dignity into the veins of civilization." This is our overwhelming responsibility.

By the end of the decade, there was great confusion. Malcolm Cowley, the dean of American literary critics, called Sara Davidson "the liveliest historian" of the generation. Her account of her sixties life and the lives of her two Berkeley roommates, *Loose Change* (1977), sold 350,000 copies in hardback, more in paperback, and was made into a television miniseries. At the end of the sixties, Sara, Susie, Tasha, and their friends looked restlessly back at their student days:

We knew what politics was then. It was marches, elections. Now politics means who you fuck, what you eat, how you cure a cold. No theory is big enough to encompass that broad a notion of politics. That's why the New Left is dying. Okay, we know we can't unlock the problems of the country without doing something about sex, the body, the blacks, the schools, ecology. But what is the priority?

The decades that followed provided no answer. Although America withdrew from Vietnam, no dominoes toppled in Southeast Asia. The Watergate scandal made Richard Nixon the first American president forced to resign, but the conservative reaction to the sixties continued and carried Ronald Reagan into the White House. The sixties began well, but it was no heroic age. Those who lived through it have strong memories. Some hate it; others mourn the missed opportunities. The sixties left many legacies. It is not yet finished.

And the Crooked Places Made Straight

1. Coming out of the 1950s

Writing in *The Sociological Imagination,* C. Wright Mills quoted from Marx's *Eighteenth Brumaire*: "Men make their own history, but they do not make it just as they please; they do not make it under circumstances chosen by themselves." Although few social scientists or political experts would have agreed with him in 1959, Mills argued that at that moment "the scope and chance for conscious human agency in history-making" was "uniquely available."

Going against the conventional wisdom of the 1950s, which saw society as stable and quiescent, the radical Columbia University professor argued the need and the possibilities for major social change. Even though young people seemed so apolitical that it was popular to call them a "silent generation," Mills predicted that they could be its instrument. Although he died in 1962, his ideas became the leading intellectual influence on the new, young political radicals of the sixties. The particular strength of Mills's analysis was the connections he drew between long-range economic, social, and cultural change. Such relationships lay beneath the social turmoil of the sixties. What went on during that decade was the product of an interaction between material circumstances; human agency; chance; and the coincidental massing of events such as the civil rights movement, the Berkeley Free Speech fight, and the Vietnam War. Together, all these things helped shape popular views of the nature of reality, and from the resulting shifts in consciousness came many of the efforts to build the organizations and institutions of social change.

TRANSITIONS

The national government that had placed 16 million men and women in uniform and spent $330 billion on its successful effort to win a global war did not leave the return to a peacetime society solely to chance. Although no comprehensive plan existed, congressional legislation provided a piecemeal shaping for postwar America. New laws affecting returning servicemen, the economy, atomic energy, and national security particularly pointed the way. The Servicemen's Readjustment Act of 1944, popularly known as the "GI Bill of Rights," provided benefits that included low-interest home loans and insurance and the chance to attend technical school or college. The Employment

Act of 1946 proclaimed the president's responsibility "to promote maximum employment, production and purchasing power," gave him a Council of Economic Advisors, and required him to make an annual report to Congress. The Atomic Energy Act of 1946 established a civilian Atomic Energy Commission (AEC) to supervise a governmental monopoly over nuclear research and development and gave the president ultimate policy control. The National Security Act of 1947 sought to unify control over the armed forces under a secretary of defense. It further provided for a general command staff known as the Joint Chiefs of Staff (JCS), established the Central Intelligence Agency (CIA) as the successor to the wartime Office of Strategic Services (OSS), and created the National Security Council (NSC) to advise the president. In the midst of the demobilization of the war economy and state, in a number of crucial areas, the structure for an activist national government was being put in place.

After surprising the pollsters and just about everyone but himself by winning the 1948 election, President Harry Truman proposed federal aid to education, a compulsory national old-age health insurance program, and legislation against racial discrimination in employment. Congress refused, but these major social changes had now reached the argument stage on the national agenda. Although no one predicted it, an activist federal judiciary, in various combinations with the Congress and the national administration, would soon be replacing local ways, not only in health and education, political representation, and the operation of criminal justice systems, but also in race and sexual relations and standards.

PRODUCTION

Production and reproduction were the underpinnings of the events of the 1960s. World War II had finally pulled America out of the Depression and created massive production and full employment. With the war's end, billions of dollars of wartime savings were spent on goods unavailable during the war or unaffordable during the Depression years. Initially there were many consumer shortages. There was a black market in meat; white shirts were not available; and when your name came up on the dealer's list, you could sell your brand-new car at a profit to a used-car dealer. Backed-up demand was so great that the end of the war produced inflation rather than recession.

In 1945, former vice-president Henry Wallace dared to write a book called *Sixty Million Jobs*. Continued high levels of consumption and spending made these jobs a reality. Although there were cyclical variations, from the 1950s through the later 1960s both unemployment and inflation remained low, commodity prices were stable, and per capita productivity improved between 2.5 and 3 percent annually. Between the end of the war and 1960, the total real value of goods and services produced increased 250 percent. Living standards also rose steadily. Most people expected to own a car and a house, and believed that life for their children would be even better.

America's new prosperity was built on cheap oil. At the beginning of the century, coal produced 90 percent of the nation's power; now it provided only 25 percent. Oil cost three dollars a barrel at the wellhead and less than thirty cents a gallon at the gas pump. Cheap oil from the Middle East combined with American Marshall Plan aid underwrote the recovery of Western Europe. Research and development, stimulated by the war, produced dynamic new industries based on chemistry and electronics. The booming automobile and building industries struggled to meet the accumulated backlog of Depression and wartime demand, as well as the needs of new families. Big business grew bigger through corporate mergers, diversifying into conglomerates run by professional, public relations–conscious management.

It was an age of technology, which saw the arrival of the transistor and the solid-state computer, stereo, Dacron, nylon pantyhose, tranquilizers, oral contraceptives, and antibiotics. James Watson and Francis Crick won the Nobel prize for decoding the molecular structure of DNA, which governs genetic inheritance. Tuberculosis had all but disappeared, and Jonas Salk's vaccine was wiping out polio in the United States. Cancer and heart disease, the afflictions of a prosperous consumption society, were the greatest killers; and for teenagers, the greatest killer was the automobile.

The changes occurring in the workplace and at home indicated how much of a corporate, middle-class nation America was becoming. Ownership of a car and a home in the suburbs no longer distinguished a factory worker from an office manager. A 1967 poll would show that almost half of the nation's union members, and three-quarters of the younger ones, lived in the suburbs. As the labor historian Robert Zieger summed it up, "the teeming neighborhoods of the vast industrial cities, with their union halls, saloons, social clubs, and traditions of solidarity and cultural cohesion, gave way to new, transient, fragmented patterns of life."

There were more salaried, white-collar employees, selling and record-keeping, dealing with paper and people, than there were blue-collar wage earners producing goods. The number of self-employed shopkeepers and small businessmen declined. Only 4 percent of the population was in agriculture. A specialized, capital-intensive, cost-effective agriculture, based on gasoline-powered machinery, fertilizers, pesticides, herbicides, vitamins and antibiotics, and hybridization of seed and breed, more than doubled agricultural output and increased the rate at which farming as a way of life was being replaced by agribusiness. The world-dominant American steel and automobile industries had not yet been threatened by the more modern postwar German and Japanese miracles, but many of the traditional ways of life were in decline. The railroads, the general magazine as national medium, and the great American city, like life on the farm, were losing their accustomed place.

The federal government, reconciled to big business through their wartime partnership, was committed to a Keynesian policy of managing taxes and government spending to control the business cycle. For business, reconversion to a peacetime economy meant release from controls; the sale of government plants and assets; and tax cuts and special tax benefits. Both Democratic and Republican administrations accepted the mandate of the Employment Act of 1946 to maintain the proper level of employment and business activity. In 1953, when the Republicans controlled both Congress and the White House for the first time since the Depression, they did not dismantle the New Deal's intrusions into the economy. The only major programs to go were the last remnants of wartime price control and the Reconstruction Finance Corporation, which had been set up under Herbert Hoover. Republican president Dwight Eisenhower launched a $26-billion spending program known as the National Defense Highway System. Government expenditures, which had been substantially less than 10 percent of the gross national product during the prosperous 1920s, reached a level of somewhat more than 20 percent during the affluent 1950s and 1960s. The economically conservative Democrat John Kennedy would come to believe that deficits were not a bad thing and would push for an economy-stimulating tax cut that Lyndon Johnson would persuade Congress to pass in 1964. In 1972, Henry Luce's *Time* magazine would feature John Maynard Keynes on its cover, and Richard Nixon would intone, "We are all Keynesians now."

While there was substantial poverty in America, it was taken as a matter of course, not as a reason for controversy and national concern. As Michael Harrington was to point out in his influential little 1962 book *The Other America,* poverty was hidden away from the sight of most Americans. From the new suburban communities to the shopping malls to the overcrowded college classrooms, America was apparently doing well and felt good about it. It was an age of prosperity. More people had more money than ever before, and the situation was obviously going to continue. The typical American was a consumer, and consumption meant having money enough beyond the basic needs to be able to spend it on "things" and enjoyment. Despite the complaints of contemporary cultural critics and the denunciations by the rebels who were to come in the 1960s, these were "good times" for the visible people of the 1950s. The astute social historian William O'Neill, who had called his account of the sixties *Coming Apart* (1971), perceptively picked *American High* (1986) as his title when he later wrote about the 1950s. It was this taken-for-granted margin and consumer affluence that lay behind much of the youth culture and the student movements of the 1960s. Looking back from the 1980s, one-time SDS leader Todd Gitlin ruminated that the rebellion had come from "the fat of the land."

POPULATION

Americans were a people on the move. The population was shifting from the country to the city, from the city to the suburbs, and from the Northeast and the Midwest to the West and the South. Each year, one out of every five families packed up and left for somewhere else. At the end of the war, professional sports were beginning to catch up with American demographics. The racial barriers started to go down. Standout black college players Kenny Washington and Woody Strode were signed by the National Football League's Los Angeles Rams, and Marion Motley by the new All-American Conference's Cleveland Browns. Jackie Robinson put on the spikes of the Brooklyn Dodgers, and Chuck Cooper became Boston's first black Celtic. A football circuit that in 1946 extended only as far south as the whites-only Washington Redskins and had just reached beyond Green Bay, Wisconsin, to include Los Angeles could hardly continue to consider itself the "national" league. A similarly restricted major league baseball system, in which the Giants, the Dodgers, and the Yankees all called New York City home, while there were no teams west of St. Louis, was also due for change.

The movement of black Americans from the country to the city and from the South to the North and the West accelerated. By 1960, half of all black but only one-third of white Americans lived in the central cities. Washington, D.C., was the first major city to have a black majority. While the larger cities, aside from Los Angeles and the South, were losing population, the suburbs were doubling, and their residents were overwhelmingly white, by a ratio of more than thirty to one. The keys to the suburban shift were the automobile, and home ownership. Veterans Administration (VA) and Federal Housing Administration (FHA) mortgages were a new Homestead Act more potent than the post–Civil War one had been. The people of the suburbs drove to work on the newly built expressways, as their jobs and shopping centers moved outward to meet them. Reading the signs of shifting population and wealth, the big downtown department stores anchored the new shopping centers with branches in the suburbs. The wide-open, bulldozed spaces provided room for the national supermarket chains to build their big stores and dominate food-buying patterns. The first modern, enclosed, thermostatically controlled shopping mall was opened on the outskirts of Minneapolis, and malls, along with drive-in hamburger stands, became the new afterschool teen playgrounds.

It was in the suburbs that the greatest population increase in American history was being born. The national population had grown by 17 million during the boom years of the 1920s and by only 9 million during the Depression 1930s. Now, in the 1950s, it soared by 28 million. From the mid-1950s to the mid-1960s, more than 4 million babies were born each year. With the economy booming, couples were marrying younger, having children sooner, or giving birth now to the families postponed during the Depression and the war years. At 179 million in 1960, the American population was twice what it had been at the beginning of the century. As the demographer Landon Jones (*Great Expectations* [1980]) summed it up, the cause was not the usual reason—decreased mortality—but rather increasing natality. Like the visual metaphor of a whole pig being swallowed by a python, the postwar generation of the young, nurtured to a large extent in middle-class suburbs, was making its way through an exploding school system. The population aged fifteen or under had increased at almost twice the rate of the rest of the population and numbered 56 million in 1960.

The number of college students doubled in the 1950s and would almost do so again in the 1960s. The GI Bill of Rights, together with American affluence, changed college from an elite privilege to a mass higher-education system and a consumer necessity. At the beginning of the 1940s, the state of Florida, for instance, had three public universities. The University of Florida was male, Florida State was female, and Florida A&M was black; there was a junior college in Palm Beach, and there were private colleges. By 1972 the state system had expanded to nine public universities and twenty-eight community colleges. Reaching out for so large, and growing, a portion of the youth population, college was to be where the action was in the 1960s. A baby born the first year after World War II would have been likely to be entering college in 1964, the year of the Mississippi Freedom Summer, the Berkeley Free Speech Movement, riots in Harlem and Rochester, New York, and Tonkin Gulf.

TELEVISION

Particularly significant for the events of the 1960s were the explosive growth of this affluent youth generation and the simultaneous emergence of television as the new national media, which not only reported but also influenced events. In 1950 only 10 percent of American families had a television set; ten years later, only 10 percent did not. Since 1890, general news and story magazines had been the national media. In the 1930s, radio joined them. Now television was taking over. With a superior cost ratio, it delivered the national audience to the advertisers. *Collier's* (1885–1957), *Saturday Evening Post* (1821–1961), *Look* (1937–71) and *Life* (1936–72) were dying. Only *Reader's Digest* remained as a mass-readership, general-interest magazine. Specialty journals directed at select clienteles, such as housewives, young careerwomen, automobile or camera buffs, runners, skiers, and scuba divers, prospered.

The success stories of the 1950s were *Playboy*, a specialty journal that offered sex as a consumer disposable for the affluent, nonmonogamous male, and *TV Guide*. The decade's viewers watched Milton Berle and Lucille Ball, quiz shows, the Kefauver Crime Committee investigations, and the Army-McCarthy hearings. When the media's hero of the mind, Charles Van Doren, tearfully confessed that his victories on the "$64 Thousand Question" quiz show were prearranged, Columbia University fired him, and the Westerns such as "Gunsmoke" and "Have Gun Will Travel" took over prime time. The struggling young ABC network tapped nostalgia for the 1920s with its crime-fighting "Untouchables."

The real shootout, however, was not on the streets of Dodge City or at the O.K. Corral but between the news divisions of CBS and NBC. Under orders from the chairman of the Federal Communications Commission to increase news programming, the scandal-stained networks competed in their newly expanded coverage. In July 1962, five months after the astronaut John Glenn had been the first American to orbit the earth, AT&T sent up its Telstar I communications satellite. Within a year, the system was in place for the instant relay of news from around the globe. Television showed the confrontation between Martin Luther King Jr.'s marchers and Public Safety Commissioner "Bull" Connor's dogs and firehoses in Birmingham; the admission of the first black students at the University of Alabama; President Kennedy's "A Time to Act" civil rights address; and King's "I Have a Dream" speech at the Lincoln Memorial in Washington, D.C. In September 1963, CBS invented the anchorman and extended its "Evening News with Walter Cronkite" from fifteen to thirty minutes. NBC soon followed. Less than three months later, a stunned nation watched the coverage of the assassination and funeral of the president and actually saw live the shooting of his murderer, Lee Harvey Oswald, in the basement of the Dallas police headquarters. According to the polls, a majority of the American people were getting their news from television. The action of the 1960s was to flood into American homes and consciousness through the picture tube: campus demonstrations, urban riots and burning neighborhoods, Vietnam (often characterized as America's "first television war"), the words and promises of presidents, and the murders of more leaders—Malcolm X, Martin Luther King Jr., and Robert Kennedy.

The relationship between television and the people was more than passive. The media forced images into the minds and triggered the emotions of its viewers. It was a dramatic, hot media that spread the news while it was still happening. It was not just, as the police often claimed, that television cameramen actually incited violence for the sake of dramatic footage or encouraged it by their presence, but that the message on the television screen produced action by contagion. Like a brush fire out of control, the television image jumped the barriers of time and distance and raced across the nation carrying implicit suggestions of what to emulate: what's in, what's hot, the latest beat, and what to wear; the news that the people were out in the streets, and the question of why the local college administration building had not yet been taken over. Television introduced the Beatles, covered the "be-ins" and "happenings," and made instant celebrities. To an important degree, television undercut organization and itself became the leader. The important thing for a cause or movement was to get on television. The voice that shouted the loudest received the most attention. The Students for a Democratic Society and the Black Panthers would both be catapulted to stardom by the media which attracted members and enemies for them that they could not handle. Efforts to develop common goals and ideology, recruit members, establish leadership, define lines of authority, and decide on tactics were preempted by the media. The actions of the antiwar movement, the New Left, and the counterculture too often became media-focused rather than organizational.

THE SEARCH FOR SECURITY

Alongside of America's new consumer society, there marched the cold war competition with the Soviet Union. Its prime symbol was the atomic bomb. World War II had killed 50 million. Nuclear weapons could kill everybody. The first bomb had been tested in the desert of New Mexico, early on the morning of July 16, 1945. As the dazzling mushroom of fire bleached the desert, project director J. Robert Oppenheimer remembered a line from the Indian epic the *Bhagavad Gita*: "Now I am become death, destroyer of worlds." A Harvard physics professor standing beside him said softly, "Now we are all sons-of-bitches!"

The initial American reaction to the news that atomic bombs had been dropped on Hiroshima and Nagasaki was public jubilation. The GIs who were to take part in the invasion of Japan felt that the bombings may well have saved their lives: the war was won, and the Japanese had it coming to them. In a Gallup Poll later that August, 85 percent of those questioned approved. Then, as Americans settled down to live with the atom, that coexistence became more complex. The good side was that the atom seemed to promise unlimited peacetime energy and make future war unthinkable.

The negative side was that anything possible was possible. In 1946, the Russians rejected the American-sponsored Baruch Plan for international control of atomic weapons. Three years later, the *Washington Post* cartoonist Herblock drew a picture of an American bomb, dressed up like Robinson Crusoe on his lonely island, discovering naked footprints on the sand which told him he was no longer alone. On a Friday late in August 1949, President Truman announced that

Sep 49—On the news of the first Russian atomic explosion

FIG. 1. From *The Herblock Book* (Beacon Press, 1952).

the Soviets had tested their own atomic device. A "doomsday clock" soberly guarded the cover of the *Bulletin of the Atomic Scientists,* the public affairs journal published by the wartime scientists who had developed the American bomb. Now the scientists reset the hands on the clock at only three minutes to midnight.

The race was on to develop a more powerful bomb. It was a time of suspicion—of the arrest and conviction of the atomic spies Klaus Fuchs and the Rosenbergs, of loyalty oaths and blacklists, of the hearings of the House Un-American Activities Committee (HUAC) and the Senate Internal Security Committee—and Senator Joseph Mc-Carthy's newest charges of disloyalty spread across the headlines of the daily newspapers. An anti-Communist hysteria swept the nation. The public prestige of the atomic scientists declined. Security clearance was denied to J. Robert Oppenheimer, who had directed the building of the wartime bombs. Controversy raged over whether nuclear war was winnable. Those who argued that there could be no winners coined the acronym MAD to represent an inevitable "mutual assured destruction." Fallout from atmospheric tests, in the form of the deadly strontium-90, began to show up in milk. A British visitor, noting the appearance of bomb shelter and evacuation signs, commented that the ones from World War II had just been taken down in England. A nuclear awareness and anxiety had become deeply anchored in the American consciousness.

The psyche of the American fifties was one of domestic optimism and international power, underlaid with suspicion. No one could predict where the growing confrontation with the Soviet Union and world Communism would lead. Students of international relations generally identify the Truman Doctrine as the beginning of the cold war. In the spring of 1947, President Truman asked Congress for aid for Greece and Turkey, and framed the request in a promise to support free people anywhere "who are resisting attempted subjugation by armed minorities or by outside pressures." In a long cable from the American embassy in Moscow, the Russian expert George Kennan named Truman's policy "containment." Later that year, the National Security Act put the operating system in place by creating the Department of Defense, the Joint Chiefs of Staff, the National Security Council, and the Central Intelligence Agency. In 1950, containment became official policy when President Truman approved a secret National Security Council recommendation, NSC-68, for worldwide American action against Soviet expansion and influence.

Behind the walls of the containment policy's global mission, there seemed little room for thoughtful debate. "Loyalty" programs and the denunciatory rampages of Wisconsin senator Joseph McCarthy narrowed the range and drained the intellectual intensity of American politics. Political sociologists were talking about "the end of ideology." As the one-time Marxist sociologist Daniel Bell summed it up, "The tendency to convert concrete issues into ideological problems, to invest them with moral color and high emotional charge, is to invite conflicts which can only damage a society. . . . It has been one of the glories of the United States that politics has always been a pragmatic give-and-take rather than a series of wars-to-the-death." What he meant was that no one now really dreamed of going to battle in the streets in an attempt to create an ideal society. Hitler and Stalin had destroyed the idea of perfection, and millions of lives had paid the price.

The New Deal reforms and the wartime achievements of the American industrial system showed that a pluralistic, pragmatic, reform way was best. The Chicago historian and future librarian of Congress Daniel Boorstin, (*The Genius of American Politics* [1953]) wrote that Americans were nonideological. Yale's David Potter (*People of Plenty* [1954]) explained that American national character had been shaped by an historically unique abundance, rather than by scarcity. Harvard historian Louis Hartz's explanation in *The Liberal Tradition in America* (1955) that the absence of a feudal past had permitted the United States to escape from deep class conflict was widely accepted as a primal explanation of American history.

The degree to which homage came to be paid to the existing social arrangement prompted a note of at least questioning concern. Practically all college students read George Orwell's *Nineteen Eighty-four* (1949), and many of them were acquainted with Aldous Huxley's *Brave New World* (1932). It was fashionable to talk about the dangers of "modern mass society," in which people could be manipulated by power, conformity, bureaucracy, and mass communications. Erich Fromm's *Escape From Freedom* (1941); David Riesman's *The Lonely Crowd* (1950); William Whyte's *The Organization Man* (1956), with its appendix on how to cheat on personality tests; C. Wright Mills's *White Collar* (1951) and *The Power Elite* (1956); and Vance Packard's *The Hidden Persuaders* (1957) were sociological best-sellers. None of these were calls to resistance or revolution. The American literature of the 1950s did not feature novels of proletarian or social concern. The focus was on the individual searching for identity and self-fulfillment. James Dean, with Sal Mineo and Natalie Wood (all of whom would die violent deaths in real life) in the movie *Rebel without a Cause*, and on his own in *East of Eden*, was only seeking a decent middle-class family life. J. D. Salinger's preadolescent hero of *Catcher in the Rye* (1951), Holden Caulfield, wanted a nonphony relationship, and the adult hero (played by Gregory Peck in the movie version) of Sloan Wilson's *The Man in the Gray Flannel Suit* (1955) abandoned preferment in Manhattan's executive office rat race for contentment in suburbia.

The prewar critique of a bourgeois society had subsided into criticism of the quality of life in a middle-class world of consumption and material success. In contrasting the 1950s with the 1960s, the reporter and historian Milton Viorst (*Fire in the Streets* [1979]) summed up the essential theme of the 1950s as "security: internal security (McCarthy), international security (massive retaliation), personal security (careerism)."

In 1962, Professor Thomas Kuhn published what was to be a highly influential little book entitled *The Structure of Scientific Revolutions*. Normal science, he explained, went about its work within the boundaries of major established theories, or world views, which he called "paradigms." Much useful knowledge is gained by working within the rules the paradigm sets forth, but over time problems develop which the paradigm cannot handle, and a younger generation of scientists emerges who question the old paradigm and see old things differently. A crisis erupts in which a free-for-all struggle takes place, with rules and values broadly debated. Eventually, quiet returns with the emergence of a new paradigm, which gains acceptance and becomes the new normal science.

The political paradigms of postwar America were liberalism and the cold war. By the mid-1950s, competition with the Soviet Union had settled into its containment rut. The Korean War had subsided into an uneasy truce. Senator McCarthy overreached himself and was censured by his Senate colleagues. President Eisenhower, the leader of victory in Europe, reigned serenely in the White House. Domestic pluralism and economic growth provided boundaries within which piecemeal, pragmatic reform could meet the Republic's needs and provide leadership for the anti-Communist world. This was to be "the American Century." The emerging challenges to these paradigms would underlie the history of the 1960s.

THE ADJUSTED PSYCHE: GRAHAM, PEALE, SHEEN, AND LIEBMAN

The 1950s saw no warning of impending change. Middle-class America seemed secure. Its mental health was represented by and ministered to by a quadrumvirate of media preachers: Protestants Billy Graham and Norman Vincent Peale, Monsignor Fulton J. Sheen, and Rabbi Joshua Loth Liebman. In church and temple, with the written and spoken word, in the millions of copies of their books, to the tens of millions who read their words in the *Ladies' Home Journal* or the *Reader's Digest,* and the even more millions who listened to them on the radio and watched their weekly television programs, they offered a message of personal reassurance.

Billy Graham and Fulton J. Sheen were traditional. Both began with the wicked world. Sheen counseled in his best selling 1949 book, *Peace of Soul*, that man could gain peace through a sense of guilt which led him to seek the ever-available grace of God. In response to Rabbi Liebman's psychoanalytical *Peace of Mind* (1946), Sheen warned, "Unless souls are saved, nothing is saved." The Baptist Billy Graham filled auditoriums, ballparks, and television screens with the message of mainstream Evangelicalism. Not touched by the Pentecostal fervor of speaking in tongues and healing, or limited by fundamentalist or denominational boundaries, he preached the inspiration of the Bible and the salvation of souls in preparation for the Second Coming and eternal life.

If Sheen and Graham were traditional and salvational, Rabbi Liebman and Dr. Norman Vincent Peale were therapeutic. Liebman's prescription for "*peace of mind*" was that the spiritual serenity of the good life could be gained by escaping from psychic anxieties. Having made its peace with Copernicus and Darwin, he wrote, religion would have to do the same with Freud. The traditional way of dealing with evil had been repression. "The psychologically mature God idea" meant facing neurotic fears and other emotional problems and transcending them. No one was better at showing the way than Norman Vincent Peale. Following up on the success of *A Guide to Confident Living* (1948), he offered *The Power of Positive Thinking* (1952) to suggest techniques for "peace of mind, improving health, and a never-ceasing flow of energy." It was, he wrote "a practical, direct-action, personal-improvement manual." He had come to his pastorate at New York's Dutch Reformed Marble Collegiate Church in 1932, in a time of "fear, anxiety, insecurity, disappointment, frustration, and failure." Now, in better times, he taught people how to be happy and successful. "The words of the Bible," he wrote, "have a particularly strong therapeutic value." With hundreds of stories—aimed particularly at managers, directors, and businessmen—of people cured of inferiority, lethargy, anxiety, emotional distress, not being liked, and irritation with others, he taught his "compound of prayer, faith, and dynamic spiritual thinking." For none of the four great media inspirationists of the 1950s was religion a call to social change or action.

THE REFUSAL TO GO ALONG

There is always dissent from prevailing attitudes and commitments. Often as not, it is cultural rather than political. In any age, there are those who find themselves disconnected from their times. The Beats who gravitated toward Lawrence Ferlinghetti's City Lights Bookshop in San Francisco's North Beach district were not elitist expatriates like the lost generation of the 1920s or political leftists like the radicals of the 1930s. Not trying to change anyone else's life, the Beats sought to tear loose, in individual spontaneity, from all the demands and constraints of America's "straight" society. Allen Ginsberg's famous "Howl,"

> I saw the best minds of my generation destroyed by madness, starving
>   hysterical naked,
> dragging themselves through the negro streets at dawn looking for an
>   angry fix,

contained neither social commentary nor program.

Coming of age and emerging from the world of childhood and dependence is often one of the most difficult of human passages. There was not only the classic path of setting out on the road, but also in affluent postwar America a youth culture was beginning to emerge which acted as a halfway house to separation. Robert Zimmerman—soon to be Bob Dylan—in Hibbing, Minnesota, and Tom Hayden in Ann Arbor read Jack Kerouac's *On the Road,* and Omaha high-schooler Nick Nolte asked himself, "You mean you can just do that? Pick up and go?" For those going nowhere in particular, there was Bill Haley and the Comets, with a new kind of driving, "rock-around-the-clock" beat for the 1955 movie *The Blackboard Jungle.* A Memphis promoter who was looking for a white boy who could sing like the black musicians found a local truckdriver named Elvis Presley. Elvis made it big on the "Ed Sullivan Show" and in a matter of months sold more copies of "All Shook Up" than Harriet Beecher Stowe ever did of her earlier liberation statement, *Uncle Tom's Cabin.*

Yet there were other roads that would lead from the 1950s with unimagined consequences. By the time of the French defeat at Dien Bien Phu in 1954, the United States was already paying 80 percent of France's war costs in Indochina. Beginning in the next year, for 379 days, the black people of Montgomery, Alabama, walked rather than ride the segregated city buses.

C. WRIGHT MILLS: AMERICAN JEREMIAH

One person who sensed the gathering forces of change was a professor of sociology at Columbia University. C. Wright Mills's importance was that he differed from, rather than represented, his contemporaries. Born in Waco, Texas, in 1916, Mills made his way East to the Columbia University faculty by way of Texas A&M, the University of Texas, graduate school at Wisconsin, and a teaching stint at Maryland. Like Thorstein Veblen, whom he greatly admired, he was an outsider. Coming to class on his motorcycle, dressed in his leather jacket and boots, critical of his profession for its bland acceptance of the normative order of things, he offered a stinging critique of American society. He lamented the decline of the old entrepreneurial middle class, the independent professionals, the family farm, the loss of pride in work and craftsmanship, and popular involvement in society's decision making. The society he described in *The New Men of Power* (1948), *White Collar* (1951), and *The Power Elite* (1956) was one of a mass, salaried, white-collar middle class, "dependent and anonymous," in a big-corporation, bureaucratic world where decisions were by manipulative, interconnected elites. There was little place for the independent individual, and people were "estranged from community and society."

The Texas maverick was a populist, but a sophisticated one. His populism was influenced by the great German sociologists Karl Marx, Karl Mannheim, and Max Weber. What particularly concerned him was less class than social stratification and power. More like Weber than Marx, he focused his attack on ruling elites rather than on a ruling class, and argued that a combination of powerful, centralized state, business, and military hierarchies had come to dominate society. The Enlightenment hope for the rule of freedom and reason had failed. The intellectuals had failed, and Mills's fellow sociologists did not have anything relevant to say about "the enormous enlargement and the decisive centralization of all the means of power and decision." It was the duty of sociology to deal with such problems, to help the people regain their role in decision making; in George Orwell's phrase, to "get outside the whale" and "become their own men."

The leadership would not come from the liberals, who had become blind and acquiescent, or from the Old Left, which was hung up on a nonrevolutionary proletariat. After *The Sociological Imagination* (1959), Mills was no longer writing academic sociology. The concept of "the power elite" had made him famous, and he was on the world lecture and conference circuit. The Cuban revolution excited him, and he hoped that it meant a "pluralized Marxist" alternative to American imperialism and Soviet ideology. His *Listen Yankee: The Revolution in Cuba* (1960) sold half a million copies, and twice as many people bought *The Causes of World War III* (1960), in which he set forth his fears about worldwide militarization and the nuclear arms race between the bureaucratic Soviet and American states.

Who could stop it? That same year, the British *New Left Review* printed his "Letter to the New Left," in which he identified the radical agency of change as "the young intelligentsia." Even by 1962, when he died of a heart attack at the age of forty-five, young intellectuals such as Students for a Democratic Society (SDS) founders Al Haber and Dick Flacks were reading him with excitement, and Tom Hayden chose Mills as the subject for a master's thesis, which he titled "Radical Nomad."

Mills's critique of the "power elites" and the passive, anonymous, middle-class masses was not an appeal for the restoration of economic competition and possessive individualism. The young intellectuals who read his works were seeking social commitment and community. The civil rights activists of the Student Nonviolent Coordinating Committee (SNCC), coming from their "beloved community" in Nashville, out to "free" Mississippi, set the pattern of group-centered decision-making and leadership. The Students for a Democratic Society gave it the name "participatory democracy." They placed it at the heart of the manifesto they wrote at their Port Huron retreat, and went off to live in the Northern big city ghettos in small communal groups to try community organizing among the poor. Both the idealism and the escapism of the 1960s were manifested in a new world of struggle and excesses, and of causes, communities, communes, collectives, "nations," and "families."

2. Marching in the Streets

The classic mid-twentieth century works on race and Southern politics were written by a Swedish sociologist, Gunnar Myrdal, and an American political scientist, V. O. Key. Both described patterns so deeply rooted that most people accepted them as immutable. Although many Americans agreed with the conclusions of Myrdal's massive 1944 Carnegie Foundation study, *An American Dilemma*, that the treatment of the Negro violated the American creed of equal opportunity, few had any expectation that it was likely to change. Ten years later, the U.S. Supreme Court's 1954 school desegregation decision in *Brown* v. *Board of Education of Topeka, Kansas* became the cornerstone of sweeping changes. Within a decade, a virtual revolution was taking place which moved racial change to the center of national concern. "The most striking error of omission in Myrdal's delineation of the course of race relations in the United States," Martin Luther King Jr. asserted in 1965, ". . . was his failure to recognize that the greatest peaceful pressure for change would come from Negroes in the South." In the creation of that pressure, King, Southern black church people, and the young had taken the lead.

It was not easy. In *Southern Politics in State and Nation* (1949), V. O. Key had described the institutions of disfranchisement, malapportionment, one-party politics, and segregation which dominated and crippled Southern politics. The white leadership of the Deep South denounced the *Brown* decision and promised resistance. Bankers, lawyers, physicians, judges, and businessmen joined the politicians in pledging to protect "states' rights and racial integrity" against any change. Much of the responsibility for the racial intransigency rested on the leaders, who encouraged resistance and often sparked violence. In 1957, Arkansas governor Orval Faubus brought a screaming mob to Little Rock's Central High School when he used the National Guard to block peaceful integration and keep nine black teenagers from entering. Eventually, President Eisenhower had to federalize the guard and use the Hundred-and-First Airborne Division to enforce the court's order. In 1962, at the University of Mississippi, two people died in rioting and President John Kennedy was forced to send in the army to protect the first black student, James Meredith, when Governor Ross Barnett heated up the opposition and then welched on his agreement with Kennedy to maintain order.

James W. Silver, who left the chairmanship of the University of Mississippi's history department after the 1962 riot, explained what it was like to live in a closed society. When people were continually told "that no authority on earth can legally or morally require any change," this created conditions that exploded into violence. When change came, it was "seen not as a legitimate outcome of classic American values, but as a criminal conspiracy against sanctified institutions."

Like Governor Barnett, other Southern leaders also encouraged resistance. Most of the congressmen and all but three of the senators (Albert Gore Sr. and Estes Kefauver of Tennessee, and Lyndon Johnson of Texas) signed a "Southern Manifesto" calling for resistance. "The Deep South Says Never" was the way the press headlined it. While it is difficult to conclude that the leaders were more racist and reactionary than the generality of white Southerners, they appealed to emotions of prejudice and paranoia that a united support of peaceful compliance might have diluted.

By 1960, six years after the *Brown* school desegregation decision, no black children were attending public school with white children in the states of the deep South. Alongside the political resistance, a violent guerrilla war was being fought in Mississippi. Eventually, once some degree of desegregation became inevitable and the more sophisticated Paul Johnson succeeded Ross Barnett as governor, organized resistance declined. A decade later, the public schools would be at least formally integrated, the voting booths open, and Mississippi would have more black officeholders than any other state in the Union.

At the beginning of the 1960s, litigation in the Supreme Court by the National Association for the Advancement of Colored People (NAACP) was practically the only path used or imagined. Within less than a decade, the way had led from the city streets and country roads of the South through the presidential offices and the halls of Congress into the laws of the land. Black marchers and demonstrators were the crucial prompting force. The struggles in Montgomery, Birmingham, and Selma, Alabama; in Greensboro, North Carolina; and in the state of Mississippi were particularly important. Black demonstrations and white violence, headlined by the press and carried into the American conscience by television, helped push the administration, Congress, and the courts into action.

MONTGOMERY

On December 1, 1955, Rosa Parks refused to give her seat to a white man on a Montgomery, Alabama, bus. Racial etiquette and the laws of Montgomery said that she was wrong and must be punished to remind black people of their proper place. Mrs. Parks had not intended to create an issue; she had paid her fare at the front, had stepped back off the bus to make the prescribed rear-door entrance, and had taken a seat toward the back. White people filled the front seats, and in time a white man was left standing. The white bus driver threatened her with arrest if she did not yield. She would not. At that moment, as Black Power activist Stokely Carmichael later described it, "somewhere in the universe, a gear in the machinery had shifted."

The most commonly told version of the story is that Rosa Parks had been shopping after a day of work, and that her feet hurt. It was probably true, but behind the chance occurrence there was a history of stirring and concern that gave birth to the civil rights movement in Montgomery and in black communities across the South. In 1953, a year before the school desegregation decision, there had been a successful church-led bus boycott in Baton Rouge, Louisiana, which awakened memories of the fight against streetcar segregation in other Southern cities at the beginning of the century. Rosa Parks was the longtime secretary of Montgomery's NAACP, founded by E. D. Nixon, who had learned social activism from the black labor leader A. Philip Randolph's Brotherhood of Sleeping Car Porters. The efforts of the White Citizens Council to get blacks who petitioned for school integration fired had led to the black boycott of a local dairy. E. D. Nixon had brought New York congressman Adam Clayton Powell in to talk about it to the Progressive Democratic Association. There had been other incidents over bus seating, and the Women's Political Council, formed when black women had been denied membership in the League of Women Voters, joined other organizations in urging change. Nixon made bond for Mrs. Parks and got on the phone to organize a boycott meeting. Professor Jo Ann Robinson, a council member, ran off the call on a mimeograph machine at Alabama State College. It was from such worlds of black community activity that the civil rights movement emerged.

Although seldom as united as they became in Montgomery in 1956, the black churches of the South provided a nurturing culture and the institutional resources from which the civil rights movement grew. As Aldon Morris pointed out in *The Origins of the Civil Rights Movement: Black Communities Organizing for Change* (1984), from this culture came the songs, prayers, oratory, testimonies, meeting places, organizing experience, fund-raising, the charismatic preacher-leaders, and mass base of participants. Interracial organizations such as the Southern Conference for Human Welfare (SCHW) and its offshoot, the Southern Conference Educational Fund (SCEF), the Southern Regional Council (SRC) and its local councils on human relations, and the Highlander Folk School, in Monteagle, Tennessee, where for almost three decades Myles Horton taught whites and blacks how to organize against segregation, helped with networking, voter education, and the training of grass-roots organizers. The pacifist Fellowship of Reconciliation (FOR) brought the Gandhian message and its own committed workers. In addition to NAACP Youth Councils, and Congress of Racial Equality (CORE) chapters, there were the various Southern Christian Leadership Conference (SCLC), affiliates, including Rev. Fred Shuttlesworth's Alabama Christian Movement for Human Rights, the United Christian Movement of Shreveport, the Nashville Christian Leadership Council, and Rev. Wyatt Walker's Petersburg Improvement Association.

Indigenous resources, local people, and community roots provided the foundation on which the civil rights movement was built. Missing from the ranks of the struggle was the contribution of black Southern unionism. It had once been a rising force, but the militant and egalitarian unionism of the packinghouses of Ft. Worth, the docks and food processing plants of Memphis, the mines and steel mills of Birmingham, and the R. J. Reynolds tobacco factories of Winston-Salem had been crushed in the anti-Communist drives of the 1950s.

The boycott of the Montgomery buses was a crucial point in the history of black America. For more than a year, despite every legal harassment the city government could devise, the black people of Montgomery car-pooled or walked until the Supreme Court ruled that the buses must be desegregated. The struggle produced a civil rights activism within the black churches of the South, and a new leader, in the person of the young minister of the Dexter Avenue Baptist Church, Martin Luther King Jr. When their boycott began, the black people of Montgomery asked only to be treated politely, and they were refused. The result was not only the desegregation of the buses but also the creation of a movement.

The path was peaceful confrontation and a willingness to suffer violence and imprisonment by publicly violating unjust laws. The basic inspiration came from Christianity, from Jesus' ministry and the witness of the black churches. King's theological studies at Crozier Theological Seminary and at Boston University had added both Walter Rauschenbusch's social gospel faith in personal goodness and brotherhood, and Reinhold Niebuhr's social activism. The radical pacifists Bayard Rustin and Glen Smiley, coming to aid the boycott, brought their experience with the teachings and practice of the Indian independence leader Mahatma Gandhi. From all of these, King fashioned the path of nonviolent resistance, which sought to change the attitude of the white majority by forcing it to face the moral issue of segregation and discrimination. The bombing and harassment by white supremacists, which continued even after the Supreme Court struck down Montgomery's bus segregation, showed that there was a long way to go.

National attention had been focused on race relations in the South, and a new moral dimension had been added. Martin Luther King Jr. took the lead in organizing the Southern Christian Leadership Conference to help develop and coordinate the civil rights activities of local communities. Although President Eisenhower had reluctantly used the army to uphold the court-ordered integration of Little Rock's Central High School, he had no intention of going further, and the SCLC had no particular plan for pushing him to do so. There had been attempted bus boycotts here and there, but the SCLC was a board of directors for a company that was yet to be organized. Despite Montgomery, the beliefs and institutions of a white supremacist society seemed unyielding. The next of the events that mustered black resolution and reached out for the national conscience came from an unexpected source.

GREENSBORO AND SNCC

On February 1, 1960, four black freshmen from North Carolina Agricultural and Technical College sat down at a Woolworth's lunch counter in Greensboro and politely requested service. When it was refused, they remained seated until the store closed. The next day they were back again, joined by more black students and a few white ones, well dressed, doing homework, while crowds, friendly and hostile, grew outside on the sidewalk. Something unexpected and exciting was taking place, and it drew national attention. A columnist in the segregation-minded *Richmond News Leader* set forth his puzzled reaction. "Here were the colored students in coats, white shirts, and ties," he wrote, "and one of them was reading Goethe and one was taking notes from a biology text. And here, on the sidewalk outside was a gang of white boys come to heckle, a ragtail rabble, slack-jawed, black-jacketed, grinning fit to kill, and some of them, God save the mark, were waving the proud and honored flag of the Southern States in the last war fought by gentlemen. Eheu! It gives one pause."

In the weeks that followed, there were sit-ins across the South and sympathy demonstrations in the North. By the end of the year, thousands had taken part, and had often gone to jail for doing so. The Greensboro students had read about Montgomery and had heard King speak, but the sit-in was their own idea. They had no organization and no greater plan. With the sit-ins spreading, an organization of student activists was formed under the general sponsorship of the SCLC. Its name was the Student Nonviolent Coordinating Committee. Within SNCC, the leading forces were students such as John Lewis and Diane Nash from the black colleges of Nashville, moved by Christian idealism, and politically minded students such as Stokely Carmichael, from Howard University and the North, who accepted nonviolence as a tactical weapon.

The sit-ins and the formation of SNCC produced a broadening confrontation with Southern segregation and a growing involvement of young people in nonviolent protest. Before Greensboro, there had been only an occasional demonstration; now a decade of action in the streets began. Under the guidance of the longtime activist Ella Baker, they had separated themselves from the SCLC and adopted a group-centered leadership, but here again, as with King and the SCLC, they were not sure what their next step was to be.

This question was answered by the Freedom Rides undertaken early in 1961 by the Congress of Racial Equality, a biracial Northern direct action group, formed in 1942 by the pacifist Fellowship of Reconciliation. In the early years of the 1960s, while the NAACP fought the long, slow battles in the courts and the Urban League talked with Northern industrialists about jobs for black people, an interacting group of direct action organizations had emerged. SCLC, SNCC, and CORE were cadre, not mass-membership, organizations. They were deeply touched by Christian nonviolence and a sense of in-group brotherhood that they saw as a "beloved community." Joined together by moral fervor and extraordinary courage, they brought the civil rights movement out into the streets and kept it there through the middle sixties.

The small, racially integrated group of men and women from CORE who set out to ride the interstate buses in May 1961 were badly beaten in Anniston, Alabama, and one of the Greyhound buses burned. In Birmingham, Police Commissioner Eugene "Bull" Connor gave the Ku Klux Klan fifteen minutes to work over the riders with clubs and chains. The police had been absent, he later explained, because it was Mother's Day and his men were all visiting their mothers. It was just as bloody at the bus station in Montgomery. After that, the federal government was forced to protect the bus riders, who, with King, were besieged overnight in the First Baptist Church by a large white mob. With the administration in Washington reluctantly pushing the even more reluctant governors of Alabama and Mississippi to promise protection on the highways, young SNCC members from Nashville joined the battered remaining bus riders to complete their trip to Jackson. Followed by other riders, they went to jail in Mississippi for entering the white waiting room in the Jackson bus station.

In a process that had deeply involved President John Kennedy and his brother Robert, the attorney general, the Freedom Rides forced the Kennedy administration to provide protection, as it did again the next year when the president used the army to ensure James Meredith's safety at the University of Mississippi. Apart from pressing the Interstate Commerce Commission into desegregating interstate bus facilities, the national government was not willing to directly challenge Southern segregation. President Kennedy was primarily interested in order and politics. Wherever possible, he avoided antagonizing influential congressional committee chairmen, who were predominantly Southern. When violence against black demonstrators became a public scandal, the administration did what was necessary to regain public order, but little more. As it saw things, the best path for civil rights was voter registration. This would not only get the demonstrators out of the streets and the headlines, it would mean votes for more liberal congressmen and senators who might support the administration's policies.

The later experiences of SNCC in Mississippi and in southwestern Georgia, where it was joined in Albany by King and the SCLC in 1962, strongly indicated that "out of the streets" was "out of mind." The experience of the Freedom Rides and jail in Mississippi changed SNCC from part-time students to full-time radical organizers. If the white establishment in Mississippi had only permitted the riders to pass through the white bus station waiting room and cafeteria in Jackson and on to New Orleans, the history of the state, and perhaps the South, might have been different.

At the end of the summer of 1961, Robert Moses began a voter registration project in McComb, Mississippi. At first there was much argument within SNCC over whether the efforts should go into working on desegregation or voter registration, but the disagreement faded in the face of the violence that threatened both projects equally. Although not interested in power for himself, Moses realized its importance for black America. Integration was not power: organization was power; the vote was power, and leadership must come from the people, not be exercised for them. Among the black poor of Mississippi, SNCC was attempting to integrate grass-roots structure and consciousness.

BIRMINGHAM

The year 1963 saw the high tide of a nonviolent, biracial civil rights movement and a shift in the role of the national government. The crisis point was Birmingham, Alabama. After the failure of its campaign in Albany, Georgia, the year before, SCLC needed a success and a way of inducing the federal government to provide active support. A month of mass marches, which came to include Birmingham schoolchildren, lured Police Commissioner "Bull" Connor into using brute force against the demonstrators. Pictures of flailing nightsticks, police dogs, and high-pressure fire hoses used against the nonresisting blacks filled the screens of the nation's television news broadcasts.

A public letter from Birmingham's leading Protestant, Catholic, and Jewish clergymen criticized the demonstrations as untimely, unwise, unnecessary, and illegal, the unjustified extremism of unwanted outsiders. Martin Luther King Jr. responded with a moving justification for the civil rights movement. Written on scraps of paper in his cell, his "Letter from Birmingham Jail" explained, in both classic Judeo-Christian and historic American terms, why, after three hundred years, black people were not prepared to wait longer for their freedom.

"I am in Birmingham because injustice is here," he wrote, "just as the prophets of the eighth century B.C. left their villages and carried their 'thus saith the Lord . . . and just as the Apostle Paul carried the gospel of Jesus Christ to the far corners of the Greco-Roman world . . . I must constantly respond to the Macedonian call for aid." "Injustice anywhere is a threat to justice everywhere," he continued. "We are caught in an inescapable network of mutuality, tied in a single garment of destiny. . . . Anyone who lives inside the United States can never be considered an outsider anywhere within its bounds. . . .

"For years now I have heard the word 'Wait!' It rings in the ear of every Negro with piercing familiarity. This 'wait' has almost always meant 'Never.' We have waited more than 340 years for our constitutional and God-given rights. . . . Perhaps it is easy for those who have never felt the stinging darts of segregation to say 'Wait.' But when you see the vast majority of your twenty million Negro brothers smothering in an airtight cage of poverty in the midst of an affluent society; when you suddenly find your tongue twisted and your speech stammering as you seek to explain to your six-year old daughter why she can't go to the public amusement park . . . and see ominous clouds of inferiority beginning to form . . . when you have to concoct an answer for a five-year old son who is asking: 'Daddy, why do white people treat colored people so mean?' . . . when your first name becomes 'nigger,' your middle name becomes 'boy' (however old you are) . . . and your wife and mother are never given the respected title of 'Mrs.'; when you are harried by day and haunted by night by the fact that you are a Negro, living constantly at tiptoe stance . . . when you are forever fighting a degenerating sense of 'nobodiness'—then you will understand why we find it difficult to wait."

Quoting Saint Augustine and Saint Thomas Aquinas to justify breaking segregation laws, he explained that an "unjust law" was one that degraded human personality and, in the words of the Protestant theologian Paul Tillich and the Jewish philosopher Martin Buber, divided humanity and reduced people to things. The person, therefore, who broke an unjust law openly and lovingly, and willingly accepted the penalty in order to reach the conscience of the community, was showing the highest respect for law. This was the kind of "nonviolent tension" that the movement had brought to Birmingham, he explained, to confront "the conscience of the local and national community."

As the street marches and the arrests mounted, President Kennedy worked behind the scenes putting pressure on business and community leaders for a settlement. More important than the mild promises forced from Birmingham city officials was Kennedy's decision to fight for a sweeping national civil rights law that not only would open up public facilities to black people but also would press for school integration, voting rights, and equal employment. Passage of such a law, which was by no means certain, would free the civil rights movement from the expensive and seemingly endless task of attacking discrimination on a community-by-community basis.

Limited though the Birmingham settlement was, facing down "Bull" Connor's fire hoses and dogs lifted the spirits and sights of the civil rights movement. Its goal was no longer local, piecemeal gains, but the end of racial segregation in America. That was clearly not going to be easy. The summer that followed was marked by spreading black demonstrations and boycotts and an escalation of white violence. Governor George Wallace put on a show for the television cameras and then stepped back while two black students peacefully entered the University of Alabama. King's "I Have a Dream" speech on the steps of the Lincoln Memorial in Washington was an exalted moment, but SNCC demanded to know why there was no protection for civil rights workers in Mississippi. That September, four young black girls were killed by a dynamite bomb at Birmingham's Sixteenth Street Baptist Church.

After President Kennedy's murder in Dallas, on November 22, 1963, his successor, Lyndon Johnson, skillfully pushed Kennedy's "public accommodations" law through Congress. As CORE continued its demonstrations in the North and SNCC worked to organize black communities in the Deep South, King went to jail in St. Augustine, Florida, and the Republican Senate leader, Everett Dirksen, provided the votes necessary to break the Senate filibuster. The new Civil Rights Law of 1964 opened up motels, hotels, restaurants, parks, and other public accommodations, and promised to do the same for all federally funded programs.

MISSISSIPPI

Winning the right to sit down and have a cup of coffee, however, did not mean that black people had suddenly become free and equal. Across the South, separation and subordination were enforced by law, tradition, and violence. The Klansman and the policeman were often the same person, and black people lacked both the vote and the economic base to assert their rights. Although race relations were bad in southwest Georgia, Black-Belt Alabama, and northern Louisiana, Mississippi seemed to be striving to maintain its one-hundred year role as the most violent champion of white supremacy.

It was in Mississippi that SNCC chose to organize the black communities and that the Ku Klux Klan became most clearly a resistance movement. The Student Nonviolent Coordinating Committee was no longer well-dressed integrationists sitting in at lunch counters; now they were a full-time, militant cadre, wearing jeans and work shirts, walking down dirt roads, and being shot at, beaten, and jailed for trying to organize the black poor of the Deep South. The civil rights struggle in Mississippi was not SNCC's creation. Although an attempt to register or encourage others to vote might cost one's job, home, or life, native Mississippians such as Medgar Evers, Aaron Henry, Amzie Moore, and Vernon Dahmer were already working through the NAACP and local voter leagues. Across the South, two-thirds of the eligible whites and less than a third of the eligible blacks could vote. In Mississippi, fewer than 7 percent of the eligible black people were registered, and in many rural Southern counties there were none at all on the voter lists. SNCC's efforts were radical on two counts. With an actual working membership of no more than two hundred, SNCC sought to change Mississippi and the South. Although the religious, nonviolent commitment still flickered, SNCC's goal was to develop a locally led, grass-roots power base in the black communities.

Frustrated by the immensity of the task and the violence of the resistance, SNCC made a hotly debated decision to recruit white college students for a "Freedom Summer" campaign in 1964. Almost literally being beaten into the ground, SNCC found that black suffering was not news. A flood of white, upper-middle-class students from prestigious universities and influential families, putting their bodies at risk, could not only provide additional workers, but might also bring media attention and government protection.

The volunteers would work with black children in the Freedom Schools and in community programs, and would help with voter registration. Like the Freedom Rides that had touched off the effort in Mississippi three years earlier, the Freedom Summer was designed to force a confrontation between Mississippi's white supremacist institutions and the national government in Washington. Among the first of the seven hundred volunteers was Andrew Goodman, who was murdered along with two CORE workers, James Chaney and Mickey Schwerner, one black and one white, by Klansmen in Philadelphia, Mississippi. They had gone to look at a black church that had been burned down by the the Ku Klux Klan. The police arrested them on a false speeding charge, held them until dark, and then released them into a Klan ambush on the road. The Klansmen killed them and buried their bodies in an unfinished earthen dam nearby. The outcry over the disappearance of the civil rights workers, and the fact that two of them were white, forced the national government into action. The FBI eventually found the bodies and identified the Klan killers, but murder was a state crime, not a national one, and Mississippi was not interested in trying them for it. Eventually convicted of the federal offense of denying Goodman, Chaney, and Schwerner their civil rights, the Klansmen went to jail for short periods, long after the Freedom Summer was over.

A Council of Federated Organizations (COFO) combined the efforts of the NAACP, SCLC, CORE, and SNCC, but SNCC directed the Freedom Summer program. At the cost of beatings, bombings, church burnings, murder, and 1,000 arrests, some 2,000 children attended the Freedom Schools, 17,000 adults attempted to register to vote, 2,000 actually got on the rolls, and 80,000 voted in the various elections that COFO held to show what would happen in a racially freer society.

The summer of 1964 was SNCC's last attempt to appeal to the nation's conscience and institutions. Its major effort was its own statewide election of delegates to the Democratic National Convention in Atlantic City. More than sixty thousand black Mississippians voted for a mixed slate that challenged the official "whites-only" Mississippi regulars. At the convention, Lyndon Johnson's concern was to hold the votes of Southern whites and to preserve harmony so that the Convention could appropriately celebrate his presidential achievements. Accordingly, he turned his vast influence and patronage powers on liberals and moderate civil rights leaders to pressure the Mississippi Freedom Democratic Party (MFDP) into accepting a compromise. The delegate-selection system would be opened up for the next national election in 1968. This time, the all-white Mississippi regulars, who had been undemocratically chosen and who were going to vote for the Republican Barry Goldwater anyway, were to be seated, along with two token Mississippi Freedom Democratic Party delegates selected by President Johnson himself.

The MFDP delegates refused to compromise and went home. For

SNCC, already skeptical of the liberals and the national government, this was the "last" betrayal. It was the same old story of white-black relations. They had not fought and suffered in Mississippi in order that someone else would decide who was going to represent them. The national government had let the Freedom Riders sit in jail over the summer of 1961, and had prosecuted black demonstrators rather than white violence in Albany, Georgia. Hoping to quiet things in the streets, it had urged SNCC to take up voter registration, only to stand by and watch while Mississippi lawmen beat and jailed them. Martin Luther King Jr.'s speech from the steps of the Lincoln Memorial was not for them. They did not share his dream, for in Mississippi and southwestern Georgia, the consciousness of the white South was a killer. With Roman Catholic Patrick Cardinal O'Boyle threatening to withdraw, the organizers of the March on Washington had ganged up on SNCC's representative, John Lewis, and forced him to tone down his speech. In SNCC's eyes, the black "followers of the dream" had been as spineless as the white civil rights moderates. The only path was the organization of black people to take control at the community level. Reaching far beyond integration and electoral politics, SNCC's goal was the radical transformation of black politics and life.

SELMA

In 1964 Lyndon Johnson won a sweeping electoral victory (losing only Mississippi, the rest of the Deep South, and Arizona to Senator Barry Goldwater) that increased his power in Congress. Although President Johnson intended to extend black suffrage in the South, it took pressure in the streets to produce the Voting Rights Act of 1965. To accomplish this, King, home from Norway with his Nobel Peace Prize, moved into Selma, Alabama, where SNCC community organizers had been working on voter registration. While King still held to his belief in nonviolent resistance, he could hardly expect to change the consciousness of Southern sheriffs and lawmen. His strategy was to force a new law out of the national government by provoking violence from white Southern racists.

With a white minister and two more black civil rights workers dead in Alabama and black marchers ridden down in front of the television cameras at Edmund Pettus Bridge by Sheriff Jim Clark's mounted posse, Selma was now a high-profile issue. King's march from Selma to the state capitol in Montgomery was protected by the federal courts and by units of the Alabama National Guard called up into federal service. It climaxed with an enthusiastic rally on the state house steps, with Governor George Wallace peering out from behind the drawn blinds of his office.

Afterward, a white housewife from Detroit, driving marchers back to Selma, was overtaken on the road and shot by Ku Klux Klansmen. President Johnson went on television to denounce "the horrible crime." A government informant in the Klan car identified Viola Liuzzo's murderers. Although state juries found them innocent on the murder charge, they were eventually convicted in federal court of violating her civil rights. In August 1965, Johnson signed the Voting Rights Act, and before the end of the year, federal registrars were at work in selected Southern counties. By the end of the decade, more than two-thirds of the eligible black voters were on the registration lists.

The national acclaim for King after Birmingham and Selma overshadowed the disagreements and conflicts within the movement. Despite appearances and the vital role that black churches and communities had played in the South, local unity was often fragile or lacking. Conservative black leaders did not support "direct action." Rev. Joseph ("J. H.") Jackson, head of the largest black church organization, the National Baptist Convention, with its 5 million members, remained opposed to King. This was not just an aversion to the risks of taking to the streets, and all the talk of loving white people; it was something more important. It was power. In the feudal world of black church politics, each minister ruled an independent principality. From the pulpit of his Olivet Baptist Church in Chicago, the largest black Baptist congregation in America, Jackson forged an alliance of the great barons among the ministers. In an atmosphere of plots, maneuvers, and pitched battles, Jackson ruled the Convention with a naked power that Lyndon Johnson might have envied and amid annual floor fights that would have made SDS's National Conference for New Politics seem harmonious by comparison. In the Baptist wars, Martin Luther King Jr. picked the wrong side. Until the end of King's life, Jackson kept the Convention against him.

Only about 20 of Birmingham's 250 black ministers fully supported King's campaign there. Middle-class black people and college students were often hesitant to take part. One of the very real achievements in Selma was the participation of the schoolteachers, who put their jobs as well as their bodies on the line. Although the crucial audience had become national, the battle for media and governmental attention had to be fought locally. This meant local people, local organizations, and local goals. Campaigns could not be sustained for very long periods, and it was sometimes difficult for local people to understand the broader symbolic consequences of small local gains.

The irresolvable conflict between King and SNCC was that he and SCLC were using local turf to fight national battles within the system, while SNCC's young activists sought to develop local grass-roots organization and power. The SCLC ministers would come into a city such as Albany or Selma where SNCC was working, and shuttle in and out of town, and jail, to attend to other business, followed by the media, negotiate an unenforced agreement, win the adulation, and take off for somewhere else. Both SNCC and SCLC were right. The role of each was defined by its nature. Unlike a corporation, political party, or government, SCLC did not sell a product, a candidate, or the exercise of public power. It had no firmly institutionalized structure and source of income. SCLC was essentially one man: King was its policy, image, and, often, funding. He had to make the decisions, give the word on the strategy of campaigns and the tactics in the streets, and negotiate with the power structures of Birmingham, Chicago, and Washington. As a result, he was continuously in motion, not just in the South but across the country, speaking, preaching, fund-raising, planning, conferring, negotiating, persuading. Mixed in with these activities were marches, court appearances, jail time, and violence. He was the object of blows, missiles, a stab wound close to the heart, death threats, bombings, and pressure from the FBI. The combination of all these repeatedly brought him to the point of physical and emotional exhaustion.

BEYOND CIVIL RIGHTS

Over the ten-year period between Montgomery (1955) and Selma (1965), boycotts, sit-ins, demonstrations, marches, and community organizing raised black people's spirits and expectations, and greatly wounded legal segregation and disfranchisement. The South had come a long way since the black people of Montgomery had sought only more considerate treatment on the city's bus lines. The white stranglehold on the black psyche had been unalterably challenged. The civil rights movement was a biracial alliance based on Christian nonviolence, appealing to black self-esteem and the better instincts of white America. It sought the support of a broad spectrum of white "conscience groups" among the liberals, the churches, labor, the big foundations, moderate white Southerners, and students; and the national government in Washington. The movement had been liberal, nonviolent, and sectional, seeking to "bring the backward South up to 'American standards.' " It was a reform movement that appealed to the established institutions to live up to their values, rather than a revolutionary one that sought to change those institutions and values. The problems were seen as primarily legal and constitutional. The opening up of politics and public places was easier than integration of the schools. The movement had cost the rest of the country relatively little. The pride and determination loosed by the struggle were powerful forces with long-lasting consequences. For the young black student or preacher, it was exciting to talk about setting a city "on fire with the Holy Ghost," but what would the next step be?

By 1966, the mood and phase had changed. Street marches were no longer an effective instrument. The civil rights movement was breaking up. Urban riots in the North raised new and frightening questions. The failure of King's efforts to quiet violence during the Watts riot in Los Angeles and to desegregate housing in the Chicago suburbs revealed problems that went beyond the civil rights experience. King came to believe that poverty and powerlessness were the central underlying factors.

In the South, James Meredith's solitary "victory over fear" march from Memphis to Jackson to encourage black voter registration ended when he was wounded by a shotgun blast just a few miles inside the Mississippi line. Civil rights leaders hurried to take his place and complete the march. Stokely Carmichael and CORE's Floyd McKissick squeezed out the NAACP and the Urban League and then argued Black Power with King. In the small town of Greenwood, Mississippi, when asked the traditional question "What do we want?" the crowd's response was not "Freedom" but "Black Power!" Later that year, at CORE's Baltimore convention, Stokely thundered, "We don't need white liberals . . . we have to make integration irrelevant!" and Floyd McKissick proclaimed that nonviolence had "outlived its usefulness."

The academic explanation of Black Power was that the basis of politics was self-interest, not conscience. Inevitably, relations between groups of unequal power were exploitive. The essential path by which to escape dependency was group solidarity, based on black consciousness. This perception had motivated SNCC's efforts to build grassroots institutions as the necessary power base for the black people of Mississippi. The leadership of the major direct action organizations had passed roughly from the hands of the integrationists into those of the militant separatists, Stokely Carmichael in SNCC and Floyd McKissick in CORE.

For the most part, whether in the violent fantasies of the Revolutionary Action movement (RAM) and the Republic of New Africa fragments, or the self-defense exhortations of the Black Panther Party, Black Power was more rhetoric than reality. What the slogan meant was never clear. Its violent face was the product of the frustration and powerlessness of the black masses. It became more functional when it sought racial unity to aid black businesses, black political power, and local community control of schools and programs. Most important, it came to mean the cultural consciousness of black history, black art, black student organizations, black pride and "black is beautiful"; and being Afro-American.

The urban riots and the new Black Power exclusionism greatly diminished white support and brought financial crises in both CORE and SNCC. The civil rights movement had lost its uneasy unity. Black Power radicalism alienated the leaders of the NAACP and the Urban League, who also refused to follow Martin Luther King Jr. and break with President Johnson over the Vietnam War. The peace movement and jobs at antipoverty agencies drew off former activists, while rival factions struggled for control of community programs. No one talked any longer about "redeeming the soul" of the South or of America. The concern was with the power to make changes, and King was becoming increasingly pessimistic about the willingness of white America to take necessary action.

Unlike the right to vote, programs to deal with poverty would be expensive. The leaders who preached nonviolence through the democratic system were "not given enough victories," but still within its context, King searched for a new strategy. In a very real way, the civil rights movement had reached the limits of what could be accomplished by litigation. Although no one was really enthusiastic about it, King decided on a "poor people's campaign" to press Congress for a bold new economic policy. Waves of the "poor and disinherited" would descend on Washington, practice civil disobedience in the streets, and lobby and pressure Congress.

THE FAITH OF MARTIN LUTHER KING JR.

Despite difficulty and growing disunity, King had continued to pursue coalition politics based on uniting blacks, liberals, labor, and the white churches, and never gave up his belief in nonviolence. Better than anyone else, he expressed the "dreams and aspirations" of black America, tenuously serving as a bridge between conservatives and militants, and reaching out to touch the Judeo-Christian conscience of the nation. For all of its importance, Gandhian nonviolence as an instrument for social change had not become part of King's philosophy until after he was launched into the struggle in Montgomery. At the heart of his being was the experience of the black churches and a transcendant Christian faith. It was in Montgomery, sitting alone in prayer, late at night, at his kitchen table, that he found himself in the voice of Jesus, which told him to fight on and promised "never to leave me, never to leave me alone. No never alone." From this vision, which echoed through the rest of his life and helped him through his doubts and anxieties, he came to accept the role that he foresaw would lead to his death.

During the initial part of his civil rights ministry, he hoped to reach the conscience of white America. As his disillusionment with white liberals and moderates, and the white churches, grew, he came to realize how necessary the action of the national government was. Knowing that it would cost him President Johnson's favor, King held off as long as he could before openly opposing the war in Vietnam in 1967. As he went north to Chicago to agitate about jobs, housing, and education, he was increasingly concerned about the problems of wealth and class in American society. By failing to speak out against the Vietnam War, he believed that he was shirking his responsibility. Racism, militarism, and economic exploitation were all tied in together. His pessimism and his radicalism grew. The civil rights movement was too middle class, and America as a nation had never committed itself to economic justice. Although he had come from the sheltered and privileged background of upper-class black Atlanta, his concerns had broadened remarkably. More than any other leader of the sixties, King came to see the connection between unjust laws in the South, oppressive conditions in the North, economics, and the war in Vietnam. While the Poor People's Campaign was being organized, he returned to Memphis to lead the strike of the city's badly paid sanitation workers away from violence. On April 4, 1968, he was gunned down from ambush by James Earl Ray. King was twenty-six when he was called to lead the bus boycott in Montgomery; when he died in Memphis, he was thirty-nine.

Weighing the meaning of the sixties, the leading historian of the black experience in America, John Hope Franklin, points out that despite the frustration and embitterment, and the loss of a "high optimism," the sense of powerlessness and hopelessness was reversed by an enormous increase in black political power and the growing awareness in the black community of its political role in American life.

For all the importance of King as an inspiration and a national spokesman, the growing struggle was essentially a local effort, carried on in hundreds of black communities. King found himself and rose to leadership through a local bus boycott in Montgomery, which drew wisdom from a similar boycott in Baton Rouge and was copied in Tallahassee. The students of local colleges created the lunch-counter sit-in in Greensboro, and others copied it in Nashville and across the South. King and the Southern Christian Leadership Conference, SNCC, and CORE went in to register voters or help in local efforts in Albany; St. Augustine; McComb; Meridian; Selma; Danville; Fayette County, Tennessee; Lowndes County, Alabama; and other black communities. E. D. Nixon, the longtime civil rights leader of Montgomery, told of a woman who exclaimed to him, "Lord, I don't know what 'ud happened to the black people if Rev. King hadn't went to town." "If Mrs. Parks had got up and given the white man her seat, you'd never aheard of Rev. King," Nixon replied.

If King, Roy Wilkins, and others articulated the feelings of black people, spoke to presidents and the media, pushed for the legislation, negotiated the compromises and gains, and made the headlines, it was local people who initiated the efforts, called them in to help, supplied the demonstrators, and would be left to carry on after the captains and kings departed. It was they who would have to turn the new laws into local reality.

3. Through the Halls of Government

In his classic account *The Strange Career of Jim Crow* (1957), C. Vann Woodward wrote that there was an "old four-handed American game" in which the courts, the Constitution, and the South had ganged up on the Negro during most of American history, while the North looked the other way. Starting in the late 1930s, the Supreme Court began to reverse its role and struck down the enforcement of racially restrictive housing covenants, all-white primaries, and segregation in the professional schools. In eighteen Southern and border states, dual school systems remained mandated by law; in six more, segregation was left to the discretion of local school boards. The public school systems of the South became the crucial battleground.

The story goes back at least to the adoption of the Fourteenth Amendment to the U.S. Constitution in 1868. One of its provisions was that no state could deny any person the "equal protection of the laws." In 1896, in the case of *Plessy* v. *Ferguson,* which concerned a Louisiana law requiring whites and blacks to ride in separate railway coaches, the U.S. Supreme Court declared that as long as the accommodations were "equal," separation did not violate the Constitution. The doctrine of "separate but equal," applied to education and other activities, became the authorizing principle for segregation and the exclusion of black people from the public life of the South. For the next half century, "equality" was, for all practical purposes, forgotten while the South concentrated on separation. Under the American federal system, civil status and most criminal proceedings were the concern of the states, not the federal government. The Civil War and the Reconstruction Amendments had overturned slavery and established the citizenship of the freed slaves. After that neither the President, the Congress, nor the Supreme Court significantly challenged the division of jurisdiction, or how the states chose to treat their black citizens. The 1954 school desegregation decision in *Brown* v. *Board of Education of Topeka* marked the beginning of what became a major ongoing shift of responsibility and power within American federalism.

The heart of the civil rights struggle was the battle against *Plessy.* In the 1930s, the National Association for the Advancement of Colored People lawyers adopted the strategy of suing to force "equal" treatment. At the least, this "end run" could improve the education of black youth while making the South face how costly it was to fund a dual school system. After World War II, the NAACP, led by Thurgood Marshall, came to challenge segregation itself. While the NAACP argued that segregation was a denial of the "equal rights" guaranteed by the Constitution, the South made "states' rights" the bedrock of its case. The Supreme Court, headed by an unsympathetic Kentuckian, Fred Vinson, was badly divided, and no clear decision seemed possible. Vinson's sudden death changed the line-up and led Justice Felix Frankfurter to comment caustically that this had been his "first indication" that a God did exist.

In 1953, President Eisenhower appointed California governor Earl Warren to be the new chief justice. The Court had requested that the lawyers reargue what the congressional framers of the Fourteenth Amendment had originally intended about education. When no clear evidence was forthcoming, Warren carefully negotiated with his brethren on the Court to produce a unanimous decision that overturned school segregation. While public education had been in an infantile stage in the 1860s, he reasoned, it had become a cornerstone of modern life and a prime responsibility of government. To segregate children on the basis of race would do them social damage and psychological harm by placing a stigma of inferiority on them. School segregation, therefore, was by its very nature unconstitutional. The following year, the Court announced that desegregation was to proceed "with all deliberate speed" and turned over the supervision to the federal district courts in the South. Although President Eisenhower reluctantly used the army to back up the courts at Little Rock's Central High School in 1957, neither he nor the Congress offered any further support.

Unforeseen at the time, there were to be several new players sitting in on C. Vann Woodward's "old four-handed American game." As the civil rights movement marched out into the streets and forced the nation to face its racial problems, the presidency; the Justice Department and—reluctantly—the FBI; the Department of Health, Education, and Welfare; and Congress became actively involved. The U.S. Fifth Circuit Court of Appeals, with jurisdiction stretching from Georgia to Texas, emerged as the prime supervisor and often the moving force of change within the system. Together, though in fits and starts, the new players began translating the new civil rights consciousness into institutional structures and practice.

THE PRESIDENCY OF JOHN F. KENNEDY

Little of this seemed likely in 1961 when John Kennedy took office as president. "I won't say I stayed awake nights worrying about civil rights," the president's brother, Attorney General Robert Kennedy, later commented. Although President Kennedy believed that all people were created equal, he explained that "other people have grown up with totally different backgrounds and mores, which we can't change overnight." Racial justice was not the urgent problem of the moment, and time would take care of it, as time had for the Irish Americans.

In twentieth-century America, the president stands at the center of the action—or inaction. Whether the problem is drugs, preserving the environment, or coping with the soaring prices of gasoline and heating oil, the national response is importantly shaped by the occupant of the White House. Policies of social response and change are produced by the interaction of the Congress, the courts, the states and localities, the national administration, and the citizenry. The White House is the unifying force. Out of the Presidency come the selection of federal judges, the supporting briefs that jiggle their decisions, the employment of marshals, the federalization of the National Guard, and, if necessary, the use of the Hundred-and-First Airborne to uphold court orders. It is up to the president to fashion a public accommodations or voting rights law, a tax cut, or the "maximum feasible participation" of the poor, and push it through Congress. Then it is up to his administration to make the laws meaningful by instituting suits, sending in voting registrars, or withholding funds. It is the president's responsibility to negotiate with the corporate interests of Birmingham, the governor of Mississippi, or the mayor of Chicago, and to go on television to inspire his countrymen to acquiescence or effort. In most things, the president is the central mover in government and symbol in national life—the Statue of Liberty and the Washington Monument made flesh. No person sitting in the Oval Office can predict, or perhaps even imagine, the roles demanded of the president and how they will be carried out.

Particularly in the age of television, the president serves as a mirror held up to the American people. They look to the presidency to see what kind of a people they are. If they like the image they see reflected, they will reward the president with loyalty and devotion; if they do not like the picture, they will punish the president by withdrawal of support (as they were to do in the late 1960s and the 1970s with Lyndon Johnson, Richard Nixon, Gerald Ford, and Jimmy Carter).

JOHN F. KENNEDY, handsome, young, and photogenic, with his crisp Boston accent, his eloquence and wit, his elegant wife, Jackie, and his rich, glamorous family, was a made-for-media natural. The Kennedy excitement was an energizing force in the consciousness of the 1960s.

It was partly real and partly a myth, to which Jackie Kennedy gave the name "Camelot" after the then-reigning Broadway musical about the days of King Arthur and his Knights of the Round Table:

> Don't let it be forgot, that once there was a spot,
> for one brief shining moment that was known as Camelot.

The excitement touched not only Americans but also millions of people in other parts of the world.

In his memorably crafted inaugural address, which echoed—not always favorably—through the succeeding decades and became a measuring rod for future presidential oratory, Kennedy cautioned that his goals would "not be finished in the first one hundred days" nor "in the first one thousand days." The first evoked the memory of Franklin Roosevelt's New Deal; the second, unknowingly, was to define the remaining span of Kennedy's days until his death from an assassin's bullet in Dallas.

In a time of aging titans—Mao, Nehru, de Gaulle, the grandfatherly Adenauer, and the avuncular Macmillan and Eisenhower—it was exciting to have a young man, the first American president born in this century, as he reminded his inaugural listeners, at the head of a leading nation. During the presidential campaign, a Kennedy Peace Corps speech had stirred University of Michigan student newspaper editor Tom Hayden. Later, a Peace Corps volunteer explained why he had joined, saying, "Nobody ever asked me to do anything before, and then Kennedy did." In a November 1960 piece in *Esquire,* the novelist Norman Mailer projected Kennedy as the hero who could tap the "romantic possibilities" of a nation otherwise "drifting into a profound decline." In Mississippi, the day after the inauguration, air force veteran James Meredith sent in his application to attend college at the University of Mississippi.

John Kennedy was by temperament an activist. "I run for the Presidency of the United States," he explained to an election-eve crowd in the Boston Garden, "because it is the center of action." His most successful campaign themes had been action oriented: closing the missile gap and getting the economy going again. He had confidence in the national government as a problem solver and intended to be a strong president, but he did not have a developed agenda. Within existing parameters, he would deal intelligently with domestic problems and world affairs.

His primary interest was foreign policy. It dominated his inaugural address and two-thirds of the thousand pages of the 1965 Pulitzer Prize–winning biography written by his friend Arthur Schlesinger Jr., *A Thousand Days: John F. Kennedy in the White House*. Although Kennedy was imaginative in his dealings with world leaders and generally sensitive to the problems of emerging Third World nations, he accepted the cold war views that Castro's Cuba and a Communist Vietnam were perils to the United States and the world.

Controversy over Kennedy's foreign policy has continued unabated since his death. Initially, the failed 1961 Bay of Pigs invasion of Cuba was redeemed by the measured handling of the Cuban missile crisis the following year. The restrained use of American power to face down a Soviet nuclear expansion into the Western Hemisphere, which most people in the 1960s saw as the shining hour of Kennedy's leadership, would afterward be increasingly criticized as "brinksmanship" diplomacy and the cause of the Soviet nuclear build-up. A decade later, revelations about various secret overthrow and assassination plans gave an indication of the frenzies that overtake American policy whenever Fidel Castro and the Caribbean are involved. From the missile crisis, however, came Kennedy's "peace" speech at American University, the beginnings of a cold war thaw, and a subsequent treaty with the Soviet Union ending atmospheric nuclear testing. There may well also have been serious reconsideration, as various Kennedy aides have later testified, of the growing American involvement in Vietnam, but if there was, it led to no conclusions, touched no policies, and was not to be revealed until after the 1964 election.

The shape of Kennedy's role was just as unpredictable in the American civil rights struggle as it was in foreign policy. He had been elected president by a majority of only 118,000 out of 68 million votes cast, and he lacked solid support in Congress. Most of its Democratic members had carried their districts and states by larger majorities than the president's. In the Senate, Southerners chaired the crucial committees and combined with the Republicans for conservative control. When it took all the administration's strength to add two liberal members to Chairman Howard Smith's House Rules Committee, Senate citadels such as Mississippian James Eastland's Judiciary Committee seemed unassailable. Nor was Kennedy of a mind to challenge them.

The historians of his presidency generally agree that he initially approached civil rights as a matter of politics, not of morality. Although he wanted to make headway against what he considered "the nonsense of racial discrimination," he was not prepared to risk his legislative program for it. The initial strategy was to use executive action and not risk "certain failure" in Congress.

Kennedy held off making the promised "stroke of a pen" that would prohibit discrimination in federal housing. He appointed a number of conservative federal judges, including Senator Eastland's one-time college roommate, on the mistaken assurance that they would behave fairly. In return, the president was promised approval for the nomination of the NAACP's star lawyer, Thurgood Marshall, to the U.S. Court of Appeals. It was a trading matter. "Tell your brother that if he will give me Harold Cox," Senator Eastland told Robert Kennedy, "I will give him the nigger."

There was a conscious effort to open up the federal service, particularly at the upper levels, and to prohibit discrimination in employment and contracts. In the Justice Department, where the new attorney general learned that only ten of almost one thousand lawyers and none of the FBI agents were black, a major recruitment effort was made. Robert Kennedy himself wrote to forty-five law school deans asking for recommendations. The expanded Civil Rights Division of the Justice Department got busy on voting rights cases, and the White House conspicuously consulted black leaders. In 1962, a constitutional amendment banning poll taxes was sent to the states for ratification.

While black leaders appreciated Kennedy's personal openness, it was not enough. After a private talk with the president, King complained that Kennedy had the requisite "understanding and political skill," but the moral passion was missing. The civil rights strategy of the early sixties increasingly became one of forcing the issue in the streets, while the administration treated it as a problem of conflict containment. In 1961, when CORE's interstate bus riders were beaten in Alabama, the administration felt forced to provide protection on the highways, but it did not interfere when they were jailed for violating bus-terminal segregation in Mississippi. Although the Justice Department did push the Interstate Commerce Commission into ending such discrimination, the hundreds of riders left sitting in Mississippi jails and in Parchman State Penitentiary foreshadowed the growing problem of the federal government's inability, or failure, to provide adequate protection for civil rights workers.

The administration found the violence to be internationally embarrassing and sought to quiet the furor in the streets. As the demonstrators refused to accept "cooling off" periods, the administration tried to redirect the movement's activity to voter registration. This, they believed, would be less confrontational. Not only would it have the benefit of avoiding the mob violence that might force the politically costly use of federal troops, it could also provide new black votes for administration policies. As SNCC organizers learned in Mississippi, the administration was mistaken. Segregation was a seamless web, in which any pressure against the customary white hegemony was seen as threatening.

Kennedy's involvement began to shift with the battle to safely enroll James Meredith in the University of Mississippi. The president's frustration over his personal negotiations with Mississippi's buffoonish governor, Ross Barnett, turned to anger when Barnett withdrew the promised state police protection. A televised presidential appeal for order was ignored, and the riot had taken two lives on the Ole Miss campus by the time army troops belatedly arrived from Memphis to relieve the besieged federal marshals. Up to this point, the government had sought to make progress through traditional administrative and legal channels, while reserving the use of force for the maintenance of public order, not the civil rights of its citizens.

Those rights became the dominant national issue in 1963, when King's demonstrators faced "Bull" Connor's hoses, clubs, and dogs in downtown Birmingham, and the president moved to take a major role. As it had done during the crisis at Ole Miss, the administration privately put pressure on businessmen and state leaders for a compromise settlement. At the same time, Kennedy decided that the government must move beyond a reactive role and take leadership. In a television speech on June 11, 1963, which many of his historians believe was his finest, he proposed a major new law that would open up public life in the South. "We preach freedom around the world, and we mean it, and we cherish our freedom here at home," he said, "but are we to say to the world and much more importantly, to each other that this is the land of the free except for the Negroes; that we have no second-class citizens except Negroes; that we have no class or caste system, no ghettoes, no master race except with respect to Negroes?"

For the first time since Reconstruction, Congress was being asked to legislate equal rights for black Americans. In labeling this "the beginning of what can truly be called the Second Reconstruction," the civil rights historian Carl Brauer has pointed out that the president "moved from the periphery to the center of the civil rights controversy."

Starting in the late 1930s, presidential administrations had shown a growing, though sporadic, interest in the problems of African Americans. Although pressed by his wife, Eleanor, to do more, Franklin Roosevelt proposed no civil rights laws to Congress during the Depression years. In 1939, his attorney general, future Supreme Court justice Frank Murphy, did establish a Civil Rights Division in the Justice Department. Two years later, to head off a threatened protest "March on Washington" being organized by the black labor leader A. Philip Randolph, the president issued Executive Order 8802, which prohibited discriminatory practices in defense industries and the national government and set up a watchdog Fair Employment Practices Committee. After the war, Harry Truman ordered the desegregation of the armed services, and his Committee on Civil Rights issued a far-ranging report in 1947, entitled "To Secure These Rights," which recommended a legislative program to end segregation and provide protection for minorities. In 1957 and 1960, the Eisenhower administration and the Democratic Congress combined on limited efforts aimed at helping black people get to the ballot box in the South. The new laws brought no major changes, but for a civil rights law to be passsed for the first time in three-quarters of a century was itself an indication that something was stirring. Change was taking place, but not yet in the consciousness of the nation. No national leader, white or black, anticipated the rising in the streets and the changes in race relations that lay ahead.

The black migration that had been drawn to the North and the West by jobs in the war industries continued after the war. By the end of the 1960s, half of all black Americans would be living outside of the South. Black votes were becoming politically important in key industrial states, and black union membership was growing. Within the South, black people were moving to the large cities such as Atlanta and Birmingham, where the number of registered black voters was growing. The urban ghettos across the nation were expanding at the same time that an educated, middle-class and professional black leadership was emerging.

John Kennedy's call for a strong public accommodations law promised no certainty as to its results. Racial violence continued unabated. Several hours after Kennedy's televised address, the Mississippi NAACP leader Medgar Evers was killed from ambush in front of his home. His assassin not only went unpunished but drew a substantial vote when he later ran for lieutenant governor. In the school desegregation cases, the Supreme Court had based its decision on the special importance of public education, but it had not rejected the "separate but equal" principle for other state action. The administration felt it safer not to ask the Court to directly overturn *Plessy* v. *Ferguson*. Instead, it argued that open accommodations were part of the power of Congress over the flow of interstate commerce. While the administration lobbied the business community, Attorney General Robert Kennedy aggressively carried the burden of testimony before the Senate Commerce Committee.

CONGRESS

In a speech to Congress five days after John Kennedy's death, Lyndon Johnson's message was "Let us continue." "No memorial oration or eulogy could more eloquently honor the President's memory," he said, "than the earliest possible passage of the civil rights bill for which he fought." The emotions stirred by the death of the president, together with Johnson's political skills and commitment, the floor leadership of Democratic senator Hubert Humphrey, and the support of Republican minority leader Everett Dirksen, succeeded in breaking a Southern filibuster against civil rights for the first time. In July 1964, the civil rights bill was the law of the land.

If the legislative battle was intricate and intense, the results fully warranted it. The Civil Rights Act of 1964 was a landmark action. As far as a law could, it mandated the desegregation of a major portion of the public life. With the exception of some very small establishments (covered in the so-called "Mrs. Murphy" clause), it barred discrimination in public accommodations, eating places, hotels and motels, gas stations, places of sports and amusement, and all other public facilities; and it prohibited threats against anyone trying to use them. It pushed voter registration, provided federal funds to help school desegregation, authorized the withholding of federal funds from discriminatory programs, authorized the Census Bureau to collect appropriate information, renewed the Civil Rights Commission, established the Equal Employment Opportunity Commission and the Community Relations Service, and gave the Justice Department a broad mandate to take action.

There was still more. When the Fair Employment section of the act, Title VII, was under consideration, the word "sex" was added to the prohibition of employment discrimination on the grounds of "race, color, religion, and national origin." While the act, also known as the Public Accommodations Act, or the 1964 Civil Rights Law, was generally aimed at racial discrimination, Title VII carried its egalitarian and nationalizing role much further. In ruling illegal most of the major discriminatory categories, it reached far beyond race. Buttressing and interacting with the Supreme Court's broad replacement of local and state standards and behavior, it added these categories to national review. Like the Fourteenth Amendment to the Constitution, the Civil Rights Act of 1964 offered a complex and powerful heritage to the nation's future.

During the congressional battle over the law, the voting rights provisions had seemed the least controversial. Now they seemed the least successful. The students whom SNCC brought to Mississippi for the summer voter registration projects found that the law made no difference. In Selma, Alabama, King commented that at the current rate it would take "about 103 years" to get the eligible Negroes registered. Meanwhile, Sheriff Jim Clark, his deputies, and various other local whites seemed intent on reducing the number of living eligibles. President Johnson was determined to open up the ballot box. In a prime-time televised speech to Congress, he asserted, "It is not just Negroes, but it is really all of us who must overcome the crippling legacy of bigotry and injustice." With his face, seemingly larger than life, filling the television screen, he promised, "And we shall overcome!" When finally committed, both John Kennedy and Lyndon Johnson made forceful use of television to push the moral education of their countrymen.

The Voting Rights Act of 1965 suspended literacy tests, set up a formula for the government to send registrars to counties and states that blocked black access to the ballot box, and required Justice Department approval of any changes in the election procedures of suspect communities. Although there was complaint that the administration of the law was too cautious, the effort to seek voluntary compliance was generally successful. Federal registrars were dispatched to only sixty-two Southern counties, while the percentage of registered black voters quickly approached that of whites. By 1968, the black voters in Mississippi had increased from 6 to 44 percent of those eligible. The voluntary approach brought a general acceptance that helped override conservative opposition to the extension of the Voting Rights Act in the 1970s and 1980s. By the latter decade, the focus of its administration was no longer on registration but on those arrangements, such as districting, that diluted black voting strength. As with schooling, the shift had been from the removal of obstacles to the enhancement of results.

The last major congressional civil rights action dealing with race came three years later. The prohibition of discrimination in the sale or rental of housing reached beyond the South to touch the sensitive neighborhood and pocketbook nerves of the whole nation. The civil rights movement and national attitudes were in transition. Against a backdrop of ghetto riots and Black Power slogans, a growingly conservative Congress turned down "open housing" bills in 1966 and 1967 and made jokes about a proposed program for dealing with rat infestation in the urban ghettos. When the housing law did pass in April 1968, after the murder of Martin Luther King Jr., it contained a backlash provision making it a crime to cross state lines for the purpose of creating a riot.

In the federal system of government, most crimes fall under state jurisdiction. This was the case with racial violence in the 1960s. Although the FBI was able to identify the Klansmen who had murdered the three civil rights workers in Neshoba County, Mississippi; Army Reserve Lt. Colonel Lemuel Penn on the highway outside of Athens, Georgia; and Viola Liuzzo in Lowndes County, Alabama, after the march on Selma, local juries refused to convict. Eventually, under hundred-year-old Reconstruction-era statutes, federal juries sent the Klansmen to jail for short periods on lesser charges of violating their victims' civil rights. In upholding the conviction of Colonel Penn's killers (*U.S.* v. *Guest* [1966]), the Supreme Court took the unusual step of indicating that it would accept a broad congressional law prohibiting violent conspiracies to interfere with civil rights. With the 1968 law, civil rights murder became a federal crime. In the changed atmosphere at the end of the 1960s, the act's prohibition of riot incitement was used in the government's prosecution of the "Chicago Eight" for their street demonstrations at the 1968 Democratic National Convention.

Although Congress had finished what it was willing to do for the civil rights of racial minorities, the awakened spirit of the Fourteenth Amendment's "equal protection of the laws" carried over into other areas. Title IX of the 1972 Education Act broadened the 1964 Public Accommodation Law's prohibition against sex discrimination, and the Rehabilitation Act of 1973 and the Age Discrimination Act of 1975 gave handicapped and elderly people protection against unequal treatment in any federally assisted program. With these laws, the Congress had extended protection to the civil rights of racial and ethnic minorities, women, the handicapped, and older Americans.

THE JUSTICE DEPARTMENT AND THE FBI

Once the laws were on the books, their meaning depended upon the ways in which they were applied and accepted. The chief enforcement agencies were the Department of Health, Education, and Welfare (HEW), the Justice Department, and the courts. Within the Justice Department, two almost fratricidal forces, Attorney General Robert Kennedy and FBI director J. Edgar Hoover, faced each other. At the beginning of the decade, neither had been much concerned with racial justice. Kennedy's commitment became both a political and a moral one, which grew until his death. He developed the Justice Department's Civil Rights Division into a strong instrument and took the lead in the various negotiations with Southern governors. His initial strategy of turning black activism from street demonstrations to voter registration created the problem of protection, particularly in Mississippi. Administration leaders explained that under the American federal system, the national government lacked jurisdiction. Embattled civil rights workers in the South questioned how the United States could fight a war for the freedom of Vietnamese ten thousand miles across the Pacific while refusing to protect American citizens in Mississippi.

Robert Kennedy did manage to push the FBI into action, but at the cost of J. Edgar Hoover's maintaining operational control. Unlike the attorney general, the director of the FBI never became concerned about the rights of black people. He had come to depend on Southern congressmen and senators to support FBI appropriations, and on the local police forces, now accused of civil rights brutalities, who had helped build the FBI's reputation for solving crimes. When pushed, the FBI did identify the gunman or the bomber and produce the evidence, even if local juries refused to convict, but this was not Hoover's view of its proper role. When violence erupted, the FBI agent usually stood across the street, taking notes. Why had the agent not intervened to help President Kennedy's personal representative, John Seigenthaler, lying in the street in Montgomery, beaten unconscious for trying to protect two women Freedom Riders? "If the agent should become personally involved in the action, he would be deserting his assigned task and would be unable to fulfill his primary responsibility of making objective observations," the FBI explained.

With administration approval, the FBI was just as likely to spy on the civil rights activists as on the Ku Klux Klan. Robert Kennedy authorized the electronic surveillance of Martin Luther King Jr., which Hoover turned into a campaign of character assassination. Justifying a telephone tap because of King's close relationships with two former Communist party members, Hoover expanded the surveillance into an attempt to destroy King. King's biographer David Garrow has shown that the FBI's attack on King went through three stages: first, a concern about possible Communist influence; next, a belief that the black leader was a dangerously immoral person; and finally, a belief that he was a sinister, radical threat to the American social order. After King's speech on the steps of the Lincoln Memorial during the 1963 March on Washington, Hoover concluded that the whole of black America would have to be contained, and he ordered a broad program of systematic surveillance and harassment.

THE DEPARTMENT OF HEALTH, EDUCATION, AND WELFARE

Since segregation was not actually written into the legal system in the North, it was harder to attack there, but in many school districts it was just as pervasive as it was in the South. When the national government entered school financing with the 1965 Elementary and Secondary Education Act, the Department of Health, Education, and Welfare had an opportunity to put into action the 1964 Civil Rights Act's authorization to cut off funding to discriminatory programs. Since the beginning of the Republic, education had been the concern of the states, and it was not until 1918, when Mississippi finally made the move, that all of them required some measure of public school attendance. Church and state questions helped block Harry Truman's attempt to introduce federal aid to education in the 1940s, but Lyndon Johnson's sweeping election victory over Barry Goldwater and the law's focus on programs for poor children helped overcome religious and racial objections. Almost immediately it became a powerful tool for integration. President Johnson stood behind HEW's Office of Education as it applied pressure to Southern school districts. When it tried to carry the fight north to Chicago, Johnson was not willing to battle his own powerful ally Mayor Richard J. Daly. Court-ordered busing, upheld by the Supreme Court in 1971 for Charlotte, North Carolina, would have to wait a while to make its uncertain start in the North.

THE COURTS

In 1955, the Supreme Court had turned over the supervision of school desegregation to the U.S. District Courts, to be pursued with the undefined guideline of "all deliberate speed." Using redistricting, freedom of choice, and nondiscriminatory neighborhood schools, the border states basically conformed. For those district judges who tried to carry out the mandate in the Deep South, the title that J. W. Peltason gave to their history, *Fifty-eight Lonely Men* (1961), indicates that supervising school desegregation was not a happy task. Nevertheless, with proper higher court support, a committed and energetic federal judge could make his guidance felt. George Wallace's University of Alabama classmate Frank Johnson assumed supervision over Alabama's prisons, highway patrol, property-tax assessment, mental health facilities, and public school systems. "If the state abdicates its responsibilities, the federal courts are not powerless to act," he said.

All but unknown to the general public, the U.S. Fifth Circuit Court of Appeals played a crucial role in the Deep South. On that bench, four judges, Elbert Tuttle, John Minor Wisdom, Richard Rives, and John Brown (three of them Republicans appointed by President Eisenhower) combined to fight segregationist politicians and judges. In pathbreaking decisions, they removed cases from state to federal courts, provided judicial protection for civil rights workers, and tackled racial discrimination in jobs, jury selection, education, and voting. Among the landmark Supreme Court decisions whose way they pioneered were the doctrines of "affirmative duty," "one man, one vote," and the protection of First Amendment rights from the "chilling effect" of state harassment.

During the debate on the 1964 Civil Rights Act, both houses of Congress had specifically stated that school desegregation did not mean that student assignment should be used to overcome racial imbalance. If the public schools were thus to be color-blind, however, how would actual integration take place? The combined efforts of the Department of Health, Education, and Welfare and the federal judiciary supplied the answer, and it was not racially neutral.

The Fifth Circuit Court's approval of HEW's 1966 desegregation "guidelines" (*U.S.* v. *Jefferson County Board of Education*) and the Supreme Court's orders to get the process going (*Green* v. *New Kent County* [1968]), represented an accelerated new phase. In a development that would reverberate through minority groups' and women's struggles during the succeeding decades, the focus had shifted from the removal of barriers to the government's positive responsibility to promote equal treatment. The government could not pretend to be color-blind. For desegregation to become integration, affirmative action was necessary. This, argued its proponents, sometimes including the Supreme Court, meant giving special help to the formerly disadvantaged. While the political and judicial arguments of the 1980s would challenge the legal principle of affirmative action, the attention of the later 1960s and early 1970s was on how to bring black and white children together in the same schools.

The "Warren majority" on the Court was still strong enough to press forward when the chief justice retired in 1968 and President Nixon appointed Warren Burger to succeed him. The Court replaced its "all deliberate speed" guideline with an order that Mississippi immediately integrate its public schools (*Alexander* v. *Holmes* [1969]), approved busing to attain racial balance (*Swann* v. *Charlotte-Mecklenburg Board of Education* [1971]), and moved out of the South with its order to Denver, Colorado, to integrate its inner-city schools (*Keyes* v. *School District No. 1, Denver, Colorado* [1973]). Beyond this, where segregation was the product of social and economic conditions, not statute law, an increasingly divided Court found no clear path. In a pair of cases involving Detroit and Richmond, the Court struck down district court-ordered busing across school district lines that had not been drawn for racial reasons. Increasingly, the nation was being divided between minority group inner cities and "white flight" suburbs.

THE SHIFT TO NATIONAL STANDARDS

The unprecedented force of judicial activism that the courts poured into the struggle for equal treatment was not limited to issues of race. Human motivation is complex, involving chance combinations of internal and external factors such as social circumstance, events, beliefs, and personal interactions. It can be only a matter of conjecture that excitement over *Brown* and the subsequent school integration cases may have touched the internal chemistry of the Supreme Court and given at least a majority of its members an unspoken sense of responsibility to clarify crucial constitutional values. In the history of the American Republic, the impact of the "Warren Court" has been matched only by John Marshall's nationalism, the late nineteenth-century judicial advancement of corporate capitalism, and the later New Deal acceptance of the liberal regulatory state. None did as much to set the pattern of individual freedoms or created greater controversy.

In summing up his contributions to the law of the land, Warren singled out school desegregation (*Brown*), reapportionment (*Baker* v. *Carr* [1962]), and the right to counsel (*Gideon* v. *Wainwright* [1963]). The most important, he believed, was reapportionment. With its "one man, one vote" standard, *Baker* v. *Carr* went into an area hitherto considered "too political" for the courts and became the precedent for establishing equal election districts at all levels of government. Particularly in the South, where small groups of rural legislators dominated state legislatures, reapportionment meant accelerating the modernization of the whole region.

Gideon, along with *Miranda* v. *Arizona* (1966), which required the reading of rights at the time of arrest, and other Warren Court decisions, changed basic criminal procedure in the states. Their effect was to apply most of the national Bill of Rights as a limitation on state law. The "due process" clause of the Fourteenth Amendment was used to extend constitutional protection against self-incrimination and to guarantee legal counsel and jury trials. Illegally seized evidence, including the results of wiretapping, could not be used in court.

Even this was not all of the "Warren revolution." In a series of libertarian decisions, the Court broadened the reach of the First Amendment. In overturning many of the cold war restrictions of the 1950s and the "age of McCarthyism," the Court drew a line between advocacy of doctrine and advocacy of action, freeing the former from prosecution. The recognition of a congressional monopoly overturned state sedition laws, and protection against self-incrimination nullified Communist-registration laws. Concern about fair procedure, and vagueness of legislative purpose, severely limited Congressional loyalty investigations and headline hunting.

In a case rising out of the civil rights struggle in Alabama, *New York Times* v. *Sullivan* (1964), the Court broadened the press's protection from libel actions by public officials. If the standards of "actual malice" or "reckless disregard" of the truth were less than definitive, they were clear by comparison with the Court's effort to define obscenity. The justices assumed jurisdiction from the states but were not able to decide what actually was impermissible, and thus they greatly increased the permissiveness of the law. In the areas of First Amendment rights, as with race relations and criminal procedure, the Warren Court was shifting power away from local communities and the states. This underlying nationalization of standards and power was the revolution within the revolution. In handling its cases, the Court broadened its "preferred-freedoms" standard to include race, voting, and fair criminal procedure as areas in which state action was subject to a more severe federal court scrutiny and justification. In the 1980s, legislation touching on women's rights would receive closer examination, although it was not fully added to this "suspect classification."

For all the controversy these changes produced, a more intense and lasting furor arose over religion and abortion. In a series of decisions centering on *Engel* v. *Vitale* (1962) and *School District of Abington Township* v. *Schempp* (1963), the Court found prayer and Bible reading in public schools to be in violation of the separation of church and state. In overturning state opposition to the distribution of birth control information and devices (*Griswold* v. *Connecticut* [1965]), the Court established the right of privacy as a constitutional principle. In 1973, the Burger Court applied it in *Roe* v. *Wade* and *Doe* v. *Bolton* to strike down state prohibition of abortion, at least in the first trimester. For decades after, as the segregationists' "Impeach Earl Warren" billboards were a fading memory in the South, angry political and religious conservatives were still rallying in front of women's health clinics and on the steps of the Supreme Court Building as the abortion issue heated up in the 1980s.

In a time when the Supreme Court's docket was dominated by civil rights questions, the crucial measure for Earl Warren was not precedent but "fairness." "Yes, yes," he would say to the lawyers before him, "but were you fair?" Although the 1953–68 era will bear his name in history, Warren did not dominate the Court as John Marshall had done at its beginnings, and he did not match Marshall as a judicial thinker or draftsman. Despite the other justices' personal respect for him, the unity of the *Brown* school case was not typical outside of desegregation issues. What was decisive was the existence of an activist liberal majority among the justices of the Court, whose concern with equality and the rights of the individual continued to pervade the Court after Warren's retirement. In a period of economic growth and general well-being, the Supreme Court took the lead in making social and political adjustments, contradicting Alexander Hamilton's prediction in the *Federalist Papers* that the judiciary would be "the weakest" and the "least dangerous" branch of the federal government. Although it drew great public criticism, the direction taken by the Warren Court was in keeping with the emerging pattern of national history, whose consciousness and structure it helped shape.

THE LAWYERS

An important player in the game of racial change was the civil rights lawyer, hero to the intellectual radicals and generally missing from the history books. In theory, the judicial system, moving with majestic formalism, is the branch of government most remote from the popular will and passion. In the second half of the twentieth century, it became the swiftest path for the assertion of minority rights. Along with the legal staffs of the American Civil Liberties Union and the NAACP, a whole generation of movement lawyers emerged, defending civil rights activists and other social dissenters and constructing arguments with which to lever the federal courts into pressing for social change. Traditionally, it was difficult to get Southern lawyers to take such unpopular cases. Charles Morgan, who was to become the ACLU's Southern legal director, was driven from the state of Alabama for speaking out against racial violence, while accused Klansmen did not lack for counsel.

Black lawyers were too few in the South. The NAACP relied heavily on those local lawyers they could find to carry on the initial phases of litigation, and many of these lawyers were not skilled at getting appeal issues into the record. Much of SNCC's help in Mississippi came from the leftist National Lawyers Guild. As the 1960s moved on, radical lawyers such as William Kunstler, Arthur Kinoy, and Len Holt (whom a prosecutor called "that smart nigger bastard who tries to make fools of white folks") were increasingly joined by young white and black law-school graduates in fighting the traditional social control patterns of Southern politics. Their primary strategy was to try to have the case "removed" to federal court where local prejudice was less likely to prevail and where procedural rules benefited the plaintiffs. The removal authority of the federal courts, which one hundred years before had been used to protect corporate economic rights, was now an important civil rights instrument. Illustrative of the importance of the civil rights lawyers was their attack on Louisiana's Un-American Activities Committee, which the state used to harass civil rights workers. The result of their appeal was the landmark 1965 *Dombrowski* v. *Pfister* decision, in which the Court struck down state actions designed to have "a chilling effect upon the exercise of First Amendment Rights."

LOCAL STORIES

Public interest tends to focus on conflict. The piecemeal working out of change is less dramatic and receives less attention. Local history has traditionally concerned itself with the more distant past, and in the North race relations have been treated by the local historians with no more enthusiasm than by the politicians. The younger scholars whom Elizabeth Jacoway and David Colburn (*Southern Businessmen and Desegregation* [1982]) drew together to describe what happened in fourteen Southern cities provided suggestive patterns. Under pressure from Washington, the courts, and their black citizens, some business communities helped ease their cities into accepting at least a minimal start on integration. Good governors helped in South Carolina, Kentucky, and Georgia. Opportunistic racists such as Orval Faubus in Arkansas, George Wallace in Alabama, and Ross Barnett in Mississippi did not. Where there had been some interracial communication, or where dedicated individuals undertook to prepare their communities, a beginning was made relatively without serious conflict, as happened in Atlanta; Tampa; Dallas; and Columbia, South Carolina. A concern for "modernizing" a community, enhancing its national reputation, and attracting new industry helped. Black leaders were usually ministers; in the white communities, the leaders were usually businessmen. Such white leaders were basically segregation-minded themselves, and their reluctance to act often permitted, and sometimes encouraged, racial disorder. When elites did assert leadership, it was usually in the name of protecting order and preserving public education and economic growth. In more traditional cities such as St. Augustine, Florida; Louisville; Augusta, Georgia; and Memphis, where there was little growth or where the business community did not offer leadership, there was trouble.

Local history can tell interesting stories. Leaders in Atlanta consciously studied the experience of Little Rock and escaped a violent confrontation; those in New Orleans did not. South Carolina's capital city, Columbia, set a pattern for peaceful integration and "all-American-city" status. In Jackson, Mississippi, business leaders feared further extremism. Their concern about losing growth and federal aid, together with new black voting strength, brought about the election of moderates to city office. As elsewhere, institutions changed first; attitudes changed more slowly, and black poverty remained untouched.

Often traditional black leaders, such as ministers, teachers, and funeral directors, who had stayed away from the movement, now combined with white moderates to squeeze out "the radicals" and run the antipoverty programs. SNCC formally left Mississippi after the summer of 1965, and many remaining volunteers and local organizers didn't want to be brought into what they disparagingly called "the white, middle class liberal army." The Office of Economic Opportunity (OEO) in Washington, D.C., helped Mississippi's governor to build a safe "loyalist" Democratic party using antipoverty funds as patronage. Grass-roots organizations such as the Mississippi Child Development Group's head start program were pushed aside; movement opposition to the Vietnam War was denounced as pro-Communist, and male preachers and teachers replaced female activists.

Even by the end of the 1960s, the swiftness of change in social attitudes shown in studies of racial belief seemed to lend justification to the social psychologist Thomas Pettigrew's argument that the Southern enthusiasm for segregation was at least as much the product of social pressure as the result of any basic personality needs. With the level of education the leading factor in acceptance, a growing majority of Southerners appeared willing to live with a condition intermediate between segregation and integration, though they were unhappy over busing and affirmative action quotas.

While power shifts did not take place, there was a turnabout in public and political behavior. However grudging at first, there was a personal acceptance of the new conditions and relationships. Although the Robert E. Lee Motel in Jackson went out of business, Lester Maddox waved axe handles at blacks who tried to enter his Atlanta Restaurant, the holes of Birmingham's municipal golf course were filled with cement, and some Southern communities drained their municipal swimming pools and let them sit empty until the sun's rays cracked the concrete, the South accepted a new way of life.

The proportion of registered black voters approached that of whites. Moderate governors and the more careful sheriffs campaigned on issues other than race, though integration plans and methods of evading them were the central staple of school board elections. In many communities across the Black-Belt South, voting reform meant opening up the electoral process to black majorities who now struggled to wrest some say in their communities from the entrenched power structures of white minorities. Despite white flight from the public school system, HEW and the courts pushed beyond "freedom of choice" and token integration. By 1970, school desegregation, at least on some level, had proceeded further in the South than in the big cities of the North. The major problems taking shape were the quality of education and the continuing population shifts that were suburbanizing white America and leaving urban schools increasingly black.

The "elaborate structure and pervasive ethos of Jim Crow" which

V. O. Key had described in his classic analysis was fading. Its destruction did not produce a new, economics- and class-based politics in the South, but did mean at least token representation for blacks, inclusion in municipal services, and a new politeness in racial politics. The political analysts Jack Bass and Walter De Vries (*The Transformation of Southern Politics: Social and Political Consequences since 1945* [1977]) summed it up by saying that "blacks have changed their status from political object to political participant." Bass and De Vries concluded with the words of Greenville, Mississippi—and sometimes national—journalist Hodding Carter III. "I'll tell you who's really free in Mississippi for the first time," he said. "It's not the black man, who still is economically about as much in bondage as he ever was. By God, the white Mississippian is free. . . . That's the hardest thing to remember now—how tiny a thing you could do ten years ago and be in desperate difficulty."

The civil rights revolution was becoming part of law and governmental practice. The changes were a combination of command and consciousness. Statutes, litigation, court rulings, pressures, negotiations, elections, and black voter registration brought changes in rules and behavior. Laws and public policies that overtly discriminated against black people in education, voting, housing, transportation, and accommodations were disappearing. The new 1964, 1965, and 1968 national public accommodations, voting, and housing and protection laws provided civil rights litigants with the advantage of legislative standards in the place of less certain common law and equity rules. National standards, reaching far beyond questions of race, were replacing local ones across the country. The battles against discrimination were of vital importance, and the gain was great. However, the civil rights struggle was but a part of the larger and more difficult struggle for equality and opportunity. While the political revolution was beginning to open up the public life of the South, it had much less effect on the conditions of poverty which imprisoned not only blacks and other minorities but also many of the aged and the young of all races.

4. Poverty and Progress

While the civil rights revolution was removing racial restrictions, it had much less effect on the economic barriers in the South and across the nation. Although a majority of the poor people in America were not black, racial prejudice and poverty reinforced each other.

It was only in the twentieth century that poverty became more than a problem for law and order, charity, and the county purse. The urban reformers of the early twentieth-century Progressive Era sought to protect the poor and the working classes by means of building and safety codes, limitations on women's working hours and child labor, meat inspection, and a pure food and drug act. The "first" New Deal of the 1930s was aimed at fostering economic recovery, reforming the financial institutions, and providing at least a minimum of support to keep people going. After the Supreme Court overturned the National Recovery Act in 1935, the "second" New Deal attempted to stimulate the economy by attacking the power of business and building up the competitive position of labor. Only with the jobs and income programs of the Works Progress Administration (WPA) and Social Security was there a serious attempt, similar to the attention given to the land under the Tennessee Valley Authority and the Farm Security Administration, to deal with the root causes of poverty. More important than the various institutional reforms, such as the regulation of the stock market, was the government's assumption of the responsibility for ensuring the basic survival of the poor and maintaining the necessary level of economic activity and employment.

THE LEAP OF CONSCIOUSNESS

For all the achievements and good intentions of regulatory government and the anti-Depression efforts of the New Deal, it was not until the 1960s that the national government reached the radical conclusion that it should attempt to attack poverty itself. The civil rights struggle, which shook up so many customary social patterns, drew attention to the poor; and the postwar economic growth and affluence made poverty seem both wrong and unnecessary.

To attempt to do something about poverty meant fighting deeply entrenched ideas. Jesus spoke of its inevitability, and the classical economist Thomas Malthus calculated that because of human fecundity, it could not be otherwise. While modern societies responded in various ways to the problems of the poor, ending poverty was something different. A leap of consciousness was needed to arrive at the belief that poverty could be substantially eliminated. The radicalness of this effort is even more surprising because of the conventional nature of Lyndon Johnson's economic thinking. He sought to eliminate poverty without redistributing the wealth or changing the structure of American capitalism. Through growth, the free-enterprise American capitalist system would provide the resources for the government to help the poor climb out of poverty and join the system. If Johnson's economics were conventional, his ambition was not.

How was the escape from poverty to be fostered? All public efforts faced the traditional perception that the poor were in one way or another responsible for their own condition, and that any form of support would only produce more children. The conventional attitude was that the public purse should not be raided to teach the poor that indolence and incontinence paid. Given the persistence of this paradigm in the minds of both the public and the Congress, it is remarkable that so much effort came to be focused on the social welfare sector of the society.

The new conventional wisdom was that the laws of the economist Malthus could only be overthrown with the aid of the economist Keynes. With proper stimulation, the economy could produce jobs, a higher standard of living, and a surplus to provide for the indigent. The way it went was that "a rising tide lifts all boats." Prosperity would bring opportunity for everyone willing to struggle for it. John Kennedy accepted this, and proposed a tax cut to stimulate the economy. With the income that it produced, the government could do something about "the poverty and degradation" he had lamented during his presidential campaign.

Kennedy had been moved by the poverty he had seen while campaigning in West Virginia and by two books, John K. Galbraith's *The Affluent Society* (1958) and Michael Harrington's *The Other America* (1962). The Keynesian, Galbraith, argued that while production had solved the traditional tensions over inequality and insecurity, the government needed to spend more in the public sector to attack the remaining poverty. In a small book laden with statistics and passion, the Socialist, Harrington, disputed Galbraith's assertion that poverty was no longer a "massive affliction." Using four thousand dollars as the poverty line for a family of four, he described the lives of the one-quarter of the American population which lived below it. When those just above the line were also considered, almost half of the population, or some 77 million Americans, lived lives of deprivation or insecurity. The president directed his chief economist, Walter Heller, to prepare an antipoverty program, to which he planned to give first priority after the civil rights bill and the tax cut had passed the Congress.

LBJ

In his first meeting after John Kennedy's death, the new president renewed the assignment. "Go ahead," Johnson said. "Give it the highest priority. Push ahead full tilt." Selecting Sargent Shriver, Kennedy's Peace Corps director and brother-in-law, to head the program, Johnson sought something that would "be big and bold and hit the whole nation with real impact." It was to be the centerpiece of his administration. Kennedy had civil rights; the War on Poverty would be Johnson's.

John Kennedy and the man he had chosen for his vice-president each faced an historic American political handicap, Kennedy's Roman Catholic religion and Johnson's identity as a Southerner, and both were alike in their absorption in politics. Together, they reshaped the social agenda of American politics but at the same time thrust the nation into a destructive colonial war that threatened to unravel the gains. As Johnson succeeded the murdered president in the White House, he pushed Kennedy's civil rights and tax cut proposals through Congress and followed them with an extensive antipoverty program. John Kennedy's New Frontier had become the core of Johnson's Great Society.

To Kennedy's agendas Johnson added civil rights laws to open up voting and housing and increase federal protection against violence; medical insurance for the aged, medical care for the poor, and funds for medical research and training; a major federal role in education from kindergarten through graduate school; the new, cabinet level Departments of Housing and Urban Development (HUD) and Transportation (DOT); the Model Cities program, which built housing and provided rent supplements for the poor; federal endowment for the arts and the humanities; and Senator Edmund Muskie's clean air and rivers legislation. With senators of Norwegian and Irish descent, Hubert Humphrey and Edward ("Ted") Kennedy, Johnson persuaded Congress to replace the discriminatory immigration system enacted after World War I. So many important beginnings and an overwhelming 61-percent electoral victory in 1964 over his Republican opponent Barry Goldwater, did not free Lyndon Johnson from personal insecurity. He lacked John Kennedy's cool serenity and the ability to stand off from himself in detached evaluation. As Stanley Kutler writes in

The Wars of Watergate (1990), "the Pedernales did not flow through Camelot." Johnson had become his own hero in a world that he must completely intimidate and dominate. Nothing was ever enough. John Kennedy, television's first political superstar, carefully avoided overexposure. Johnson wanted to be on all the other networks at the same time, all the time. Power brought Johnson admiration but not affection. People had wanted to be like John Kennedy, but no one wanted to be like Lyndon Johnson.

Since his college days at Southwest Texas State Teachers College, Johnson had driven himself to succeed, focusing enormous energy on establishing relationships and persuading people. He came to Washington in 1931 as a twenty-three year old secretary to a conservative Texas congressman, became a Roosevelt protégé as national youth administrator in Texas and later a New Deal congressman from Austin, and developed a close relationship with the Speaker of the House Sam Rayburn. In 1948, in a hotly disputed election, he was elected to the Senate by eighty-seven votes that were discovered a week after the polls closed. As he had with Sam Rayburn, Johnson cultivated a relationship with Georgia's powerful insider senator Richard Russell. In three years he was the Senate majority leader. Overwhelming in intense one-to-one personal persuasion, Johnson poured his enormous energy into gaining an understanding of his fellow senators, their needs, and their political situations. The tart Washington columnists Evans and Novak watched him operate and named his method "the Johnson treatment" and "the Johnson network." His natural constituency was the Senate, where, as another commentator wrote, he could "work his magic in the flesh, one vote at a time," never able to equal the success of Kennedy, and later Ronald Reagan, in using television to wholesale their charm into the living rooms of America.

Although other biographers have had difficulty treating Johnson and his presidency kindly, leading Southern historians such as T. Harry Williams and Joe B. Frantz believed that his commitment to the poor was sincere and deep. The War on Poverty, they concluded, was linked to Johnson's past, and came out of his own struggles in the parched hill country of the Pedernales, combined with his experience teaching Mexican-American schoolchildren in Cotulla, his National Youth Administration days in Texas, and his New Deal experience in Washington.

Both Kennedy and Johnson saw the attack on poverty as releasing the idealism of youth. It appealed to Kennedy as a way to follow up his inaugural call for commitment and effort. For Lyndon Johnson, it fitted in with his desire to help people and to be a new Franklin Roosevelt. According to T. Harry Williams, Johnson was "overpowering in man-to-man persuasion," but "not cherished by the masses of people he had helped, and by whom he wanted to be loved." In *Decade of Disillusionment: The Kennedy-Johnson Years* (1975), Jim Heath summed up Johnson as "a proud and vain man, consumed by the desire to be a great president."

In his 1964 State of the Union Message and a special report to Congress, Johnson called for a national War on Poverty, which he included in the vision of the Great Society that he offered at the University of Michigan later that spring. The Economic Opportunity Act of 1964 was passed by both houses of Congress with remarkable speed, and was ready for signing by the end of the summer. The War on Poverty that began in the 1960s was of a complexity that went beyond a single legislative program. In various forms, the policies, the controversies, and the poverty still exist. Taken together, they have had a major impact on the role of government, the inflation of the 1970s, the budgetary deficits of the 1980s and the 1990s, and the direction of national politics.

There was a considerable difference between the recovery programs of the New Deal and the antipoverty wars of the 1960s and after. In his presidential autobiography *The Vantage Point* (1971), Lyndon Johnson summed up the distinction between a people "temporarily dislocated by the sickness of the economy" and the different "poverty in the midst of plenty" of people trapped in a "hopeless cycle from a deprived youth to a bleak and despairing old age." The War on Poverty was "an imaginative program," T. Harry Williams wrote, but not one aimed at redistributing wealth or challenging the private-enterprise system. Reaching beyond the formal War on Poverty program, generaled by Sargent Shriver in the new Office of Economic Opportunity (OEO), there were three major approaches: the Kennedy tax cut; OEO's human restructuring programs; and the income support (or transfer) payments, which were expanded in the sixties and continued to increase thereafter. Of these, the various payments and benefits were seen as the least important in the antipoverty planning but would eventually cost the most and have the greatest impact.

THE TAX CUT, OEO, AND INCOME SUPPORT

Although most government planners recognized that basic poverty was not the result of the business cycle, Johnson had reason to push John Kennedy's tax cut through Congress. The economic boom that it helped stimulate was necessary to provide both more jobs and the government income to pay for antipoverty programs. The disabled, the elderly, and many families headed by women lay outside the job cycle, and some 5 million employed heads of family brought home incomes below the poverty line. The Office of Economic Opportunity sought to provide training and support to lift at least the young out of poverty. The traditional instrument of this kind of human-capital effort in America is education. As the school system was given the responsibility of desegregating American society, so education and training were basic to the attack on poverty. Head Start would work with preschool children, usually black, and Upward Bound would offer bright high schoolers a chance at college. The Neighborhood Youth Corps was to provide inner city children with work experience and income. The Job Corps would take other young people out of their impoverished environments for intensive training and education. A domestic Peace Corps, Volunteers in Service to America (VISTA), would harness the enthusiasm of the more affluent. Community Action and later the Model Cities program set up neighborhood health centers, provided legal services for the poor, and attempted to involve the poor in program development and leadership under the mandate to seek their "maximum feasible participation." When the federal government entered the field of schooling with the 1965 Elementary and Secondary Education Act, money was set aside for students from deprived backgrounds.

The tax cut's direct benefits went to upper- and middle-income people, and it was the stronger groups, not the weaker, that benefited from a prosperous economy. Where poverty was structurally entrenched, economic growth and even improved job skills did not touch it. Crucial to the problem of poverty was direct income aid, which had more of an impact on the poor and the national budget than did the skills development programs of the OEO. From the vantage point of many sociologists, the greatest need of the poor was money. Of the transfer payments inaugurated under the New Deal, the Old Age and Survivor's Pension System (Social Security) was the most important. In addition, there were programs providing unemployment insurance and worker's compensation; public housing; and assistance for specific categories of disabled people such as the aged and the blind; most famous, there was Aid to Families with Dependent Children (AFDC), commonly known as "welfare."

Other programs, based on the recognition of need, were added during the 1960s. They provided food, housing, and health services (sometimes described as "in-kind" payments), which were not always calculated in income measurements. A food stamp program similar to that of the early New Deal was established in 1961. The 1965 law that set up the Department of Housing and Urban Development (HUD) extended support of low-cost housing units and initiated a rent supplement program. The establishment of Medicare in 1965 provided a basic health insurance plan for the aged. It consisted of a compulsory hospital cost insurance program (now made part of Social Security payments), and a voluntary supplementary program took care of doctors' bills. Coverage for the nonelderly poor was consolidated under the name "Medicaid."

In practice, the Great Society's impact on poverty went far beyond the programs of the OEO. In a way most unusual in the American experience, the government was acting to deal with a problem that had not yet become a crisis and was not represented by a powerful interest group. It sought to provide at least a minimum level of well-being (housing, food, medical care, and education) for everyone. The free enterprise system would provide sufficient funds for both increased private consumption and public programs. The lives of the disadvantaged would be altered through education and job-training programs under the guidance of the federal government. The expansion of Social Security, and the various income support or social welfare programs providing housing, food stamps, education, and medical care became part, though not always consciously, of the effort. Subsequent acts, such as the Model Cities program of 1966, reorganized or expanded existing programs.

The OEO's human-resource development plans, which were what the 1960s understood by the War on Poverty, never had a chance.

"Shine, Joe?"

FIG. 2. Reprinted with special permission of North American Syndicate, Inc.

The initial 1964 funding had been a politically cautious sum of less than $1 billion. The Vietnam War soon diverted the nation's attention and resources. It was hardly necessary for President Johnson to delay a tax increase and conceal the costs of the war to keep Congress from slashing social programs; the War on Poverty was never funded enough to make a difference. "Vietnam took it all away," Sargent Shriver lamented, "every goddamned dollar."

NIXON

In 1969, the Republican Richard M. Nixon became president. He attacked various OEO projects, particularly those that involved community action and were designed to help people work their way out of poverty, but his administration increased income support and welfare programs. In a generally combative relationship with the Democratic Congress, President Nixon actually presided over a growth in the size and the costs of antipoverty programs. California's Republican governor, Ronald Reagan, did not like the Community Action program any more than did many Democratic mayors, but Congress and the Supreme Court would not permit the destruction of programs such as Legal Services. Various parts of OEO were distributed among the old-line governmental departments, and in 1974, OEO itself was terminated. Job training was turned over to the states and local government through federal block grants under the Comprehensive Employment and Training Act (CETA) of 1973. By the end of the decade, the human-resource development programs of the War on Poverty no longer existed as a comprehensive attempt to raise the poverty underclass into the American mainstream.

Nevertheless, as the Republican party of Dwight Eisenhower had accepted—at least in practice—the New Deal, so the Republican party of Richard Nixon accepted the campaign against poverty. Even though Nixon vetoed bills, including major appropriations that contained various antipoverty efforts, curiously, it was the income support (or welfare) portion that grew the most. Early in his administration, Nixon presented a "family assistance plan" designed by his domestic counselor, Daniel Moynihan, but grew unenthusiastic about the idea of a guaranteed minimum $1,600 annual cash income for each poor family. By the time the Family Assistance Plan died in Congress four years later, an explosion had taken place in income support programs.

In Mississippi for a Senate poverty subcommittee hearing, two Democratic senators, Robert Kennedy of New York and Joseph Clark of Pennsylvania, found raw hunger in the dirt-floored delta shacks. Newspaper stories, foundation studies, teams of doctors, and congressional investigations estimated that some 10 million Americans suffered from acute hunger and malnutrition. In 1968, a prestigious Citizens' Board of Inquiry published an illustrated report, *Hunger U.S.A.*, which listed 256 counties in crisis. All a Kennedy plot to malign the South, scoffed Mississippi congressman Jamie Whitten, whose Agricultural Appropriations Subcommittee controlled the food stamp program. Basically, food stamps were a minor agricultural surplus support program, and a skeptical and distracted Lyndon Johnson had not been interested in risking his Vietnam War tax increase in order to change things. By 1969 the hard numbers were in, and it was President Nixon who asked for major changes. Senator George McGovern of South Dakota led the appropriations battle, but it was in trouble. As Senator Strom Thurmond and the conservatives on the Rules Committee moved to cut its funding, his South Carolina colleague Fritz Hollings rose to speak. Yes, as governor of South Carolina he had known that there was hunger that blighted the lives of both black and white. It had been concealed because it was bad for development, Hollings explained, but now "the hunger and the burden of the poor can no longer be ignored." Annual appropriations moved above the $1-billion mark, and food stamps were now free to welfare recipients and available inexpensively to those close to the poverty line. In 1965, the food stamp program had spent $36 million for 633,000 people. A decade later, it spent $5 billion for 20 million recipients.

The rules governing AFDC eligibility were recast, and residency and "no-man-in-the-house" restrictions were dropped. The number of AFDC recipients increased from over 4 million to almost 12 million people. With the codification of the federal programs for the support of the indigent under the 1972 Supplemental Security Income Act (SSI), social welfare expenditures soared. Social Security for the elderly was increased five times between 1965 and 1974, and reached an annual $64 billion. Altogether, by the time Richard Nixon left the White House, federal Social Security and welfare payments were double what they had been when he became president and almost four times what they had been in the mid-1960s. At $150 billion a year, they had risen from one-third to almost half of the federal budget.

A VIEW FROM THE 1990s

What were the results of the War on Poverty? The poor remained, and so did the War on Poverty. Even the 1980s conservative Republicanism of Ronald Reagan, while pushing deregulation and a crusade against big government, reluctantly promised to protect Social Security and extend a "safety net" beneath the nation's "truly poor." The American dream of the 1960s was based on economic growth, an end to racial segregation, and the solution to poverty, all with the aid of a benevolent, interventionist national government. By the 1980s, the dream was unrealized and the scholars were in disagreement not only as to the extent of success or failure but also as to whether the path itself was a mistake. Theodore White, the historian of presidential elections; Allen Matusow, the author of the New American Nation series account of the 1960s; and Vaughn Davis Bornet, a student of the Johnson presidency, all took various positions of pessimism and condemnation. Bornet, in *The Presidency of Lyndon B. Johnson* (1983), characterized the War on Poverty as rhetorical overkill. Matusow, in *The Unraveling of America: A History of Liberalism in the 1960s* (1984), declared it a failure. White, in *America in Search of Itself* (1983), denounced it as a disastrous overreaching of the national government into "every nook and cranny of national life." The historian of poverty Thomas Patterson speculated in *America's Struggle against Poverty* (1981) that the failure of the War on Poverty had played a major role in the neoconservative revival but maintained that nevertheless there had been a revolution in attitudes and programs.

In disagreement, the political scientist John E. Schwartz, in *America's Hidden Success* (1988), and Sar Levitan and Robert Taggart, in *The Promise of Greatness* (1976), defended the Great Society's programs as highly beneficial. The social welfare historian Walter Trattner showed the state of the confusion with his conclusion, in *From Poor Law to Welfare State* (1984), that "perhaps the time has come, or is coming, when most Americans will acknowledge (or be forced to acknowledge) that the poor will be with us, always, through no fault of their own, and that they, too, have a right to a healthy, happy, and secure life."

In his final reflections on the modern presidency, Theodore White pictured the dreams of the sixties, and particularly the War on Poverty, as a great mistake. The costs of food stamps, school lunches, and the like had risen into the billions. During the optimistic days of the sixties, the government had set out to "free everyone" and had created instead a world of bureaucracies and inflation, and "a nation of dependents." Allen Matusow labeled his own analysis of the poverty programs "The Failure of the Welfare State." It was, he wrote, "one of the great failures of twentieth-century liberalism." Both the human-capital strategy of educating and training people to take them out of poverty, and the welfare approach of subsidizing their food, shelter, and medical care, as well as the area-development effort in Appalachia, were flawed and unsuccessful. Usually, vested interests undercut governmental programs; the compensatory education money of the Elementary and

Secondary Education Act was not spent on the poor; Medicare doctors inflated the public bill for care that Matusow claimed they had previously provided anyway; Medicaid did not help the working poor; "fast-buck speculators and greedy developers" produced poorly restored or badly managed housing (most of whose owners or renters were not poor anyway); and the vocational training provided by the Job Corps was for low-level jobs that often were not available.

According to Matusow, Lyndon Johnson's instruction to Sargent Shriver to keep "crooks, Communists, and cocksuckers" out of the Office of Economic Opportunity overlooked the really "dangerous" element: the radicals who would attempt to promote social change. The Community Action programs sought to involve the poor in their planning, but when the mayors and local power structures realized that their control was threatened by the "maximum feasible participation" of the poor, they took over or forced the administration to curtail the Community Action efforts. Thus died what Matusow believed was the one thrust toward the redistribution of power and wealth that was essential to a real war on poverty. Even so, two decades later a survivor of Community Action, the Legal Services program, which had sent two thousand lawyers into the ghettos and inner cities, was still alive despite the continuing efforts of first Governor and then President Reagan to terminate it.

EVALUATING PROGRAMS

A major problem in the historical evaluation of poverty and the programs that attempt to combat it is the confusion between the standard of living and income inequality. Although the former has improved, the gap between classes and the relative distribution of national income have remained relatively unchanged over the past quarter of a century. In a society of rising expectations, where every medium—from billboards to television—proclaims that America is a culture of affluent consumption, the poor are not likely to measure their condition against what "Granny" used to have. Rising expectations, unfulfilled, are the stuff of social unrest and a problem for historical judgment, but the 1960s and the 1970s have had an effect on standards of living among the poor, even if not standards of contentment.

At the beginning of the 1960s, the Census Bureau estimated that nearly 40 million people, or 22 percent of the population, lived in poverty. Economic growth and government programs brought substantial improvement. By the mid-1970s, the poor numbered around 25 million, or less than 12.5 percent of the population. The population of black people who were poor had fallen from more than one-half to one-third. The figures rose during energy crises, periods of inflation, economic slowdowns, and funding reductions, until the mid-1980s when poverty claimed an estimated 33 million. The civil rights revolution of the 1960s opened up educational and career opportunities to the black middle classes. Shifting attitudes and governmental pressure, strengthened by the enforcement powers of the Equal Employment Opportunity Commission (EEOC), helped the economy to produce jobs for blacks as well as working-class whites. Statistics that show some patterns, hide others. Thomas Patterson used University of Michigan studies to show constant movement in and out of the official poverty category. Within a decade, perhaps some 70 million people, or close to one-third of the total population, moved back and forth across the fictional poverty line. Poverty statistics, he concluded, indicate only the much smaller number of people who are poor "all the time." The lives of the near poor—one misfortune away from poverty—were a hidden story. So, too, were the problems of the working poor. Badly paid work was a crucial source of poverty. One-third of those below the poverty line held full-time jobs. For a family head to be working for the minimum wage might mean that five people would be living in poverty. According to a 1984 study by Princeton University, the only change in the 1980s that had substantially affected a major segment of those in poverty had been the dropping of working poor from the welfare rolls.

The sociologists Sar Levitan and Robert Taggart categorically disagreed with what they described as "the sweeping and erroneous conclusion that the Great Society failed." Rather, they argued, "the 1960s programs and policies and their continuation had a massive, overwhelmingly beneficial impact and the weight of the evidence convincingly supports this view." The human-resources development programs of the OEO, the heart of the War on Poverty, have been the most difficult to evaluate. The publicity that inaugurated the programs inevitably raised expectations too high. In spite of the fireworks over the challenge to city bureaucracies and political machines, the Community Action programs for education, health, family planning, and legal services produced promising results. Levitan and Taggart, Patterson, and Schwartz found that community-based programs for child care and preschool education, nutrition, and health; as well as job-training and employment efforts, did benefit their participants.

Even more important were the various income support and in-kind programs (known variously as welfare, income-maintenance, and transfer payments). Although they were not formally part of the War on Poverty, they were more heavily funded and enduring, and they touched those whom economic growth and human-resource development did not. The publicity from studies on hunger in America, beginning with the 1967 Field Foundation Report, produced child nutrition programs and a major expansion of the food stamp program under the Nixon administration that substantially cut malnutrition.

During the decade of the War on Poverty, 1965–74, federal payments for Medicaid, housing, and food stamps rose from $1.2 billion to $26.6 billion. The amount of money paid out by Medicare increased from $16.6 billion for 20.8 million recipients to $54 billion for 29.9 million people. Even with the rise in the cost of living, the poor were better off. Among the modern Western nations, the United States spent the smallest proportion of its national income on social programs.

At the beginning of the 1960s, 40 percent of the aged were living below the poverty line; in 1974, only 16 percent were, and the elderly were seeing the doctor more often. Infant mortality had fallen by one-third, with particular gains among black people. Ominously, however, children were replacing the aged as the largest group among the poor. The two lines crossed in the mid-1970s—the standard of living of the elderly improving, that of children deteriorating. A decade later, almost one-quarter of all children (and almost one-half of the black and one-third of the Hispanic children), usually in woman-headed families, lived in poverty.

Among the unemployed, the underemployed, the underpaid, the elderly, and in female-headed households, in Appalachia, in the inner city, and in the countryside, poverty remained in America. After the 1960s, it was neither as invisible nor as inarticulate as it had been before. Many organizations and groups—the National Congress of American Indians and the American Indian Movement, the National Welfare Rights Organization, the National Farm Workers Association, the Political Association of Spanish-Speaking Organizations, and the Gray Panthers; black and Hispanic mayors and congressmen, social welfare programs, their bureaucracies, and the interest groups that have developed around them; and minority law-school graduates and Legal Services lawyers—expressed the emotions and pressed the claims of the poor. *In the Shadow of the Poorhouse* (1986), by the social welfare historian Michael Katz, argued that the Community Action effort nourished a growing, grass-roots citizens' involvement that was providing a new leadership in social service and government. By the end of the 1970s, no one still talked about "wiping out" poverty, but in a nation in which federal welfare and transfer payments totaled close to $300 billion, no one was forgetting it either.

5. Revolt on the Campus

In his 1960 "Letter to the New Left," C. Wright Mills criticized the "false consciousness" of complacent American liberals. It was not they or the working class who would be the new agency of change. "Who is it that is getting disgusted with what Marx called 'all the old crap'?" he wrote. "Who is it that is thinking and acting in radical ways? All over the world . . . the answer is the same; it is the young intelligentsia."

THE YOUTH GENERATION

In the 1960s, a youth generation emerged for the first time as a powerful force in American politics and culture. Its home was the university. After the 1970 shootings at Kent State and Jackson State, President Nixon's National Commission on Campus Unrest reported, "When the decade began the American public was impressed with the courage, idealism and restraint of student civil rights workers; as the decade ends, public opinion is fearful, angry, and confused." There had been isolated student protest and violence before in America, usually over such issues as food, visiting speakers, and dormitory regulations, but not a movement. Now, not only were off-campus issues added but the university itself was seen as servant, symbol, and battleground for what was wrong in national life. This development was a product of conditions and generations. Rapid social change and a massing at the universities combined with historical circumstance and a series of internal and external events to produce new involvements and consciousnesses. The campus and antiwar dissent resulted in social turmoil that did much to make the Vietnam War unbearable and topple the presidency of Lyndon Johnson, but it failed to create the theory and organizational means for developing a Left tradition or an enduring student political culture.

In the decade and a half since World War II, the number of young people had grown almost twice as fast as the general population and more than ever before were entering college. There were 1.7 million college students in 1946, 3.8 million in 1960, 6.5 million in 1965, and 8 million in 1970. The general affluence that spared them from the work force and built the new colleges and universities to house and teach them also initiated them into the consumer society and promised to provide for their future. Thus they were, for the most part, set free of the compromises that the job world forces on youthful energies and ideals, and were not yet a part of the decision-making structures of society. Liberal education transmitted the society's humanistic ideals and encouraged the student to revere them. The degree to which the means-focused world fell short of those ideals led ends-focused students to disillusionment and, sometimes, revolt. In *The Unraveling of America* (1983), the historian Allen Matusow wrote, "A minority of an idealistic and privileged generation confronted the contradiction between American principles and American realities and would not abide it." The Yale psychologist Kenneth Keniston, who had also studied the alienated youth of the 1950s, spent the summer of 1967 with the leaders of the growing anti–Vietnam War movement. Becoming radical, he wrote, did not mean that students rejected their parents or underwent a "fundamental change in core values." Anger, not guilt, produced their radicalism. The shock of confrontation with "poverty, injustice, political manipulation and institutional dishonesty" pushed them into social action.

Generations are made, not born. It was the civil rights movement that stirred the sleeping campuses. Even before John Kennedy could proclaim that government had passed into the hands of "a new generation born in this century" and call upon his listeners to consider not what their country could do for them but what they could do for their country, four black students from North Carolina Agricultural and Technical College had sat in, politely but resolutely, at the Woolworth's lunch counter in Greensboro. After that, it was a youth thing: SNCC, CORE, sit-ins, Freedom Rides, Mississippi, Birmingham, and "We Shall Overcome." There just was no way to get young people out of the streets and off the evening news. More than at any other time in American history, there was a series of characteristically youth involvements and causes: civil rights, the Free Speech movement and university reform, fighting in Vietnam, fighting against the war, and the counterculture.

BERKELEY

At the beginning of the 1960s, there was no discernible indication that a generational revolt was brewing on the Northern campuses. The cold war and McCarthyism had silenced not only the Marxist Left but also much critical discussion about the nature of American society. Left, pacifist, and peace groups were minuscule. Conflict between students and the University of California's regents over anti-Communist oaths and academic freedom, protest over the execution of the rapist Caryl Chessman, the police attack on students at the House Un-American Activities Committee hearings in San Francisco's City Hall, and the election of a so-called leftist student government (SLATE) at Berkeley could be written off as California particularism.

The University of California at Berkeley was the centerpiece of California's three-tiered higher-education system, and was possibly the best university in the nation. In 1964, Berkeley had 27,500 high-scoring students, a prestigious faculty, and an annual budget of two-thirds of a billion dollars, half coming from federal government grants and contracts, including those that supported the nuclear weapons laboratories at Livermore and Los Alamos. In a published series of lectures, *The Uses of the University* (1963), the university system president, Clark Kerr, had lamented that the modern emphasis on research resulted in the deemphasis of teaching, the imposition of endless rules, and an atmosphere of impersonality. In its service to the general society, he explained, this was the price that the multiversity paid for its role as "a prime instrument of national purpose."

It is of little wonder, therefore, that when the students came to question the national purpose, the university would also become a target. The affair that touched it all off was a battle over internal rules. Berkeley was a more volatile community than the university's administrators realized. Berkeley CORE had led students and community people in "shop-ins" and "fair proportion employment" picketing of local merchants and the Sheraton Palace Hotel in San Francisco. In the fall of 1964, students such as physics and philosophy major Mario Savio were returning from SNCC's Mississippi Freedom Summer and community organizing in the Deep South. Although not without arousing protest, the university had always told students what they could and could not do. Now it sought to reassure conservative regents and former senator William Knowland, the influential owner of the *Oakland Tribune,* by clamping down on campus political activism. The result, for the first time in American college history, was a massive student insurrection. It fascinated the press and the academy. Across the nation it stirred student imaginations, already made receptive by the civil rights movement.

It started simply with the denial of the space near the University's Sather Gate where students had traditionally collected signatures and money for political causes. From the young Communists to the Youth for Goldwater, the students joined in a "free speech" protest, and tables were set up anyway. There were suspensions, arrests, a sit-in in Sproul Hall, an early morning police bust, and massive rallies. The irresolute administration alternated between amnesties and new disciplinary charges. The students and the teaching assistants went on strike. The faculty debated and resolved, the regents rejected, and the conflict expanded. The attempt to limit off-campus picketing had become an on-campus free speech issue, a battle against university authority, and an attack on the university itself. Students protested against large classes being conducted by graduate teaching assistants while famous professors devoted themselves to research and outside consulting. The issue was shifting to one of "alienation" and the nature of the university. The IBM card used for registration became the symbol of protest against the university as a knowledge factory. "I am a UC Student," a picket sign proclaimed. "Do Not Fold, Bend or Mutilate." "We are not raw materials to be made into products to be bought by the clients of the university," Mario Savio shouted. The machine had to be controlled. Summoning the spirit of Henry Thoreau's earlier call for civil disobedience against slavery and the Mexican War, he urged, "You've got to put your bodies upon the gears and upon the wheels, upon the levers, upon all the apparatus, and you've got to make it stop."

It didn't really matter that the university eventually cancelled its political restrictions, that there was a new chancellor, that the Free Speech Movement became a "dirty speech" controversy when a non-student appeared carrying a sign reading "Fuck," and that a year later the new governor of California, Ronald Reagan, fired the president of the university system, Clark Kerr. The fight over campus rules had escalated from a limited conflict over freedom of speech to one that involved not only the quality and conduct of education but also broad off-campus social issues. The Commission on Campus Unrest named it "the Berkeley invention." By insensitivity, irresolution and overre-action, a liberal administration had produced a mass student reaction that raised large questions about the university. Over the years that followed, while most students were not radicalized, across the country large numbers of them could be mobilized in protest against the pol-icies of the university and the national government.

Jack Weinberg was a former graduate student in mathematics who was to originate the slogan "Don't trust anyone over thirty." Early in the Berkeley confrontation, the campus police arrested him for man-ning a forbidden "sign-up" table for CORE. Students spontaneously sat down in the street around the squad car. Soon there were a thou-sand bodies blocking its movement. With Weinberg and the officers inside, they remained for more than thirty hours while negotiations involved the students, the police, Clark Kerr, and the governor of the state of California. Holding a loudspeaker, Mario Savio took off his shoes before climbing on top of the police car to address the sur-rounding students. Although protestors were willing to engage in civil disobedience, initially it was non-violent. This was to change with the Vietnam War.

VIETNAM

Early in February 1965, nine sleeping American advisers were killed when National Liberation Front forces shelled the Pleiku airfield barracks in Vietnam. In response, and for the inexact purpose of "breaking the enemy's will" to fight, President Lyndon Johnson escalated American involvement in the war. Bombers flew north, and American soldiers moved out in search of kills and combat. Antiwar dissent began to grow on the college campuses of America. When a faculty debate was set up in the place of a strike at the University of Michigan, a new instrument, the "teach-in," was born.

Other campuses copied Michigan. A national "teach-in" was scheduled, with more than one hundred campuses across the nation linked by telephone. The administration's spokesman, the national security adviser and former Harvard dean McGeorge Bundy, failed to appear. That his "more pressing" assignment turned out to be involved with the use of American troops to prevent a popular uprising against a military dictatorship in the Dominican Republic seemed to confirm suspicions about American foreign policy. The campus "teach-ins" became antiwar demonstrations. The administration's views were not asked for and often not allowed to be heard.

By 1966 there were more than a quarter of a million American soldiers in Vietnam, and the draft reached out to the campuses. The decision to take the students who were not in the upper academic ranks of their classes heightened an anxiety-based anger over war policy, which became even more intense with the general termination of college deferrals. According to the polls, a majority of the students supported the government and the war, but their support was unenthusiastic and they preferred to provide it from a distance. Defeating the Communists might be important, but one did not feel a moral commitment to risk or to accept interference with one's life. Some colleges refused to supply class standings, and professors talked about not assigning grades. The growing antiwar feeling was more than a flight from military service, but the draft did increase personal awareness of the war and pushed students into taking stands.

What happened on the campuses has too often been told as the story of Berkeley, Columbia, Wisconsin, and Harvard. Their elite prominence, activism, and media coverage did make them dramatic and symbolic, but almost every college had its own story, and few of these have even been partially told. Students and recent graduates from more than two hundred colleges and universities—public, private, and parochial—took part in the 1964 Mississippi Freedom Summer. Swarthmore College students were arrested in Chester, Pennsylvania; and University of Florida students went to jail in St. Augustine. Penn State had its Committee for Student Freedom; a Campus Freedom Democratic party was organized at the University of Nebraska; and University of Texas students campaigned to desegregate college bathrooms, with the slogan "Let my people go." During 1964–65, there was some kind of protest on a majority of the nation's four-year campuses.

Vietnam and the draft changed the pattern and intensified the conflict. Militancy increased on Southern black campuses. Police and National Guardsmen shot students at South Carolina State, Jackson State, and North Carolina A&T. Black students occupied administrative offices at Chicago, Brandeis, and dozens of other colleges, and brought rifles into the Willard Straight Union at Cornell. At numerous colleges, students sat in against military recruiting and napalm's manufacturer, Dow Chemical. Campus ROTC buildings were set on fire. University officials were held hostage at Connecticut's Trinity College and at San Fernando State, as well as at Columbia University. In the final year of the decade, bombing threats ran into the thousands. People were injured in explosions at Pomona College, San Francisco State, and Santa Barbara, and a graduate student was killed by a bomb at the University of Wisconsin's Army Mathematics Research Center. There is no count of student expulsions, but the number of students arrested increased from four thousand in 1968–69 to almost twice that number the following academic year. The National Guard, which had almost no role in Southeast Asia, was called on to intervene more than two hundred times in civil disorders on American campuses.

Calvin Lee, who had been both a class president and a dean at Columbia, wrote that in the early sixties, college movements, including those on the Left, were "*for* something, *for* desegregation, *for* equality for blacks, *for* individualism." They were to become a protest against depersonalization, against alienation, against the IBM card, and against the war. Against a background of civil rights turned Black Power, ghetto riots, hassles over marijuana and long hair, and university rules, and police busts, the Vietnam War was eroding belief in reform and the commitment to nonviolence. Things were becoming nasty. A crowd in the Harvard Yard kept Defense Secretary Robert McNamara from speaking, and on the West Coast, black-jacketed members of the Hell's Angels motorcycle gang beat up students who tried to picket the Oakland Army Supply Depot.

The interminable, painful, dirty inconclusiveness of the war, brought home to the dinner table by television and the growing campus unrest, made the war increasingly difficult to bear. According to the polls, a great majority of Americans were willing to go along with national policy but felt that if the United States was not going to win, it ought to get out. Most students shared this attitude. Only a small percentage of them considered themselves "radicals," but these were the ones who organized the rallies, demonstrations, and sit-ins against recruiters, and denounced university administrations as being linked to Washington. For them, the war was not only wrong, it was the inescapable result of a repressive American system, run by the big corporations. The university, with its government contracts and military research, its ROTC and military-industrial recruiting, was also culpable. For students concerned with ideas and symbols, getting their college president to denounce the war became a moral issue.

RADICALIZATION

With the radicalized students increasingly unwilling to accept the university as neutral, it became not only their arena but their target as well. Students had historically contended against institutional rules and regulations; now for the first time they were challenging the legitimacy of the university itself. While most students had not come this far, many were interested spectators, concerned about regulations and their personal freedom, and the quality and relevance of their education. They were uneasy about the draft and troubled over the morality and the seeming endlessness of the war in Vietnam. Large numbers could be rallied on specific issues, particularly when the university seemed unresponsive and administrators could be pushed into bringing the police onto campus. Even so, classes, jobs, and social life came first; students remained students and only occasional protesters. It was exciting to be standing up against authority on behalf of moral values, to feel part of a movement that you read about in the newspaper and saw on television. Only a minority ever actually took part in demonstrations or turned out as spectators: rock concerts and celebrities drew bigger crowds, the counterculture was more "cool," and there was always an exam for which one had to study. For the small minorities for whom activism was central, there was the continuing question of what to do next to keep the excitement going and bring large crowds out again.

Rhetoric and emotion became more extreme. To administrators, the government, and much of the adult population, it seemed as though the young activists were intent on destroying the university and American society itself. For their part, the radicals questioned whether there was anything worth saving. The activists tended to be the children of well-to-do, liberal, sometimes radical (nicknamed the "red diaper" students), professional, often Jewish or liberal Protestant families. For the most part, they were attempting to apply, rather than reject, the values of their parents. Unlike first-generation college students, who were more vocationally and professionally oriented, the activists tended to be in the humanities and the social sciences. Science and engineering students were not likely to be involved. The more selective the school, the more likely it was to produce student activism.

In 1967, Richard Flacks, who had been an early leader of SDS, summed up its early sixties values as *romanticism* (the search for self-expression and a free life), *antiauthoritarianism* (opposition to arbitrary, centralized rule-making), *egalitarianism* (belief in popular participation and rejection of elitism), *antidogmatism* (rejection of ideology), *moral purity* (antipathy toward self-interested behavior and the "sell-out" of the older generation), *community* (breakdown of interpersonal barriers, a desire for relationships), and *antiinstitutionalism* (distrust of conventional institutional roles and careers).

Although the activists probably never numbered more than 5 percent of college students at the most, the college population had become so large that this could mean tens of thousands across the country. In addition, hundreds of thousands more might turn out for a national day of protest. With the threefold expansion of higher education since 1950, this was a sufficiently large critical mass to create explosions on the campuses and in the streets. They could push their colleges both to policy changes and to punitive reactions that increased support for the dissidents. The activists possessed two particular advantages. They possessed the explanations and the initiative. Almost in a vacuum, it was they who defined the meaning of what was going on and provided the names for it. By sudden precipitate action they could create, if not control, situations. Although the Harvard SDSers repeatedly voted against it, their Progressive Labor faction suddenly occupied a university building and produced a police bust that resulted in broad campus outrage.

If the activists could have reached out and convinced other groups of the identity between a "wrong" war and "the system," their radical dissent might have had a chance of building a movement. It already drew support from older peace organizations, some professors, and groups such as Clergy Concerned and Women Strike for Peace, as well as from the street people of the growing counterculture. Almost always, there were faculty involved as advisers and sometimes as leaders. Potential allies and recruits might have been found among as yet uncommitted teachers and students, parents, concerned professionals such as doctors and lawyers, and members of the press.

NINETEEN SIXTY-EIGHT: NO REVOLUTION

Nineteen sixty-eight was the year in which the insurrectionary potential of the United States was tested. Perhaps not since labor's riotous year of 1877 had the possibility of revolution seemed so great. An increasingly discredited national administration suffered a major psychological defeat in a distant, interminable, bloody, and unpopular war. Alienated racial and generational cohorts talked about revolutionary violence. A series of domestic explosions threatened popular faith in the system, and everything showed up nightly on the television screen. Against a background of student demonstrations and strikes, the destruction of draft board records, and the sedition trial of Yale chaplain William Sloane Coffin and baby doctor Benjamin Spock for encouraging draft resistance, there was the Viet Cong's surprise Tet offensive in Vietnam. Eugene McCarthy and Robert Kennedy challenged Lyndon Johnson's reelection from the antiwar Left, as did George Wallace from the populist Right. Johnson withdrew from the presidential race. The ghetto riots that followed the murder of Martin Luther King Jr. sent palls of smoke over the White House. Robert Kennedy was murdered. Columbia University experienced a new kind of student takeover and an old kind of police bust, and the protests at the Democratic National Convention in Chicago stirred up a police riot. In Europe, there were student riots in Berlin, a student uprising in Paris almost toppled the French government, and Russian tanks put down the attempt to create "Communism with a heart" in Prague.

At Berkeley four years before, Mario Savio had politely removed his shoes so as not to scratch the top of the police car while standing on it to make his speech. Now the radical message was that civility and reform were gone, this was revolution. A professor on the edge of the crowd interrupted Columbia University SDS leader Mark Rudd. "What is your program?" he asked. "I don't have a program," Rudd replied, "but I have a vision, and my vision is better than your vision, you motherfucker!" Out of the intense heat of the conflagration that would burn away the old world, a new, as yet unimagined society would emerge.

For the radicals who had provoked and led the Columbia take-over, the university was hostage for the general society. After six days, the university called in the police. The black students quietly marched out. The white students barricaded in the remaining buildings were roughed up, dragged out, and arrested by the New York City police. The specific issues, Rudd later admitted, did not count: the goal had been to radicalize the students. "Two, three, many Columbias" would lead "the long march" through the institutions of a repressive corporate America. The war, inept university administrations, and police violence convinced many of the young that they were being victimized by a society that was unresponsive and needed to be changed. Most of the rest of society praised the police.

Nineteen sixty-eight produced no revolution. The four years between the Berkeley Free Speech movement in 1964 and the 1968 riots at Columbia and in Chicago carried a growing youthful dissent from reform to what appeared to be the edge of insurrection. The next four years, from the election of Richard Nixon to his reelection and the withdrawal from Vietnam in January 1973, quieted the youth rebellion and brought an end to the politics of the sixties. It did not look that way at first. The war continued for four more years, at the cost of another twenty-five thousand American and uncounted Vietnamese lives. Having come to believe that society had entered into a revolutionary state, and increasingly frustrated over how to capitalize on it, the radical Left turned to sectarian and nihilistic violence. Classes were disrupted, the research of an unsympathetic Columbia University historian was destroyed, campus ROTC buildings were burned, and dynamite bombs were set off.

The now-revolutionary New Left sectarians had lost touch with the expanding opposition to the war. Among college students and faculty who rejected both the war and revolution, it was an agonizing situation. The marches and protest seemed to have no effect. The Vietnam Moratorium Committee dissolved in the spring of 1970. Its chief coordinator, Sam Brown, explained that he thought that mass demonstrations were no longer effective. Then, at the end of April, President Nixon sent American troops into Cambodia. The burst of anger on the campuses became an explosion when National Guardsmen fired into a crowd, killing four students and wounding others at Ohio's Kent State University. Ten days later, in an unrelated incident, police fired into a women's dormitory at Mississippi's black Jackson State University and killed two more. There were strikes and protests on nearly one-third of the nation's twenty-five hundred colleges and universities, and tens of thousands of student protestors converged on Washington to gather around the White House and the Lincoln Memorial.

Michigan University president Robert Fleming testified to the newly appointed Commission on Campus Unrest, headed by Pennsylvania governor William Scranton, that violence was not caused by campus problems. "We can handle those," he said. "What we cannot do is deal with problems like war." President Nixon was unsympathetic to the message from the politically hostile campuses. The fundamental cause of unrest among the young, he maintained, was not the war, poverty, or race, but the "sense of insecurity" that came from the loss of traditional religious and family values. According to the polls, a majority of the American people agreed with him. Across the country, the feeling was that the students who were shot at Kent State had "gotten what was coming to them"; and it was students, not the National Guardsmen, against whom Ohio grand juries brought in their indictments.

THE QUIETING OF THE CAMPUSES

By the early seventies, the fire had gone out. Most basically, it had died with the American withdrawal from Vietnam. The slowdown of the economy and an emotional exhaustion helped to turn the attention inward from society to self. The "Age of Aquarius" seemed to have become the "Age of Narcissus." The American student emerged from college into a job market that was more fluid and less predictable than in most other societies and which made large demands on the individual's psychic energy. Although many people joined the antiwar protests, no sector of society accepted the radical premise that basic changes were needed in the system. Like the working class in Werner Sombart's classic explanation of the failure of socialism in America, the college students also preferred "roast beef and apple pie"—consumption rather than political ideology.

Nonetheless, campus consciousness did change during the 1960s, and the best measure of this change was to be found at the center rather than at the extremes. Student politics is ordinarily a specialized activity in which a majority do not take an active part. At large universities, only a minority trouble themselves to vote in student elections. Socially conservative fraternities and their politically satellite sororities play a disproportionately large role. On the whole, the growing challenge to institutional authority was focused on academic requirements, disciplinary rules and proceedings, and the opening up of the women's dormitories. Students rallied against the right of administrations to impose on-campus penalties for off-campus activities such as civil rights arrests, and to control student dorm hours and sexual arrangements. Only very rarely was a radical party or coalition, such as Berkeley's SLATE in the early 1960s, elected to office. A resolution about the draft, or the election of black student presidents and homecoming queens, was a more common way of showing that times were changing.

Although no more than 20 percent of the nation's twenty-five hundred campuses were represented in the National Student Association (NSA) and the competing Association of Student Governments, NSA was much more representative than SDS ever was. It had been formed in 1949 to counterbalance the Communist youth organizations, whose effectiveness American students had seen at the World Student Congress in Prague the year before. In 1952 the CIA secretly came on board, as the radical journal *Ramparts* was to reveal in 1967. It guided NSA's participation in international student congresses and exchanges, and did intelligence gathering on the side.

At home, for the most part, NSA functioned freely and took forthright stands on civil rights and campus issues. This made it too controversial for many student governments, but it did provide an opportunity for student interaction and recruitment. In the early sixties, civil rights activists and intellectual radicals mingled with campus politicos, editors, and student body presidents. Early 1960s NSAers included SNCC members Charles McDew, Bob Zellner, and Sandra Cason; SDS leaders Al Haber, Tom Hayden, Paul Potter, and Rennie Davis; the feminist Gloria Steinem; the future football union leader Ed Garvey; Barney Frank, headed for the Mississippi Freedom Summer and the U.S. Congress; and famous magazine editors-to-be Willie Morris and Ronnie Dugger.

For the radicals of the later 1960s, the mainstream student leaders were too conservative and trapped within the system, but NSA's Association of Student Government Presidents did not mince words in telling legislators that the campus disorders were the product of misgovernance. Allard Lowenstein, who had headed NSA in 1950, stayed in touch. In 1966 he got one hundred student leaders to sign an open letter telling President Johnson that they were "deeply troubled" over the unfairness of the draft and the widening of the war in Vietnam. The next year, Lowenstein was a speaker at NSA's national convention, where he launched his campaign against Lyndon Johnson's reelection. From within the system, Lowenstein recruited for Eugene McCarthy's 1968 presidential campaign, as did Sam Brown for the anti–Vietnam War Moratorium.

According to the opinion polls of the late sixties and early seventies, when campus conflict was most intense, two crucial patterns were apparent. The first was that although students were becoming doves on the war and expressed little confidence in the government's ability to handle problems, most of them continued to see themselves as moderates. The second dividing line was between college and the rest of society. As the graduates went out into the job and career world, their replacements from the high schools generally shared the more conservative views of the general society.

THE RISE AND FALL OF THE NEW LEFT

Despite the turmoil of the 1960s and the rejected war in Vietnam, the United States did not approach the edge of revolution or even a general campus insurrection. Although the students, as President Nixon reminded them, were only a small percentage of the population, they were enough to affect national policy and play a crucial, though unmeasurable, role in making the Vietnam War unendurable. Why then did they not create a radical tradition on the campuses and among the American young? It is not possible to say what might have happened if the war had lasted another decade and produced a radical culture that was shared in a postgraduate overlap between the campuses and the general society. In other times and countries, student parties have acted as recruiters for adult organizations, but this did not happen in the American sixties. The Old Left, composed of Communists, Trotskyites, various kinds of Maoists, and within-the-system Socialists, was minuscule and chronically moribund. There was no labor party, as in Great Britain, into whose left wing the students could graduate. Marxist analysis had only minor standing in the American academy, and anti-Stalinism was the leading preoccupation of most Left intellectuals.

For the first time, a youth movement seemed to be developing on the American Left which was not an adjunct to an older, adult party. Where the strength of Marxist parties in other countries had come from the scientific claims of their ideology and the promise to overturn traditional elite and class domination, the initial appeal of American campus radicalism was the freshness and utopianism of its philosophy. Where radicalism abroad promised disciplined modernization, in postmodern America it looked to the image of a simpler past and a tradition of communal anarchism. If it were to endure and flourish, the New Left would have to find a way to translate its ideology and goals into programs and organizational structure, and reach out for its constituency. The Vietnam War produced a massive and angry opposition to the policy of the national government. The New Left's opportunity was to convince its potential followers that the war was the product not of mistaken policies but rather of basic faults and contradictions in the American political system and society.

In a major history of generational revolt, *The Conflict of Generations* (1969), the Freudian sociologist Lewis Feuer argued that when society's institutions fail to adjust to social and cultural change, oedipal drives combine with the conscious rejection, or "de-authorization," of authority to produce a rebellious younger generation. If Feuer's historical perceptions can be disengaged from his image of "the primal sons destroying their Father" and his tendency to report the worst about the New Left, he presented a suggestive model. From the initial study group, or "Circle," concerned with questions of ultimate meaning, the student moves to the search for fighting issues. Next come the demonstration and the strike, followed by a now-revolutionized populist, or back-to-the-people, stage. ("*V narod!*" cried the nineteenth-century Russian revolutionary Alexander Hertzen: "To the people!") Rebuffed by "the people"—proletariat or peasantry—the frustrated revolutionists turn away from democracy to elitist nihilism or underground violence.

The New Left—or, as its members sometimes called themselves, "the Movement"—included SDS, SNCC, CORE, the Berkeley Free Speech movement, the Mississippi Freedom Democratic party; the various Mobilization, Moratorium, Vietnam Day, and Vietnam Summer committees and caucuses, Resist, the Resistance, Women Strike for Peace, SANE, and other peace groups; the magazines *Liberation, Studies on the Left,* and *New Left Notes*; the Liberation News Service, and the underground press. Its self-defined membership was dependent on a commitment to "direct action," outside of channels. If you were willing to "put your body on the line," you were part of the movement. Of all of the participants, only SDS seemed to show promise of encompassing and consolidating the intense individual campus, racial, and antiwar activities into a general movement. Where the consciousness of labor intellectuals and leaders had been formed by the experiences of the 1930s and the cold war, the young New Left saw McCarthyism as the greater danger.

TOM HAYDEN AND SDS

Breaking away from its Socialist party sponsor with the rejection of an anti-Communist stance, Students for a Democratic Society produced the analysis, the vocabulary, and much of the early energy for campus radicalism. However, it failed to develop an organizational praxis that would create the leadership and cadres to guide the antiwar momentum and establish a lasting radical movement or tradition. The history of the rise and fall of Students for a Democratic Society is the essential case study for the failure of the American Left in the 1960s. SDS began with the Port Huron Statement communitarianism, went through a momentary fame that it could not handle, and ended in traditional Old Left sectarianism and a self-destructiveness that Black Panther critic Fred Hampton aptly called "Custeristic violence."

Tom Hayden had spent the spring of 1962 working on the draft of a position paper to be discussed by the Socialist party's youth organization at the United Auto Workers' Port Huron camp near Detroit. As finally adopted, the statement began its "Agenda for a Generation" with a self-identification: "We are a people of this generation, bred in at least modest comfort, housed now in universities, looking uncomfortably to the world we inherit." Brought up to believe in American power and values, college students had become troubled by racism, the cold war, the bomb, world poverty, the military-industrial complex of the warfare state, the mindless paranoia of anti-Communism, the cumbersomeness and triviality of the universities, the hypocrisy of American ideals, and the dominance of society by the elites who ran business, foreign affairs, and labor. Although the statement also criticized Stalinism, its focus was on the United States, particularly the failure of the liberals. SDS began as a small group of young radical intellectuals who wanted to create a humane, nonexploitative American society, free of domination by corporate power or Stalinist bureaucratic rigidity.

The new society must break through the alienation of manipulated and depersonalized man to build open and creative human sharing and community. This meant people interacting with each other and having a real influence over the direction of their lives. The political key and resonating phrase was "participatory democracy." The term itself came from a University of Michigan philosopher, Arnold Kaufman; the transforming example from the Student Nonviolent Coordinating Committee in the South. Participatory democracy faced the external question of how to politically combine individualism and face-to-face relationships with radically reforming the modern leviathan national industrial state. The internal question was how to live intimately together both as a community and as a political movement. What happened in the accelerating history of the movement was that SDS quickly came to accept participatory democracy as a replacement for representative democracy, rather than a linkage with it. The result was that when SDS grew beyond its small-group intimacy, it did not develop an organizational structure to make necessary policy decisions. The experience of working out the final statement in the frenzied three days at Port Huron combined with the example of SNCC's brave anarchistic purity to produce this triumph of idealistic optimism. For both SNCC and SDS, the search for purity would lead to exhaustion and chaos.

More than anyone else, Tom Hayden, the draftsman of the Port Huron statement, was the prime political activist of New Left America. Named for St. Thomas Aquinas, coming out of divorced, middle-class, Catholic Middle America—and Father Coughlin's parish in Royal Oak, Michigan—Hayden's vision of the 1960s was one of a secular apocalypse. He admired Holden Caulfield, James Dean, and Jack Kerouac, and read existentialism and C. Wright Mills. At the university, the center of his life was the *Michigan Daily.* In 1960, as its incoming editor, he hitchhiked out to the West Coast to cover the Democratic National Convention. On the way, he stopped off in Berkeley to write about "the new student movement." The editor-to-be of the *Michigan Daily* was a valuable property, and the SLATE activists showed him the territory, from the Livermore Laboratories, where he interviewed Edward Teller, to the stoop-labor world of the Mexican farm workers. At the convention, John Kennedy's acceptance speech excited him, as would the president's words on the Peace Corps the next year in Ann Arbor. In a picket-line interview, Martin Luther King Jr., told him, "Ultimately, you have to take a stand with your life."

On the way back, Hayden attended the National Student Association congress at the University of Minnesota. There he met the SNCC delegation and a young University of Texas student, Sandra Cason, nicknamed "Casey," who had come to SNCC from an intentional Christian community at the University of Texas. Returning to Ann Arbor, he edited the *Michigan Daily,* read political science and philosophy, and was drawn into the SDS orbit. He was twenty-one. He wrote well and took ideas seriously. He went south and helped deliver food to the black sharecroppers who were evicted from their homes for trying to vote, and wrote about it for the *Daily.* At the next year's NSA congress, in Madison, he was blacklisted as a "militant" by the secret CIA control group, but he continued to build his network of friends. He and Casey were married. SDS sent him to Atlanta as Southern field secretary, and Casey returned to work with SNCC. Hayden and NSA vice-president Paul Potter were beaten in McComb, Mississippi, and Hayden went to jail with the movement in Albany, Georgia.

The Port Huron statement was a generational manifesto, a compound of C. Wright Mills's social criticism and SNCC's organizational principles. It combined an attack on university bureaucracy and rule-making, like that which would infuse the Berkeley Free Speech fight and campus protest across the nation, the excitement of the civil rights struggle, and the foreign policy analysis that would underlie the antiwar movement. The next year's SDS convention brought another manifesto and gave a name to the enemy: it was "corporate liberalism."

Gathered together now, mostly in graduate school at the University of Michigan, they were a campus-bred movement, but they could not remain students forever. Al Haber, who had recruited Hayden and generally nourished the movement, argued that the first necessity was to continue working out their radical critique, but inspired by the civil rights struggle and particularly by SNCC's young workers in Mississippi, they decided to "go to the people." In 1964, SDS's Economic Research and Action Project (ERAP) groups went off to live communally, for the "freedom" of shared sacrifice, in white and black inner-city neighborhoods of the North. "Ghetto fever," Al Haber called it. Their task was to organize the poor and help them develop grassroots community power in nine cities, including Boston, Newark, Philadelphia, Cleveland, and Chicago. Tom Hayden chose Newark, which had a black majority. ERAP worked best in Cleveland, but its successes were meager.

By 1964, SDS had only a few dozen college chapters and fewer than fifteen hundred members, and was not particularly going anywhere. Then came the Berkeley Free Speech fight and the escalation of the war in Vietnam. The Berkeley legend, along with the civil rights struggle, created a common cause. When the government started drafting students off the campuses in 1966, it intensified awareness of the war and made it personal. In the spring of 1965, SDS had led the first march in Washington, D.C., against the war and was discovered by the media. Although it never exercised continuing leadership of the antiwar cause, SDS became national news, a "dangerous" dissenter from government policy. New members flooded in and overwhelmed the old leadership.

THE CHANGING OF THE GUARD

A rapid generational change took place. The new SDSers were younger, more inclined to take to the streets, and more into the dawning counterculture. Kirkpatrick Sale (*SDS* [1973]) described them as "moral activists," less Jewish, less well-read, less intellectual, and uninterested in "all that thirties horseshit," more anarchistic and strongly opposed to organizational centralization. "Blowing in the Wind," not "We Shall Overcome," now represented the SDS spirit. The "new" New Left edged aside its "elitist" founders, who moved off elsewhere into the growing antiwar movement.

With no tradition or guidelines, the new leadership had defined the war as the natural outcome of "the system," but was unwilling to try to confront it with an opposing institution. The anarchistic tendency of the new SDSers was too strong. Instead, they carried their ideal participatory democracy to its logical, antiorganizational conclusion by weakening SDS's national office and refusing to set a national policy. In the name of "student power," the local chapters would pick their own causes and directions. SDS took part in the national antiwar and antidraft protests, but it was not the leader. Leadership was left to SANE, the National Coordinating Committee, the Moratorium's Vietnam Summer, the various Mobes, the antidraft Resistance, and others. These antiwar efforts could produce a march on the Pentagon or could draw three hundred thousand protesters into the streets of San Francisco and New York, but could not build cohesive, enduring membership organizations. At its 1966 peak, SDS had more than thirty thousand members on several hundred campuses and was the only organization that seemingly might have built a radical culture and tradition. The war was the crucial issue for students and the Left, but SDS did not know how to deal with it. It chose instead to jump beyond the antiwar movement to revolution.

The new cry was "student as victim," or "student as nigger." In times of crisis, generations change quickly. The new SDS was more Left and more militant. SNCC and CORE had rejected biracialism and turned to Black Power, summer riots were shaking the black ghettos and had ended ERAP's effort to build a movement of the inner-city poor, and the Marxists were moving in. The search for authenticity and community had long since become a search for the correct revolutionary constituency. In the search for a surrogate proletariat that has so beset the American Left, SDS decided to concentrate on the college students who were being trained to become the salaried technicians of American capitalism. The place to reach them was on the campuses. Through local struggles over on-campus recruitment interviews by the armed services and napalm manufacturer Dow Chemical, dorm hours, and the "free university," a new "Student Power" working class would be created, capable of consciousness and revolution.

By 1967, however, the idea of students as the prime revolutionary class had faded, and SDS was looking to the outside world again. The success the next year at Columbia in using the University to attack the general society led SDS leaders to misread their own power and the national temper. The Tet offensive, the student uprising in Paris, the ghetto riots after the murder of Martin Luther King Jr., and the violence at the Democratic National Convention in Chicago convinced them that the country had come to the brink of revolution. "Columbia," the historian Allen Matusow wrote, "began the New Left's decline into madness."

THE DECLINE INTO MADNESS

SDS had turned away from New Left humanism. It now rejected participatory democracy in favor of Old Left ideological rigidity and sectarian conflict, and sought to bring down American society by warring against it in the streets. The SDS leadership had turned to an idolization of Che Guevara, Ho Chi Minh, and the revolutionaries of the Third World. In the spring of 1965, as new members drawn by the anti–Vietnam War parade streamed in, SDS had removed the antitotalitarian restriction from its membership. The youth group of the Communist party's Maoist splinter, the Progressive Labor party (PL), formally disbanded and moved into SDS. Armed with ideological certainty, dialectical experience, and tight discipline, they began their struggle for control. In the rapidly changing and increasingly frustrating world on the Left, the Marxists had the advantage of possessing the only comprehensive analysis of revolutionary change. The result was mass seduction.

In 1969, at the Chicago Coliseum and in Flint, Michigan, factions vied within SDS over who was the most faithful to Marxism-Leninism. "Do you consider yourself a socialist?" Bernardine Dohrn was asked. "I consider myself a revolutionary Communist," she replied, and was elected to the National Office. The newly emerged Weatherman faction and Progressive Labor fought bitterly over whether students must tie themselves to the working class or the Third World to produce revolution. Chanting "Mao, Mao, Mao Tse-tung" and "Ho, Ho, Ho Chi Minh" at each other and denouncing the "white-skin privilege" of PL's working class heroes and the sexism of the Revolutionary Youth Movement's (RYM, pronounced "rim") Black Panther allies, they fought for the carcass of the movement.

The Weathermen next tried recruiting blue-collar youth, by showing their fighting spirit through disrupting high school classes and slugging it out with teen gangs on the streets and lake beaches in preparation for returning to Chicago to take on the police. At the end of 1969, the last remnants went underground in small "affinity groups," to discipline themselves through destroying their last remnants of bourgeois morality ("killing the pig inside"), and to make bombs and wage guerrilla warfare against "pig Amerika." When the campuses exploded in anger after the 1970 spring invasion of Cambodia and killings at Kent State, there was no organization on the Left to make something more lasting out of the events. Two months before, a Weather Underground group preparing antipersonnel bombs for use uptown on the Columbia University campus had blown themselves up in a Greenwich Village townhouse.

There is much wisdom in the former SDS leader Todd Gitlin's argument (*The Whole World Is Watching: Mass Media in the Making & Unmaking of the New Left* [1980]) that SDS was overwhelmed by attention and pushed into too rapid a growth before it could properly define itself and begin building a supporting base and a Left tradition. The media aggressively pursued the happenings and dissidents of the sixties. For the New Left and the antiwar movement, the temptation was to do what would make headlines and be shown on the television evening news. Media publicity took priority over organizational efforts. The demonstration in the streets was "where it's at." The Vietnam War was both an opportunity for the Left and its fatal entrapment.

In both France and the United States, the working classes wanted no part of student insurrection. In Paris, it was the Communist party's striking industrial workers who refused to join hands with the students. In the United States, the Maoist PL was not wrong in believing that the New Left, which it did so much to destroy, needed a broader base than the campuses. Unlike the traditional Left, which sought to win over working-class and peasant majorities, SDS and the New Left reached out from the universities to seek support from the ghetto poor and the minorities, who together still added up to a minority of the American people. The early SDS's Port Huron statement had spoken the moral language of the American people. In a very short time, the New Left had moved outside those shared values and aspirations that made communication possible, and lost contact with both the American majority and the minorities for which it sought to speak. Increasingly isolated and irrelevant, it became more self-destructive. As the political sociologist Seymour Lipset wrote in *Rebellion in the University* (1971), "the New Left groups . . . had no clear concept of any road to power, of a way of effecting major social change." Although the civil rights movement came close to finding a Jesus in Martin Luther King Jr., and the New Left produced a Pilgrim in Tom Hayden, it never produced a Marx, and nowhere a St. Paul or a Lenin.

6. The Counterculture

While marchers in the streets were attempting to reform social conditions in America, there were others who were attempting to change "the human condition," or to escape from it. These others came to be called the "counterculture." The counterculture has been seen both as a current that ran parallel to and then diverged from the political movements of the sixties, and as an integral part of their rapidly changing phases. It was fed by a developing youth culture that was more expressive than rebellious and by an adult higher culture that took its lead from the popular and youth cultures.

A decade later, in an insightful analysis in *Theory and Society* (1976), the sociologists Daniel Foss and Ralph Larkin argued that the youth movement that confronted society at the social, cultural, and psychic levels had gone through "alternating processes of political confrontation and cultural intensification" before declining rapidly in the early seventies. During a decade of growing social turmoil, a conspicuous fraction of America's white, middle-class youth and its allies attacked— when they were not ignoring—the dominant institutions and social values. They not only questioned what the broader society said was reality, they took delight in scandalizing its morality and in dreaming up new ways to do so.

Foss and Larkin saw the youth movement as going through four alternating phases of overt politics and cultural intensification: (1) between 1960 and 1965, the "old" New Left of the civil rights and Berkeley Free Speech movements sought community and humanitarian social reform; (2) between 1965 and 1967, the hippie phase intensified the cultural aspect with a revolt built around music, sex, drugs, and mysticism; (3) emerging in 1967, the "new" New Left moved toward revolutionary confrontation in the streets of Chicago; (4) the youth movement as a whole lapsed, exhaustedly, in 1969, into a mellow "freak-radical" period of collective personal liberation, or "Woodstock Aquarian" phase. For Foss and Larkin, the normative figures of the counterculture were first the SNCC, SDS, and Berkeley leaders; then, for the hippie phase, the communitarian Diggers, Timothy Leary, Ken Kesey, and the acid-rock groups such as the Grateful Dead and the Jefferson Airplane. For the "new" New Left phase, they were SDS and the Yippies; and in the weary end-of-the-decade Aquarian phase, the various communes and collectives. In the electronic age of the sixties, radio and television raced to turn local action into national patterns as the pace of change accelerated.

In 1969, the California philosopher Theodore Roszak, in *The Making of a Counter Culture,* gave the emerging counterculture its name. What was happening, he wrote, was that generational disaffiliation was being transformed into "a major lever of radical social change." The young were getting dissent "off the adult drawing board." In a dialectical way, the young had emerged as a new social class, rising out of and in opposition to a mature industrial society whose world view was based on rationality and technology. When Tom Hayden made a similar case in SDS's Port Huron statement, he spoke for a small, advanced sector of college socialist dissent. Seven years later, Roszak maintained, cultural dissent had come to identify a generation. For the first time, a national youth culture had emerged in the United States, but it was not possible at the end of the sixties to tell how much of its behavior was generational and how much was social alienation and political revolt, and how far it was all going to go.

YOUTH

By the beginning of the sixties, the Baby Boom had produced a consumption-oriented, teen-aged nation of 25 million people. They lived, primarily, outside the work world, gathered together in large educational institutions. By mid-decade, the college population had nearly doubled to 6.5 million, occupying an extended interval between adolescence and adult membership in the job market. With the preentry period thus extended for so large a number, the postadolescent "youth" stratum of society became an important social factor. If a class is traditionally identified by its relationship to the means of production, this new "youth generation" was characterized by the absence of such a relationship. In *A Troubled Feast* (1979), the modern U.S. historian William Leuchtenburg described the "special circumstances" of the sixties as "the emergence of a generation of young people endowed with a superabundance of worldly goods, locked into an educational system for two decades or more, cordoned off into multiversities, roiled by the draft and the Vietnam War, troubled by its prospects in a world that seemed increasingly bureaucratized and technologically driven." While the world of adolescence and youth is not necessarily one of alienation, a special stream of social consciousness converged with youthful self-consciousness in the 1960s to create the counter culture.

ROCK

Music was central to the life of the young. It was immediately accessible, the most important consumption item: turned up loud on the radio, bought at the record store, traded or borrowed. It could belong to you as an individual, alone in your room—with Father pounding on the door—or dorm, as a personal mystical experience or in common communion. In the 1930s and 1940s, "Your Hit Parade" touched the heart, and folk music moved the collegiate social conscience; by the mid-1960s, rock tapped the autonomic system. Before this, popular music had generally been written by distant professional songwriters and played from a score by older men, all wearing jackets of the same color and usually led by someone who played a horn or a woodwind. The critic and *Partisan Review* editor Richard Poirier (*The Performing Self* [1971]) wrote that for people of school age, it was the first time that their music was invented by "their own near contemporaries," with whose "lyrics, manner and dress" they could identify. Rock was something that belonged only to them. Where before they had been adolescent, their music made them tribal.

In February 1964, the variety show host Ed Sullivan brought the Beatles to the United States and presented them to the national television audience. The result was electrifying. Their well-scrubbed look, their Teddy Boy dress and the hair down over their ears, their wit, their ensemble performance that did not submerge the individual personalities, their compelling but not overwhelming acoustical beat, and their lyrics of love and holding hands created a powerful personal chemistry. They came across as real. Particularly for an age group who had perhaps been the most vulnerable to the shock and insecurity caused by the murder of their young president in Dallas only three months before, there was now a replacement in the cheerful, cheeky, talented "Fab Four" from Liverpool.

The rock sound became a rock culture. For the young, it was total immersion. According to the critic Albert Goldman in *New American Review* (April 1968), it was "part aphrodisiac, part narcotic, and part hallucinogen." By the latter part of the sixties, it had become pretty much literally all three. The Beatles' music had come out of black America. It had been named "rock 'n' roll" in the mid-fifties by the disc jockey Alan Freed and introduced in the white world by Bill Haley and the Comets, Buddy Holly, and Elvis Presley. When rock seemed moribund in the early sixties, the Beatles revitalized it with a British reinterpretation and a dynamic new group sound.

The Beatles loosened up and set the style of the sixties youth culture and countercultures. They launched the wearing of long hair by men and dressing up in outlandish fashion. Their name was inspired by the early rock heroes Buddy Holly and the Crickets, and they touched base with Bob Dylan as he was moving from folk music to rock. When the Beatles first swept into America, they were singing teen love plaints such as "I Want to Hold Your Hand." That was 1964. Two short years later, John Lennon boasted, "We're more popular than Jesus Christ now." They touched youthful loneliness with "Eleanor Rigby" and "Hey, Jude," and sang about running away in "She's Leaving Home." At their peak in 1966, while the summer of love and drugs was unfolding in San Francisco, they got high with the songs in their album *Revolver*—and higher with "Lucy in the Sky with Diamonds" and at least four other psychedelic drug songs in their *Sgt. Pepper's Lonely Hearts Club Band*. They changed the visual landscape with their *Yellow Submarine* movie, floated off to the gurus of India, land of the sitar, for more mysteries, and took a bad trip in "A Day in the Life." Their call was for peace, not violence: aggression was for Mick Jagger and the Stones. John Lennon wrote the anti–Vietnam War anthem "Give Peace a Chance," but the murderous Charles Manson "family" misread the message of "Helter Skelter" in the *White Album* as a prophetic call for racial war—and horror. The range and excitement of the Beatles' musicianship and creative talent were part of the bridge that brought the high culture into a loose combination with the popular culture of the sixties. The constant experimentation with dress, drugs, life style, and musical form both reflected the frenetic pace of change in the second half of the sixties and also influenced the many young people, who took the Beatles as cultural heroes and models.

Music had strengthened the resolve of the civil rights movement— singing, clapping, holding hands, swaying, marching. "We Shall Not Be Moved," "Ain't Nobody Gonna Turn Us Around," "Woke Up This Morning with My Mind Stayed on Freedom," "We Shall Overcome," and "Oh, Freedom!" were sung in hot, crowded black churches in southwestern Georgia, in jail in Mississippi, or on the road in Alabama. The freedom songs were essentially religious. They came from deep in the heart and the black experience, and made commitment.

The message of the folksingers such as Pete Seeger, Phil Ochs, Joan Baez, and Bob Dylan was political. Seeger, who had belonged to the older Left, brought word of people's causes and struggles in other places and times. Joan Baez, with her silver-pure voice, was always there, sitting-in at Berkeley's Sproul Hall, married to Stanford draft resister–student president David Harris, waiting alone in bus stations late at night to catch the bus to the next day's antiwar concert. Dylan's politics were deeply personal, and in his own searching he gave others a handle, if not the meaning, for their own paths. In 1962, he was asking, "How many roads must a man go down?" measuring the Cuban missile crisis with "A Hard Rain's A-Gonna Fall," and writing "Oxford Town" about James Meredith at Ole Miss. At the end of 1963, John Kennedy was dead, and Dylan was singing "The Times They Are A-Changin'." The story is that when the Beatles visited Dylan on their first American trip he turned them on to marijuana, although it is difficult to believe that the bars and cafes of Liverpool and Hamburg had not already performed an introduction. In July 1965, as Lyndon Johnson was committing American troops in Vietnam and bombing north of the seventeenth parallel, Dylan was booed when he showed up at the Newport Jazz Festival in high-heeled boots and a black leather jacket, playing rock on an electric guitar. They booed him, but he was right. Rock was "where it's at." Although he never mobilized marchers in the streets, Dylan's lyrics were a scriptural resource for the sixties. "Like A Rolling Stone" provided a name for both the magazine and Mick Jagger's group. In the line "You don't need a weatherman to know which way the wind blows" (from "Subterranean Homesick Blues"), the SDS militants found their name. As they turned to violence and went underground, they thought they saw their path in the line "The pump don't work 'cause the vandals took the handles."

LIBERATION

Somewhere about 1967, the year of the great Be-In in Golden Gate Park and the March on the Pentagon, the hippie culture turned into the counterculture. San Francisco gave birth to it. In a trend copied in New York's East Village and in student ghettos across the country, sex, drugs, and rock found a crash pad in Haight-Ashbury. Life was psychedelia. Country Joe and the Fish, the Jefferson Airplane, and the Grateful Dead played their acid rock and lived communally. Before *Hair* acted it out on stage, they were already a tribal-love-rock musical. The model had been created.

Drugs had always been around, but in the eyes of most white, middle class Americans, they belonged to the outlaw classes—blacks, Mexicans, Chinese, and jazz musicians. In respectable America, housewives took tranquilizers, businessmen sipped martinis, long-distance truck drivers popped pep pills, workingmen drank beer, and Seagram's and 7-Up was the national standard; but that was "different." In the mid-sixties, marijuana and LSD tapped into the new, affluent world of the white, middle-class youth generation. Marijuana—"pot," or "grass," made from the female hemp plant, the forbidden "reefers" that their parents had been warned against in their youth—had been around for a long time. The properties of lysergic acid diethylamide, synthesized from rye wheat fungus, were discovered by a Swiss chemist in the 1940s. Both marijuana and LSD were mind-altering drugs, or hallucinogens. "Pot," except in heavy doses, gave most people a relaxed, euphoric feeling, while LSD, or "acid," jumbled perceptual and cognitive experience, relaxing emotional controls, intensifying color and sound, distorting time, space and the sense of self, and causing heightened body awareness. Neither pot nor acid was physiologically habit forming, although you never knew just what you might be taking, and acid could turn a neurotic person psychotic and even suicidal.

"Getting stoned" on pot or "tripping" on acid was the thing to do. It was an escape from the hassles and stress of the everyday world, an expansion of consciousness, an intensification of euphoria, and a new kind of community ritual and world, with incense, strobe lights and surrealistic posters, cushions on the floor, and the Beatles, the Jefferson Airplane, or the Doors (who found their name in Aldous Huxley's use of William Blake's "Doors of Perception" to describe his discovery of mescaline) on the stereo. Following defrocked Harvard professor and LSD's self-appointed high priest and publicist, Timothy Leary's, advice to "tune in, turn on, and drop out" was not why parents had sent their children off to college.

Too little was known about the long-run effects of the drugs, and there were conflicting reports about genetic damage. A different kind of damage was possible penalty if you were "busted" for dealing or possession. Marijuana and—after 1966—LSD were illegal. Punishment, although erratic, could be severe. Parents argued that using pot often led to harder and more dangerous drugs, and it frequently did. Stimulants and depressants, "uppers" and "downers," were part of the culture. In the hippie and dropout worlds, people often took whatever came their way, including heroin. Cocaine was not yet a youth or a black thing. "Coke" was part of the "fast life" of society— movie stars and musicians—and it cost too much. Amid all the comings and goings and confusion, drugs had entered the world of youth and white middle-class America.

Hallucinogens did not increase sexual potency, but when in 1966 Timothy Leary told *Playboy* that "LSD is the most powerful aphrodisiac known to man," he did wonders for its reputation. Pot did relax inhibitions, and often the capacity to do anything about it. Sex had hardly had to wait for the 1960s to make its appearance. In the hothouse world of youth, the obstacles had been moral principle, disease, pregnancy, parental disapproval, the dean of women, inexperience, and lack of opportunity. With affluence; penicillin; the pill; the campus population explosion; off-campus living; and the generational challenge to existing patterns, restraints, and values, the sixties became a world of greater permissiveness, less guilt, and more sex. The old campus rules—visiting hours, open dorm room doors, and curfews, along with the college acting *in loco parentis*—were a thing of the past. *Life* magazine's May 31, 1968 story about "The Arrangement" reported that the Judicial Council at Barnard College had voted to suspend the snack bar privileges of a student for living with her Columbia University boyfriend. Along with couples at Louisiana State, Florida, Wayne State, and Berkeley, whose pictures *Life* also displayed, Barnard sophomore Linda LeClair and her roommate Peter Behr had reached the "fifteen minutes of celebrity" that artist Andy Warhol predicted would be allotted to everybody in the new pop culture world.

To whatever degree it was adopted, the mode of the counterculture had been established. The range and extent of youthful participation were wide and varied, but the anguish of parents and the hostility of the police were intense. While some, in Allen Matusow's words, "abandoned the rhetoric of love for the politics of rage," the counterculture was more of a value shift and a withdrawal than a political assault. Janis Joplin summed up its antipolitical side, saying, "My music isn't supposed to make you riot. It's supposed to make you fuck." With the counterculture, sexual language had come out of the closet. By the end of the decade, not only were truck drivers wearing their hair down to their shoulders, but young women were talking like truck drivers. The real question for those who, like Theodore Roszak, saw the counterculture as a lever for radical social change, was whether it could be "political" without being political. Could societal liberation be achieved by self-liberation? While Roszak argued the futility of a politics that concentrated on changing institutions ("redesigning the turrets and towers"), his East Coast counterpart, Yale Law School professor Charles Reich—in the best-seller *The Greening of America* (1970)—saw the hip world of beads, bells, and music easing America into Consciousness III.

Although the counterculture did not produce a revolution that reshaped America's turrets and towers, it did have a marked impact on values and standards. In the sixties, the literary critic Morris Dickstein explained, the line between the high and the popular cultures gave way. Appropriately using Dylan's song "Gates of Eden" as the title for his 1978 book, he pointed out that "rock was the culture of the sixties in a unique and special way." The arts of the sixties were kinetic, full of energy and intensity. They made you want to move. If you didn't like rock, you would not like what was going on in the other arts either.

HIGH CULTURE

A distinguished spokesman for the New York intelligentsia, the Social Democrat Irving Howe, decried what he saw as a debasement of high culture's role. "Alienation has been transformed from a serious and revolutionary concept into a motif of mass culture," he complained. In reality, he was protesting against the shift in consciousness that had come to characterize the culture of the sixties: the emphasis on taste, experience, and emotion, instead of rationality and cognition. Part of the evolving high-culture mode known as Postmodernism, which focused on how the audience experienced the work of art, had challenged the rational, analytical analysis of the previously dominant New Criticism. Immediacy and immersion replaced aesthetic distance. This new sensibility led to a Dionysian attack on standards and restraints. No wonder the counterculture's values were so threatening to authorities and parents.

NORMAN MAILER

"Change the prevailing mode of consciousness," Roszak had proclaimed, "and you change the world." At the end of the fifties, in a book appropriately titled *Advertisements for Myself* (1959), the novelist Norman Mailer explained that he was out to make "a revolution in the consciousness of our time." He tried out the possibility that John Fitzgerald Kennedy might be the archetype of romantic possibilities that would tap the subterranean river of emotion inside us ("Superman Comes to the Supermarket," *Esquire,* November 1960, reprinted in *The Presidential Papers* [1963]). Not unpredictably, Mailer had to settle for himself, the artist, as the center of sixties existentialism.

Mailer was of an earlier generation. Born in New Jersey in 1923 and raised in a middle-class Jewish family in Brooklyn, he was a child prodigy in search of fame. Entering Harvard at sixteen, he earned a degree in engineering and "discovered modern American literature." He was drafted, soldiered in the Philippines during the latter part of World War II, and afterward quickly wrote the war's best American novel. *The Naked and the Dead* (1948) was a big, complex, 1930s-style naturalist account of the brutalities of war and the corruption of power in a failed campaign on a jungle island in the Pacific.

The 1950s were not a good time for Mailer. He was as much a celebrity for his boozing and brawling as for his writing; the successful second novel did not come, as he mixed sexual fantasy with a warning against totalitarianism both in the Soviet Union and in Senator Joseph McCarthy's America. By the end of the decade, he increasingly turned away from social commentary to dig more deeply into the irrational and instinctual depths of the psyche in search of the repressed vital forces that could break through the dull conformity of American life. Shaking himself loose from the sex, violence, and power compulsions that had occupied him in *An American Dream* (1965), he found his voice in his Pulitzer Prize–winning account of the 1967 protest march on the Pentagon in *Armies of the Night* (1968). Here Mailer's subject, presented in third-person narration, was the initiation of Norman Mailer, speechmaker and jailed demonstrator, existential activist and cosmic fool. In "the Pentagon," Mailer found a symbol for the "oncoming totalitarianism" and the cultural oppressiveness that lay at the base of American politics. Now he was marching to assault it: "High church of the corporation, the Pentagon spoke exclusively of mass man and his civilization; every aspect of the building was anonymous, monotonous, massive, interchangeable." At the great Pentagon be-in, Mailer was exploring his own consciousness along with that of a "new generation" that hated authority and, he wrote, "believed in LSD, in witches, in tribal knowledge, in orgy, and revolution. . . . [and] had no respect whatsoever for the unassailable logic of the next step."

AGAINST INSTITUTIONS

Psychologist-prophets led by R. D. Laing proclaimed "the holy mystery of madness" and the insanity of ordinary life. The most-read postmodernist novelists, Joseph Heller (*Catch 22* [1960]), Ken Kesey (*One Flew over the Cuckoo's Nest* [1962]), and Kurt Vonnegut (*Slaughterhouse-Five* [1969]), wrote of a society of institutional insanity, with little distinction between Milo Minderbinder's air force, Big Nurse's hospital, and Billy Pilgrim's world that killed and maimed. Susan Sontag summed up for sensibility in *Against Interpretation* (1966) that art was aimed not at stimulation of moral sentiment but at giving pleasure. It was based on sensation, not ideas. The theater and the movies—which were, along with rock, the prime art forms of the young—became sexier, nuder, more political, more violent, and more cruel.

"Off Broadway" and guerrilla theater playwrights went in for everything they could think of that could be performed on the stage. The cast of *Hair* took off all their clothes for a brief moment of total nudity, although the audience could see nothing because it was impossible to focus with so many bodies on stage. In *Paradise Now,* Judith Malina and Julian Beck's Living Theater tried to get the audience to undress, and the cast of *Che* either did or pretended to do on stage everything that *Hair* sang about:

Join the Holy Orgy
Kama Sutra Everyone.

The most mentioned, if not most read, social philosopher of the later sixties was the Frankfurt School dogmatist Herbert Marcuse. Marcuse combined radical political and cultural dissent with his concern about alienation and the oppressiveness of American materialistic success in *One-Dimensional Man* (1964). In *Eros and Civilization* (1954), he had coupled the revolutionary Marx with the conservative Freud to explain that advanced industrial society imposed more sexual repression than was necessary to maintain civilization. End this surplus repression and a new reign of sexuality and joy would infuse society. Having been adopted by the radical students, Marcuse discovered and toasted them in *An Essay on Liberation* (1969), but his influence was not a lasting one. C. Wright Mills had helped shape radical thinking; Marcuse was quoted more for what he justified than for what he stimulated.

Throughout the counterculture, the rejection of organization ran strong. Liberation, whether in the arts or in life, was opposed to established institutions and authorities. The political radicals delegitimated authority and cast about for alternatives. For some, the old ways would have to be destroyed before the new, whatever it might be, could emerge. For the Yippies, the communalists, and the vast body of Aquarians, the political meaning of the counterculture was that only through self-liberation could society be made better.

The Yippies were not a movement. They were a "put-on" trip created by Jerry Rubin and Abbie Hoffman, who got high, got bored with counterculture politics, and drifted into a guerrilla war against the establishment. As long as the media coverage held out, they were a sensation, attempting to levitate the Pentagon, dressing up in Revolutionary War uniforms to appear before the House Un-American Activities Committee, and playing games in the streets of Chicago with a pig that they presented as their presidential candidate. As Jerry Rubin described it, they were Marxists out of the revolutionary tradition of "Groucho, Chico, Harpo, and Karl."

COMMUNALISM

Beneath the sixties' efforts to reform society's institutions and ways, or to escape from them, lay a search for values and for a change in consciousness. In an effort that seldom has become so widespread and so manifest in American history, people were seeking a different way to relate to each other. The heart of SDS's Port Huron Statement was the call for a change in human values and relationships. The depersonalization and loneliness of a power-oriented society were to be replaced by a new, humane, world of interactive communities which the SDSers called "participatory democracy." The young students who formed the Student Nonviolent Coordinating Committee carried into it the religious idealism of the Nashville civil rights movement's "beloved community." Drawn together, supportively, under pressure, as missionaries of a new faith in a hostile land, their "freedom houses" in Mississippi were the first communes of the 1960s. Inspired by SNCC and the Freedom Summer, a portion of the New Left sought its Mississippi in the black ghettos of the North. Leaving their Northern campuses, SDS activists moved into spartan inner-city collectives in Baltimore, Newark, Cleveland, Chicago, and Oakland to live together and organize the poor for power.

By the end of the sixties, the hopeful idealism was gone on the Left, and community had become bizarre and coercive. SNCC left Mississippi and "that interracial crap." When the Weathermen went underground after the failed violence in Chicago, their communal "cadre" cells sought to discipline themselves harshly to destroy all lingering traces of bourgeois individualism that would unfit them for the revolution.

In the exhaustion of the end of the decade, Tom Hayden, who had been part of the early SDS Economic Research and Action Project collective in Newark, joined the Red Family, one of many small communes in Berkeley. Even in the politically oriented collectives, the mood had turned inward. Having failed to conquer the world in the streets, activists now had to reconstruct themselves and coercively change their own consciousness, to be ready when their time for the streets came again. The free, loving community of the early sixties had been replaced by ideological discipline and recrimination. In the consciousness-raising power struggles of the Red Family, Hayden was judged too aggressive and male chauvinist, and was expelled.

As the political potential for creating a new society was being burned out by the seemingly endless war in Vietnam and the revolutionary fantasies of New Left factionalism, a nonpolitical communalism emerged. For a moment, it seemed to some that they might be utopian pioneers out beyond Vietnam and LBJ's Great Society, who Theodore Roszak hoped would "discover new types of community, new family patterns, new sexual mores, new kinds of livelihood, new esthetic forms, new personal identities on the far side of power politics, the bourgeois home, and the consumer society." At the end of the decade, there was more going back and forth than ever before in American communal history. Perhaps several thousand communes, urban and

FIG. 3. From *Feiffer: Jules Feiffer's America from Eisenhower to Reagan*, edited by Steven Heller. Copyright © 1982 by Jules Feiffer. Reprinted by permission of Alfred A. Knopf, Inc.

rural, variously explored all of Roszak's hopes. They existed in all imaginable forms of meditation, craft, drug, occult, Christian and Oriental mysticism, and sensual and ecological self-exploration. The movement to the commune peaked around the turn of the seventies. Despite problems of authority and continuity, some communes have endured, while other intentional and alternative life-style communities continue to be formed. Over the following decade, much of the new communalism was expressed in religious seeking. Many cults, and particularly the Asian-bred ones, such as the Divine Light Mission, the Moonies, and the Hare Krishna society, sprang from a counter-counterculture search for doctrine and order.

WOODSTOCK AND BEYOND

The counterculture and the youth and pop cultures came together for three days in August 1969 near Woodstock, New York. There, jammed together on the hillsides of Max Yazgur's farm, more than a quarter of a million young people, clothed or naked, got turned on in the rain by pot, drugs, rock, and being together, and shut out the rest of the world. *Time* magazine got in on the spirit and wrote that "the festival turned out to be history's largest happening. As the moment when the special culture of U.S. youth of the '60s openly displayed its strength, appeal and power, it may well rank as one of the significant political and sociological events of the age." It is now a cliché that the "Woodstock Nation" died four months later on the

Altamont drag strip east of Berkeley, California, with bad acid, hate, and violence. The Hell's Angels motorcycle gang, hired as security guards, terrorized the crowd, and while Mick Jagger and the Stones performed, the Angels beat to death a pudgy, naked, drugged-out youth who had ventured too close to the stage.

Pot, hash, acid, uppers and downers, sex, rock, youth festivals, and happenings were all absorbed into the American free-market culture. Probably only comparatively few people withdrew completely from the straight world. Most of the rest, the young in particular, were touched by some part of the counterculture. Where they were, it was as much a consumption experience as it was radical alienation. The counterculture produced freer expressive behavior, but not a broad new culture of opposition or the new world it had once seemed to promise. Two low-budget movies of 1969 summed up the failure to remake America. Was there ever a chance? "We blew it," Peter Fonda's *Easy Rider* acknowledged in a lucid moment during its drug trip across southside America. In *Alice's Restaurant,* Ray stood forlornly in the doorway and Alice was left with the dirty dishes in the kitchen as all the others went on their way after dinner — probably to a rock festival, but not an antiwar demonstration. Vietnam was a lyric to the counterculture, not an all-encompassing cause. The most important political concern at the end of the sixties was the war, and the counterculture was antipolitical.

7. President's War, Media War

In his much-admired book *Dispatches* (1977), the correspondent Michael Herr told of an incident in which Ambassador Henry Cabot Lodge, visiting the Saigon Zoo in 1963, was pissed on by a tiger through the bars of its cage. Lodge joked with his accompanying newsmen to the effect that "he who wears the pee of the tiger is assured of success in the coming year." Herr's comment was less reassuring. "Maybe nothing's so unfunny as an omen read wrong," he wrote. Never in the history of America's wars did the presidents of the United States read their situation so wrongly as they did during the Vietnam War.

Wars have been hard on American presidents. James K. Polk, exhausted from the handling of the war with Mexico, did not stand for reelection and died two years later. Lincoln was assassinated just as the Civil War was drawing to a close. Wilson suffered what was probably a mild stroke during the Versailles Peace Conference and a more severe one during his unsuccessful fight for the ratification of the treaty. Franklin Roosevelt died of a stroke just a month before victory in Europe, and Harry Truman stepped down, discredited by the stalemated struggle in Korea. In Vietnam, once American ground troops were committed, little went well for the occupants of the White House.

Like none other, Vietnam was a president's war. Usually, after the surprises or the diplomatic maneuvering, a president would go to Congress for a declaration of war, and the armed services would then set about trying to win the war. Although Congress was never asked to declare war, the Korean conflict was a comprehensible one whose progress could be followed on the map. The war in Vietnam was an undeclared "limited war" on behalf of an uncooperative client in Saigon, against a misread foe in Hanoi, for unexamined reasons, with contradictory goals and covertly changing strategies. It was fought with no clear battle lines, by presidents who agonized over maintaining limits, tried to fine-tune the battlefield efforts, and struggled to hide the war from the American people. After Hanoi's surprise 1968 Tet offensive, with more than half a million American troops already in Vietnam and after the aerial war in which more bombs had been dropped than in all of World War II, the generals asked for 206,000 more men, enough to require a calling-up of the civilian reserves. When the new defense secretary, Clark Clifford, went into the "battle room" of the Pentagon and asked what could be accomplished with the additional troops, no one could tell him.

THE FAILURE TO UNDERSTAND

There were few corners of the world about which Americans and their leaders knew less than they did about Vietnam. Ignorant of the history of the Vietnamese people and their millennial battle against Chinese, French, and Japanese colonial domination, American policy makers misread the postwar renewal of that struggle as a part of a worldwide Sino-Soviet thrust. Franklin Roosevelt had somehow been convinced that French rule was a sorry disgrace and should not be restored, but he was now dead, and the cold war guided American understanding. France was a crucial ally that had to be supported. With the triumph of the Communists on the Chinese mainland, and the war in Korea, the cold war policy of containment moved to Asia in the form of the "domino theory." If French Indochina fell, the reasoning went, the Philippines would be threatened and all the nations of Southeast Asia would topple. In the 1950s, the United States was paying 80 percent of France's war costs and had even considered atomic intervention when a French army entrapped itself at Dien Bien Phu. At the 1954 Geneva Conference, the weary French agreed to withdraw. Under Russian and Chinese pressure to compromise, Ho Chi Minh accepted a temporary division of Vietnam at the seventeenth parallel, with the country to be reunited by a national election in two years.

The Americans, misreading the strength of Vietnamese nationalism and seeing only the Communist aspect, hoped to create a separate state in the South. In the resulting Saigon power struggle, Ngo Dinh Diem, a rigid, mandarin representative of the landlord class and a member of the Roman Catholic minority, emerged victorious. Diem and his American backers refused to hold the promised reunification election. As the Kennedy administration took office in the United States, the war had begun again on a guerrilla level in the South.

To John Kennedy, Vietnam was a bothersome sideshow. It was also "a test" of American strength in holding back Communism, winning wars of national liberation, maintaining commitments, and showing toughness. For Secretary of State Dean Rusk, it was always a matter of containing Chinese expansion. The Diem government and its successors in South Vietnam were no worse than the static and repressive regimes of privileged elites that the withdrawing colonial countries were leaving behind them all over the world. What the successive American presidents failed to understand was that they were faced by the dynamism of war-hardened, disciplined, Communist-led forces that represented anticolonial nationalism and a desire for social change.

The deteriorating situation forced both John Kennedy, in 1961, and Lyndon Johnson, in 1965, to escalate the commitment of American forces to prevent a South Vietnamese collapse. In doing so, they changed the nature of the American involvement in the war. Johnson inherited Kennedy's advisors and sixteen thousand troops in Vietnam, presumably not engaging in combat. Five years later, there were more than half a million, bearing the major share of the fighting and supported by an awesome aerial technology, from helicopter gunships to B-52s. With the attention of the American people caught by pictures of Buddhist monks incinerating themselves on the streets of Saigon and stories of the murder of President Diem during an American-supported army coup, there was no quiet path open for the president. As the political and psychological stakes increased, first Kennedy, then Johnson, then Nixon, chose to expand the war to escape being tagged as having lost it.

At no time before the Tet offensive in 1968 did the various presidents and their top aides undertake serious, long-range consideration of what they were doing. The national security advisors believed that their role was to tell the president what he wanted to hear. Basically, American purpose was characterized by a series of negatives. Lyndon Johnson's goals were to keep South Vietnam out of the hands of the Communists, avoid bringing China into the war, and escape a backlash at home that would endanger the Great Society legislation in Congress. This meant avoiding heavy American casualties, not calling up the reserves, and not increasing taxes or formally declaring war. The fighting was to be kept limited, short, and relatively painless. Hanoi was to be forced to accept a permanent partition of Vietnam, and a non-Communist government in Saigon. All the various American bombing halts and negotiation offers were based on these conditions, which were directly contrary to the cause for which North Vietnam's ruling League for Vietnamese Independence (the Viet Minh) was fighting. Since their purpose was to unite all of Vietnam under communist leadership, it is not surprising that Hanoi and its southern arm, the National Liberation Front (the NLF, or—as the Americans deconstructed the term "Vietnam Communists"—"Viet Cong") refused to cooperate.

ESCALATION

The reports of an attack on American ships in the Gulf of Tonkin and the shelling of the American officers' billet at Pleiku provided the excuse for committing American planes and troops in a protective-preventive reaction policy that kept expanding. The air force, the navy, and President Johnson overrated the effectiveness of airpower. The army wanted to mobilize the reserves and use full force on the enemy. The CIA, which had challenged the official view that the renewal of the war in the South had been imposed by Hanoi, questioned the effect of the bombing, and was again ignored. The president's advisors, the cream of the Ivy League universities and the foreign policy elite, misread Hanoi's will and staying power. With the exception of Under Secretary of State George Ball, they urged the president onward.

President Johnson chose "the slow squeeze," a graduated increase in the use of ground and air power, which became "Rolling Thunder's" bombing in the North and the war of attrition, with its "search and destroy" missions and "body counts," in the South. Following Johnson in the White House, Richard Nixon adopted a strategy of pressuring Hanoi by bombing ferociously, and reducing American casualties by turning over the ground fighting to the South Vietnamese army. All of these steps were designed to force agreement from Hanoi by increasing the pain—a pain which, as the CIA reported, Hanoi was apparently willing to endure. As early as 1966, in a note to Defense Secretary Robert McNamara, his aide John McNaughton offered a summary of the trap into which American policy had worked itself. The purpose, he wrote, had come to be 70 percent to avoid the humiliation of defeat, 20 percent to keep South Vietnam out of Chinese hands, and 10 percent to provide a better way of life for the people of South Vietnam. As much as possible, this confusion of purpose was kept hidden from the American people by the administrations of presidents Kennedy, Johnson, and Nixon.

Along with the other disagreements that always come with an unsuccessful war, there have been at least five major controversies over why things turned out as they did in Vietnam and whether they could have been different. The *"full and fast squeeze"* argument is that the armed services could have won the war had they been permitted to do so through unrestrained use of military force. The *"Tet"* argument is that what was ultimately a major military victory for the American and South Vietnamese armies was undercut by media-abetted defeatism on the home front. The *"aid and comfort"* argument is that antiwar dissent in America had encouraged Hanoi to continue the fight. The *"hearts and minds"* argument has focused on the question of a political as opposed to a military solution through winning the support of the civilian population. The *"slippery slope"* or *"quagmire,"* dispute centers on whether the deepening involvement stemmed from the failure to "foresee consequences" or the deliberate covert scripting of an unfortunate escalation. One point on which the subsequent critics agreed was that the American people should never be expected to sustain a prolonged, undeclared war, and should not be asked to do so.

The underlying assumption in the first four arguments was that some sort of a limited military victory had been possible which would have forced Hanoi to accept an independent, non-Communist state in the South. Once American armed forces were committed, General William Westmoreland and the Joint Chiefs of Staff maintained, they should have been allowed to do whatever was necessary to win. Despite evidence to the contrary, many of the military leaders continued to believe that airpower could have been decisive in North Vietnam and that failure to use its full potential doomed American forces to an unavailing war of attrition in the South.

Other critics have argued that heavier bombing would not have been effective in destroying Hanoi's willingness and capacity to fight. They hold that the key to success was not in the North but in the South. The core of nation-building in South Vietnam was the safety and allegiance of the people: the winning of "hearts and minds." Although the U.S. Army preferred an offensive strategy, an alternative plan to interdict supplies and troops from the North while the South Vietnamese forces protected the villages and cleared out the Viet Cong would have fitted within the traditional role of the military. Providing population security and community development for the villages would not, and successful counterinsurgency might have necessitated basic changes in how the army operated. The angry comment of a frustrated senior officer, "I'll be damned if I permit the United States Army, its institutions, its doctrine, and its traditions to be destroyed just to win this lousy war," has been widely quoted by those who believe that Vietnam showed that the American military was not prepared to deal with unconventional wars.

Vietnam's postwar economic failures, corruption, and oppressiveness, and the flood of boat refugees have made Hanoi seem less invincible in retrospect. American troops did fight well, particularly in conventional battles, and the countryside did not rise in support of Hanoi when it launched the Tet offensive. The South Vietnamese soldiers, on occasion, fought resolutely, and villagers preferred to be left alone rather than have their sons conscripted by the Viet Cong. Nevertheless, all the years of bombing the North, the two intensive campaigns of 1972, and the various incursions into Laos and Cambodia failed to disrupt the flow of men and supplies to the South. The successive regimes in Saigon never found—or seemed much interested in seeking—a way to reach out to the people and the villages, in order to build a South Vietnamese nation. The incompetence, corruption, and oppressiveness of Saigon's governmental and military systems, which indiscriminately bombed their own people, tortured and killed prisoners, and made unit commanders and hamlets pay for artillery support, would be difficult to equal. The American commanders and ambassadors, such as Generals Paul Harkin, William Westmoreland, and Maxwell Taylor, and those around them who told them what they wanted to hear, never understood what was happening. During the American Civil War, it had taken President Lincoln long, painful years to find the right generals for the Union armies. The Vietnam War presidents never found a Ulysses Grant or a William Tecumseh Sherman.

THE PROLONGED and costly inability to either win or withdraw should leave no doubt that Vietnam was indeed a quagmire for the United States. The air assault on North Vietnam was no hasty improvision. The attack on the American helicopter base and army barracks at Pleiku served as an excuse to put plans into operation which the administration believed necessary to prevent the collapse of the South Vietnamese war effort. The commitment of ground forces had not been part of the administration's plan or intention, but with the bombing of the North, it had set its foot further down the "slippery slope." The next step was to send in marines to protect the airbases; in two years there were half a million American fighting men in Vietnam.

THE MEDIA AND THE WAR

From the return of the French in 1945 to the fall of Saigon in 1975, the Vietnamese revolution stretched out over thirty years. From the major introduction of American troops in 1965 to the "peace" agreement in January 1973, the direct American involvement lasted seven of those years, and the media reported its events as they had never before covered a war. Although the distaste of generals for newsmen has a long history, it has, for the most part, been without reason. The traditional role of the press is that of a well-censored, patriotic cheerleader. As long as the war in Vietnam was small and the prospects favorable, media coverage was limited and generally supportive. When American troops went into action, the coverage grew. There was more about the war in the press, and it came into everyone's home via television every night. "The living-room war," Michael Arlen, the *New Yorker's* correspondent, called it. Although Washington always reported that the United States was winning, it never won, but it was not until the war became more clearly out of control that the coverage even partially followed suit.

The first generation of Vietnam newsmen represented the print media. They were a skilled, post–World War II cohort that included David Halberstam, Neil Sheehan, Charles Mohr, Homer Bigart, Jerry Rose, and Malcolm Browne, mostly representing *Time,* the *New York Times,* and the Associated Press. They did not question the war, but they refused to "get on the team" and accept the view—presented at the official briefings—that the situation was promising and all was going well. Instead, they went out into the field with American advisors such as Colonel John Paul Vann, later the subject of a brilliant Pulitzer–Prize winning biography by Neil Sheehan (*A Bright Shining Lie: John Paul Vann and America in Vietnam* [1988]), and reported back that Diem and the generals were corrupt, the villages were not secure, and the South Vietnamese Army was not willing to fight. This created problems back in the editorial offices in New York. Henry Luce, the mandarin ruler of the *Time-Life* empire, never doubted the vital necessity of saving Asia from the Communists and refused to support his Saigon staff. The *New York Times,* on the other hand, was not going to water down its coverage, as it had done in 1961 with Ted Szulc's story of the planned Bay of Pigs operation, and it did not accept President Kennedy's complaints that Halberstam needed "a change in assignments." Even so, when the news desks in New York checked their newsmen's reports through their Washington bureaus, there was a strong tendency to accept the word of the State and Defense Departments that the reporters were too close to their stories and were losing objectivity.

Television Arrives in Vietnam. With the commitment of ground forces in 1965, the television reporters arrived. Just as the path to a general's rank in the army led through troop command in Vietnam, so the rising stars of television news earned their place by covering the war. Sam Donaldson, Charles Kuralt, Garrick Utley, Ed Bradley, Morley Safer, Ted Koppel, and Dan Rather all reported back from Vietnam. The evening news had been newly born in 1963, with its time increased from fifteen to thirty minutes. Color television came two years later. Working with cameramen carrying new, lightweight cameras with synchronized magnetic sound, the reporters sent their best tapes back to New York by the newly available satellite, to be reshaped into useable stories and presented by the "anchorman" sitting at the big desk in the middle of the newsroom studio. By 1968 there were almost two hundred print and television reporters covering the war.

While the argument continues over how good their coverage was, the best path to understanding how the American people received their picture of the war has come from the political scientist Daniel

Hallin's 1986 study *The "Uncensored War": The Media and Vietnam*. Hallin defined three levels of media coverage, running from *consensus*, through *legitimate controversy*, to *deviance*. Initially, there was only "consensus" about Vietnam. The United States was defending the security of the Free World by containing Communist aggression. It was "us" against "them," and *they* were fanatical, cruel, and ruthless. Only the official U.S. government view was reported. The Communist side, and the objections to American involvement, lay beyond respectability, in the sphere of *deviance*, and did not need to be explained or presented.

When there was consensus in the government, the media reflected it. When there was bad news and disagreement within the administration, or when questions were raised by recognized authorities, the media became more detached, questioning, and even adversarial. The news was not good, official policy was not succeeding, and the government failed to control the definition of the situation. The NLF was winning, Diem was attacking the Buddhists, American troops were taking a combat role, and Washington was considering escalation. The administration's contradictory effort to signal Hanoi that it was willing to raise the military stakes, while at the same time trying to assure the American people that it was not doing so, created major problems for news management. Differences within the administration were leaked. Leading senators asked questions. Only then, in the realm of "legitimate controversy," did coverage approach objectivity.

When there was confusion in Washington it was mirrored in the press. The war always had its supporters. The hard-liner Joseph Alsop questioned whether President Johnson was "man enough" to use the necessary force, and the *Washington Post* remained hawkish until 1968. When *New York Times* correspondent Harrison Salisbury sent reports from Hanoi about the damage to civilians from American bombing, colleagues criticized his dispatches. Although the Pulitzer Prize judges recommended him for the prize, the publishers' committee overruled them.

The most respected of American newspaper columnists, Walter Lippmann, brought back advice to Johnson from French president de Gaulle that military victory would be impossible. Lippmann's argument that Vietnam was not within America's sphere of vital interest brought him scorn from President Johnson but influenced press and congressional opinion. In 1964, Senator William Fulbright had guided the Tonkin Gulf resolution through the Senate almost without dissent. By the spring of 1966, his Foreign Relations Committee hearings offered a forum for respectable questioning of the war, but it was not until after the Tet offensive, two years later, that "our war" had become "the war," and nonelite dissent was gaining "legitimate controversy" coverage. The *New York Times* began to carry congressional criticism of the war on the front page, but kept its own critical analysis for its columns and editorials on the inside pages. While *Times* editorials, and national columnists such as Lippmann and James Reston, were important in New York and Washington, what the national audience read was the headlines. In the American tradition, this was the place for "news." What was elsewhere, if one wished to look for it, was opinion. While national administrations may lose the battles of the editorial page, through their ability to "make news" they dominate the headlines and thus monopolize the nation's attention.

The "Hot Medium." Television has its unique problems in presenting the news. Television is a "hot medium," offering a dramatic image to a very large and diverse audience, and capable of producing a highly emotional reaction. Television news is more costly than other forms of coverage and, in the days before Watergate, it was more cautious. Large portions of its audience, as well as its advertisers and the owners of its affiliate stations, dislike any movement away from conservative, "consensus" values. To hold the attention of the channel switchers and pass the viewers on to the network programming that follows, television news combines information with entertainment. With eight minutes devoted to commercials, the half-hour evening news has only twenty-two minutes to divide among some seventeen or eighteen items, usually only half of them illustrated by film. Even a feature story lasting more than a minute can not handle several different or contradictory elements. "Keep it simple" is the correspondent's guideline. As a result, each story is organized around a single well-defined theme, and the stories, like those from the wire services, are often more concerned with human interest than with political analysis. They report "what happened today," but not how things came to this point.

A series of images frozen in the minds of the viewers back home helped to define the Vietnam experience: the burning Buddhist monk, the Vietnamese mother and children swimming across the river to escape the war, the little, napalmed girl running naked down the road, the marines at Cam Ne setting fire to the village roofs with their Zippo lighters, the wounded American soldier on the stretcher being given a blood transfusion, the fighting inside the American embassy compound during the Tet offensive, General Loan killing a prisoner in the Saigon street, the family welcome for the returning American prisoners of war, the girl in black kneeling over the dead student at Kent State, the chaotic helicopter evacuation of the roof of the U.S.

embassy as Viet Minh forces captured Saigon, and, years later, the thousands of names on "the wall" of the Vietnam Veterans Memorial in Washington, D.C.

There can be little doubt that the news photographers and the television cameramen showed what a hard, dirty war it was. Even assuming that the American public was not already case-hardened to blood and violence on its television screens, the war of attrition, with all its search-and-destroy missions, free-fire zones, kill ratios and body counts, provided relatively few battle pictures. The Viet Cong's jungle units rarely waited for the helicopters and the cameramen to arrive.

The Tet offensive was different. Having drawn American forces to the support of remote bases, the Viet Cong launched a coordinated attack, under the cover of a Buddhist New Year (Tet) truce, on more than 150 cities, provincial and district capitals, and hamlets throughout South Vietnam. The American embassy compound in Saigon was penetrated, and the ancient capital of Hue was not recaptured until after almost a month of hard, house-to-house fighting. For months, the administration had been offering an optimistic analysis of the progress of the war and the weakening of the Viet Cong resolve. The media's first response to the surprise, the ferocity, and the magnitude of the Tet offensive was to portray it as a disaster for the Americans and South Vietnam. A little more than a week after it began the CBS anchorman Walter Cronkite went to Vietnam to have a look for himself. On his return, he presented a half-hour "special" on the war, talking about the destruction, the casualties, the refugees, and the damage to the pacification program. Three years before, after an earlier trip to Vietnam, Cronkite had reported that the United States had "made the courageous decision that communism's advance must be stopped in Asia and that guerrilla warfare as a means to a political end must be finally discouraged." Now his message was that the United States was not on the edge of defeat but that the North could match any escalation. "It seems now more certain than ever," he concluded, "that the bloody experience of Vietnam is to end in a stalemate." Watching the broadcast, President Johnson reportedly lamented, "Well, if I've lost Cronkite, I've lost Middle America."

Cronkite. By 1967, "The CBS Evening News with Walter Cronkite" had passed NBC's "Huntley-Brinkley Report" in the ratings and become the nation's leading news program. Until the management of CBS began cutting costs in the 1980s to pay for defeating a take-over bid by the Atlanta broadcasting mogul Ted Turner, the CBS news staff was clearly television's best. According to press polls in the aftermath of Watergate, Walter Cronkite was "the most trusted man in America."

Born in 1916, the son of a St. Joe, Missouri, dentist, Cronkite had dropped out of the University of Texas in his junior year and worked as a radio sportscaster, and then as a reporter for the *Houston Post*. In 1942 he went off to London to cover World War II for the United Press International (UPI) wire service. Edward R. Murrow was making his reputation with his nightly broadcasts amid the bombing: "Hello, America, this is London calling." Murrow sought to add Cronkite to CBS's stable, which included William L. Shirer, Eric Severeid, Charles Collingwood, Richard Hottelet, and Howard K. Smith, but UPI gave Cronkite a twenty-five-dollar raise and he stayed on, making the crisp, fact-filled wire-service style his own. He covered the North African invasion, flew in a bomber raid over Europe, and reported the war in France and the low countries, and afterward the Nuremberg war trials. For two years, he was UPI's man in Moscow. Returning to the United States, he found that his $125 a week was not very much for a married man, and when a raise was not forthcoming, he returned to Kansas City and signed up with the local CBS radio affiliate, which sent him to Washington. Murrow picked him up for the network, though he was never one of "Murrow's boys." He did the live television coverage of the Democratic and Republican nominating conventions in the 1950s, and in 1962, with Murrow running the U.S. Information Agency for John Kennedy, Cronkite took on the newly named role of "anchorman" for CBS.

For nineteen years, as managing editor and anchorman, Walter Cronkite offered his television viewers a low-key, solid, deliberately middle-of-the-road report of the day's news. Much in the style shaped by his wire service years, he sought to avoid offering his own opinions and creating controversy. The image of the anchorman, sitting at the big desk in the middle of the newsroom, calmly and authoritatively tying together the reports coming in from all over the world, offered reassurance, if not coherence. Cronkite's graying hair and moustache, wrinkled face, calm manner, rich voice, and midwestern accent, and his mixture of what seemed a combination of objectivity and optimism about America, inspired confidence. As fellow newsman David Halberstam summed him up in a fascinating "soap opera" of a history of the contemporary media, *The Powers That Be* (1979), "in a difficult time, people had a sense of his being a good man, worthy of their trust." When one heard the nightly sign-off "And that's the way it is," a lulling sense of belief remained. In 1968, when Walter Cronkite spoke on the meaning of the Tet offensive, and again in 1972 when he focused attention on the Watergate break-in intrigues (which resulted in a backstage battle with CBS's top management over the coverage), the reporter was pushing the course of history.

Tet. While Lyndon Johnson was "losing" Middle America, a major portion of the Viet Cong's fighting capacity was all but being wiped out on the battlefields of Tet. The American and South Vietnamese forces suffered heavy casualties but fought well. There was neither a revolutionary uprising in the cities nor a massive defection of South Vietnamese troops. The war would continue, but it would be carried on primarily by forces that infiltrated from the North. Nevertheless, two months later, Johnson ended his televised message on the war with the unexpected withdrawal of his candidacy for reelection. The American role in the fighting would continue through the first administration of Richard Nixon, with a doubling of the casualties, but, after Tet, the U.S. policy was one of seeking a way to get out.

Many of those who believe that the results could have been otherwise, place much of the blame on the press and the media. A war that could have been won on the battlefield was lost in Washington. A major setback for Hanoi had been reported to the American people as a disaster for the United States. Johnson failed to provide additional troops, and defeatism spread across the nation. In a painstaking analysis of the Tet coverage, the *Washington Post*'s Saigon bureau chief Peter Braestrup later criticized its quality and follow-up. "Crisis journalism," he maintained, was always inadequate, and during Tet it did not convey the larger picture of what had actually happened.

From the beginning, America's Vietnam policy had lacked a satisfactory strategy for either military victory or meaningful negotiation. Tet was the point at which this was broadly realized. After years of optimistic promises, the administration could not offer a satisfactory explanation of what had happened and what lay ahead. Senator Eugene McCarthy's surprising 42 percent of the vote in the 1968 New Hampshire Democratic presidential primary, which combined the support of both doves who opposed the war and hawks who were angry at the administration for not winning, was a product of that inability. Former secretary of state Dean Acheson frankly told Johnson that he was not being correctly informed about the war. "With all due respect, Mr. President," Acheson said, "the Joint Chiefs of Staff don't know what they are talking about."

Not only were the national media questioning the president's policy, but he was also receiving complaints from the corporate and institutional elites whom he had always carefully cultivated. "What the

President needs is not a war speech, but a peace speech," Clark Clifford exclaimed on reading a draft of Johnson's proposed television address after Tet. "What seems not to be understood is that major elements of the national constituency—the business community, the press, the churches, professional groups, college presidents, students, and most of the intellectual community—have turned against this war."

Although both Johnson and Richard Nixon, who followed him into the White House, were isolated from personal contact with the antiwar movement, their advisers and the members of their cabinets were not. Relatives, wives, children, and colleagues challenged administration officials' support of war policies and gave them a sense of a society dividing against itself. Since the strongest opposition to the war came from the elite campuses, the pressures on the war intellectuals was particularly strong. Lyndon Johnson's hawkish Brandeis advisor John Roche toughed it out, and Harvard's man in Richard Nixon's administration, Henry Kissinger, devoted great effort and byzantine skill to maintaining friendly ties with journalists and university colleagues. Although muted, the sounds of the streets and a sense of the fracturing of American society were carried into the White House.

To Johnson's surprise, his longtime friend Clark Clifford, the new secretary of defense, and the group of senior advisors brought in from outside the government now offered a negative assessment. This group, known as "the Wise Men," and composed of the people who had made military and diplomatic policy in every administration since World War II, warned the president that the United States must begin to disengage itself from an effort that could not succeed, was harming the economy and bitterly dividing the nation.*

*The members of the Senior Advisory Group on Vietnam, which met in the White House on March 25 and 26, 1968, were tough-minded, highly experienced men, unlikely to have been overly influenced by the media. Townsend Hoopes, who had been Under Secretary of the air force, listed them as "Dean Acheson, Secretary of State under President Truman; George Ball, Under Secretary of State in the Kennedy-Johnson period; McGeorge Bundy, Special Assistant to Presidents Kennedy and Johnson; Douglas Dillon, Ambassador to France under President Eisenhower and Secretary of the Treasury under President Kennedy; Cyrus Vance, Deputy Secretary of Defense under McNamara and a diplomatic troubleshooter for President Johnson; Arthur Dean, chief Korean war negotiator; John J. McCloy, High Commissioner to West Germany under President Truman and Assistant Secretary of War during World War II; General Omar Bradley, World War II Commander and the first JCS Chairman; General Matthew Ridgway, Korean War Commander and later NATO Commander; General Maxwell Taylor, JCS Chairman under President Kennedy and later Ambassador to Saigon; Robert Murphy, a senior career Ambassador of the Truman-Eisenhower period; Henry Cabot Lodge, former U.S. Senator and twice Ambassador to Saigon; Abe Fortas, a sitting Associate Justice of the Supreme Court and a personal advisor to President

THE MEDIA VERSUS THE PRESIDENT

Although the failure in Vietnam was the result of national policy rather than of the way the war was reported, the media were claiming an increasingly important influence on that policy. Coping with the Depression, world wars, and the cold war had increased the role and the power of what Vietnam-era critics came to call "the Imperial Presidency." While the Congress might modify or reject the president's policies, it could not challenge his hold on the attention of the public and the national agenda. The president was the active force in government. Through his control of information he could define situations, and as the representative of the whole nation, he was the focus of national loyalty. As chief diplomat and commander-in-chief, he had the power to set foreign policy. Rare was the congressman or senator who could vote to deny support for the the brave men who were fighting and dying to defend whatever the president might define as "freedom" and "national honor."

By the 1960s, every family had a television set, and the president could reach into almost every household in America to command the attention and manipulate the national symbols. No president did it as often as Lyndon Johnson did in the 1960s. Only television itself could challenge the president's control of the national consciousness by focusing attention on particular problems and questions. Complaints about "bias" in the media were caused not by the opinions of the newscaster but rather by what topics were covered. In his account of Richard Nixon's sweeping reelection victory, *The Making of the President—1972* (1973), Theodore White rebuked the press and the media for their self-appointed role of contending with the president over what the national issues would be. Two years later, he was praising the media for helping bring to light the Watergate scandal that unmade Richard Nixon.

After Vietnam and Watergate, television and the press more readily entered the sphere of "legitimate controversy," and were more willing to press questions and to undertake investigative journalism. As Lyndon Johnson wryly commented, no one received the Pulitzer Prize for supporting the president. Even before Watergate, the presidents had become increasingly preoccupied with the media. For the most part, John Kennedy dazzled reporters and established a comradeship

---

Johnson; and Arthur Goldberg, Ambassador to the United Nations and a former Secretary of Labor and Supreme Court Justice" (*The Limits of Intervention* [1969], pp. 214–15). According to Hoopes, only Taylor, Fortas, and Murphy proposed continuing the existing policy, but with heavier bombing.

FIG. 4. From *Feiffer: Jules Feiffer's America from Eisenhower to Reagan,* edited by Steven Heller. Copyright © 1982 by Jules Feiffer. Reprinted by permission of Alfred A. Knopf, Inc.

with them; Lyndon Johnson tried to dominate them; and Richard Nixon saw them as an enemy against whom he must insulate his presidency. With television sets in the Oval Office tuned simultaneously to all three networks, Johnson tried to make the media part of his administration, promising, cajoling, complaining, and punishing. The CBS White House correspondent Dan Rather was a fellow Texan, and Johnson assured him that they would get along famously. When they didn't, Johnson refused to recognize Rather's questions at press conferences, complained about him to CBS, and demanded that he be reassigned.

In the world of large affairs, power centers do not exist in isolation from each other, and there were many personal ties between the White House and the networks. John Kennedy tapped the CBS news-chief Edward R. Murrow to head the U.S. Information Agency, and had close relationships with NBC. ABC, where Jim Hagerty, Eisenhower's former press secretary, was a vice-president, obliged Richard Nixon when it could, even to the extent of blacking out as "political" the half-time "Give Peace a Chance" show at the University of Buffalo–Holy Cross football game. Lyndon Johnson's relationship with CBS president Frank Stanton stretched back to Johnson's days as a young Texas congressman, when Stanton had helped Johnson's struggling little Austin, Texas, radio station gain CBS affiliation. Now, when CBS, after much hesitation, carried Morley Safer's film of the marine setting fire to a thatched roof in the Cam Ne hamlet with his Zippo lighter, Stanton was awakened by a call from the irate Johnson: "Frank are you trying to fuck me? . . . this is your President, and yesterday your boys shat on the American flag." In February 1966, Senator Fulbright scheduled the first serious congressional consideration of the war for his Foreign Relations Committee. Just as he had done two years before to turn media coverage away from Fannie Lou Hamer's Democratic convention testimony on police brutality in Mississippi, Johnson hastily arranged a media event, this time taking his cabinet to Honolulu to meet with Vietnamese air marshall Ky. NBC televised the Fulbright hearings in their entirety, but CBS ducked most of it in favor of reruns of Lucille Ball's "I Love Lucy". To help improve public relations, Johnson brought a former president of NBC, Robert Kinter, onto the White House staff.

Richard Nixon believed that the media and the press hated him. He isolated himself as much as he could from them and fought them. At the top of his enemies list were the *Washington Post,* CBS, and the *New York Times*. After the *Times* revealed the secret 1969 Cambodian bombing, he wiretapped his staff's contacts with reporters, and fought the 1971 publication of *The Pentagon Papers*. Avoiding press conferences, he sought to rally the owners of affiliate television stations against the network news, used television to speak to the nation over the heads of the newscasters, and pressured them to back off from instant analysis of his speeches. As the Republican candidate Barry Goldwater had so successfully done at the 1964 Republican convention, the administration improved its popular standing by overtly attacking the media and the press.

In a brilliant, televised speech in November 1969, Nixon successfully rallied "the silent majority" in support of his policy of "peace with honor" and in opposition to the liberals, the antiwar dissenters, and the press. Vice President Spiro Agnew followed up, using speechwriter Patrick Buchanan's script, by denouncing the newscasters and the Eastern press as an "effete corps of impudent snobs," out of step with America. "A small group of men, numbering perhaps no more than a dozen anchormen, commentators and excutive producers," he complained, "decide what forty to fifty million Americans will learn of the day's events in the nation and in the world . . . to a man these commentators and producers live and work in the geographical and intellectual confines of Washington, D.C., or New York . . . the most unrepresentative community in the entire United States." It was a message worth "careful consideration," the Nixon-appointed Chairman of the Federal Communications Commission told the industry that he regulated.

Although this onslaught improved the administration's standing in the polls and dampened television coverage of the massive antiwar "New Mobilization" rallies in the fall of 1970, it could not touch the basic problem, which was the increasing national opposition to the war. Years afterward, George Reedy, who had been Lyndon Johnson's press secretary, pinpointed the misconception that had underlain the American failure in Vietnam as the inability to fully realize that it had been a struggle for allegiance, rather than strategic position. *New York Times* reporter David Halberstam's comment that the Vietnam correspondents "caught the shit for the failure of reality to match American hopes" can be extended to apply to the military and political leadership as well as the men who did the actual fighting in the swamps, rice paddies, and jungles of Vietnam. In 1989, the U.S. Army historian William Hammond published the first volume of his study *The United States Army in Vietnam: The Military and the Media*. "The media didn't turn people against the war," he summed up. "The war turned people against the war."

8. The Antiwar Movement

While a growing number of newspapers and national magazines opposed the war on their editorial pages, television praised the sincerity of American peace initiatives and took a very cautious line on the antiwar movement. Coverage of antiwar coverage activities increased after Tet, but only within-the-system activities, such as the campaign of Senator Eugene McCarthy's clean-shaven volunteers in New Hampshire, were given favorable comment. If there was anything more unpopular than the war itself, it was the antiwar dissenters in the streets, but they put intense pressure on two emotionally insecure presidents and helped make the war unbearable for the American people.

The antiwar movement was a rebellion and an anarchy, rather than an organization. Its members were primarily white and middle-class. They were ministers, pacifists, professors, housewives, intellectuals, civil rights activists, professionals, and students. Since significant opposition to the war did not develop in Congress or either of the political parties until Eugene McCarthy and Robert Kennedy sought the Democratic presidential nomination in 1968, the antiwar movement lacked access to the political system and developed as a guerrilla assault from the outside. This did much to shape its nature. It came to life in the spring of 1965 with a "teach-in" at the University of Michigan as the combat troops moved into Vietnam. When twenty thousand marchers unexpectedly showed up at its Washington protest, Students for a Democratic Society drew its first national attention and a flood of new recruits. The poet Robert Lowell publicly declined an invitation to a White House Festival of the Arts, and many of those who did attend used the occasion to take exception to their host's policy on Vietnam. A young member of the Catholic Workers burned his draft card, and a Quaker protested the war by burning himself to death on the steps of the Pentagon.

Intellectuals, professors from the prestigious Eastern universities, Rhodes scholars, returned Peace Corps volunteers, student body presidents, and college newspaper editors signed protest ads in the *New York Times.* An antidraft movement calling itself the Resistance, led by David Harris, a former Stanford student body president, spread east from California. Harris refused to register and went to jail. The heavyweight boxing champion Muhammad Ali refused induction and had his world championship taken away. The nation's most famous pediatrician, Benjamin Spock, and Yale chaplain William Sloane Coffin were convicted for obstructing the draft. The Jesuit priest Philip Berrigan went to jail for setting draft records on fire with homemade napalm in Catonsville, Maryland, and pouring blood on draft files in Baltimore. The folksingers Joan Baez (who married David Harris as he went off to prison), Pete Seeger, Arlo Guthrie, Phil Ochs, Judy Collins, and Peter, Paul, and Mary sang at the rallies; and the various coordinating committees, mobilizations, and moratoriums organized massive protest demonstrations. There were no prerequisites for membership. The *moratorium* committees organized the moderates; the *mobilizations* reached out for the radicals. If you marched in the streets, you were a part of the antiwar movement.

ORGANIZING THE ANARCHY

The 1967 Spring Mobilization to End the War in Vietnam rallies in New York and San Francisco drew more than a quarter of a million people. Draft calls were up to thirty thousand a month, and students publicly burned their registration cards. *Ramparts* magazine revealed that the CIA had been financing the National Student Association and the Michigan State University programs in Vietnam. Ignoring more cautious advisors, Martin Luther King Jr. took his stand against the war; and when President Johnson went to Los Angeles to speak, police clubbed protesters outside the Century Plaza Hotel. The antiwar action was in the hands of the Vietnam Summer, which involved some twenty thousand volunteers across the country in a propaganda and community-organizing campaign modeled after the 1964 Mississippi Freedom Summer. Its leadership was becoming convinced of the failure of liberalism and was moving toward the Left.

The antiwar movement could no more be reduced to order than it could be kept out of the streets. The 1967 attempt at a National Conference for New Politics to unify Left and other activist groups fell apart in the face of a Black Power takeover. After that, no one attempted to put it all together. In addition to the countless local groups and committees, antiwar intellectuals, peace liberals, and radical pacifists, the New Left and the Old Left searched for ways to confront or to use the war. Never unified as an organized political party or force, the movement found that its anarchy and wildness became an asset. Although it could not challenge the president for control of policy or win popular approval, it raised the price of the war, not only for the president but also for the Congress, and for local political and community leadership across the nation. Despite high levels of violence in American life, the American people were accustomed to having the streets of their towns and cities politically peaceful. Of all the purposes the Founding Fathers wrote into the preamble to the American Constitution, the goal of ensuring "domestic tranquility" has been the one most taken for granted. Now, coming on top of the civil rights demonstrations and summers of urban rioting, the antiwar movement produced a challenge that could not be ignored.

The moderates sought to work within the system, pushed for a negotiated settlement, and recruited antiwar candidates. Seeking to change national policy, *liberal antiwar intellectuals* such as Arthur Schlesinger Jr., John K. Galbraith, and Joseph Rauh organized Negotiations Now to gather a million signatures on a petition to stop the bombing. New York congressman Allard Lowenstein, a former president of the National Student Association, was a genius at getting things started, particularly among the young. He was always recruiting volunteers for Mississippi; or seminarians, student leaders, and college editors to sign letters against the war. Committed to working within the political system, he set out in search of an antiwar candidate to challenge Lyndon Johnson for the Democratic presidential nomination in 1968. Robert Kennedy feared that his own candidacy would be seen primarily as personal self-aggrandizement and could not make up his mind, and so Lowenstein's Concerned Democrats found their man in Senator Eugene McCarthy of Minnesota, who was willing to take on the president and the war. In a time of overheated rhetoric and passions, McCarthy's low-key campaigning, which concealed the lack of a real desire to be president, seemed refreshing.

The *peace liberals* were represented by the Committee for a Sane Nuclear Policy (SANE); the Student Peace Union (SPU); Women Strike for Peace (WSP); the Catholic Workers and Peace Fellowship; the Quakers; and Clergy and Laymen Concerned about Vietnam (CLCV). Their leaders, including the *Saturday Review* editor Norman Cousins, the Harvard professor H. Stuart Hughes, and the socialist Norman Thomas, chose the path of persuasion, not civil disobedience, and refused to march with the Communists and those who carried the North Vietnamese flag. WSP and Dr. Spock differed from other peace liberals in their unwillingness to exclude anybody. Women Strike for Peace had emerged in 1961 in a protest against both Soviet and American nuclear testing and the arms race, and the Cuban missile crisis added to their sense of urgency. The House Un-American Activities Committee (HUAC) subpoenaed them and demanded membership lists, but WSP had none. When HUAC asked Dagmar Wilson, a housewife and children's-book illustrator, who the leaders were, she giggled and replied, "We're all leaders." Across the country, the press joined the WSP's middle-class, middle-aged housewives in making fun of the committee.

The *radical pacifists* who followed the Fellowship of Reconciliation leader A. J. Muste and the tireless organizer David Dellinger, editor of the peace journal *Liberation,* rejected no one who was against the war.

Both the *Old Left* and the *New Left* saw the unjust war in Vietnam as the product of corporate capitalism in America. A victory for Hanoi would be liberating for America. The SDS Washington march in the spring of 1965 was the first major demonstration against the war. It brought a flood of new members, but participatory democracy, carried to an extreme, immobilized decision making, and SDS turned away from leading the antiwar movement. The tightly disciplined, Maoist Progressive Labor (PL) and the Trotskyite Socialist Workers party (SWP) had no such problems. Progressive Labor chose to bore from within SDS, made it ideological, and in the battle for control, helped destroy it. The Trotskyites focused their drive for power on the various mobilization (Mobe) committees that, under David Dellinger, organized the 1967 March on the Pentagon and other major demonstrations, including the confrontation with Mayor Richard Daley and the Chicago police at the 1968 Democratic National Convention.

CHICAGO, 1968

The radical pacifist Dellinger and the displaced "old" New Left activists Tom Hayden and Rennie Davis, who had gone to Hanoi and seen the effects of American bombing, had no trust in the Democrats. They went to Chicago not to influence delegates but to make a militant protest both against the Democrats as a "war party" and against the whole of American politics. The National Mobilization Committee to End the War in Vietnam set up headquarters and applied for permits to camp in the city parks and stage its own counterconvention in the streets. The city refused. Mayor Richard Daley had consolidated the most powerful Democratic political machine in the nation out of Chicago's white working-class ethnic communities, its black southside ghettos, and its dynamic State Street business community. Nobody was going to "come to our city and take over our streets, our city and our Convention," he told the press. The riots that spring following the murder of Martin Luther King Jr. had set the black West Madison Street commercial district ablaze. Shocked by the violence and the devastation, Mayor Daley and the *Chicago Tribune* denounced the restraint shown by the police. The mayor's new orders were to shoot to maim looters and kill arsonists. Peace marchers were handled roughly by the police, and with the clear prospect of violence, most of the antiwar organizations decided to stay home.

Abbie Hoffman and Jerry Rubin were not concerned. The Yippies were going to Chicago, they announced, to stage a "festival of life" in contrast to the Democrats' "festival of death." Hoffman had worked with SNCC and the civil rights movement; Rubin, with a talent for public relations, had been a West Coast antiwar leader before David Dellinger tapped him to organize the March on the Pentagon. By 1968 Hoffman and Rubin had both dropped out of the straight world and entered the long-haired world of pot, acid, put-ons, and happenings. They represented only themselves and a circle of friends, and their "thing" was dramatic ridicule of the system. Now they were in Chicago, with a pig they proposed to nominate as their candidate for president. Although Tom Hayden and the serious political revolutionaries disliked their antics, the media loved them. In their own way, they represented the opposition to the war among the counterculture young on the East and West coasts and in the hippie ghettos that gathered around the nation's colleges and universities.

Inside the Chicago Amphitheater, with Robert Kennedy having been murdered in California and Minnesota senator Eugene McCarthy only passively contesting the platform plank on Vietnam and the nomination, the Democrats picked Vice-President Hubert Humphrey as their candidate. Downtown, across Michigan Avenue from the hotels and the business district, the protesters rallied in Grant and Lincoln Parks. Amid showers of rocks and bottles, the police, backed up by the National Guard, used Mace and their nightsticks to clear the parks, indiscriminately beating demonstrators and spectators. On edge from twelve-hour-a-day duty, the policemen reacted angrily to obscenities and resistance from the demonstrators. At an afternoon rally on the third day of the convention, when the American flag was pulled down, the police charged the crowds flailing away at anyone they could reach. That night, the convention moved through the nominations and the vote; and the police faced would-be marchers on Michigan Avenue. As the police attacked both the demonstrators and spectators crowded up on the sidewalks against the buildings, the window of the Hilton's cocktail lounge gave way, and the police moved in through the broken glass, beating the bleeding victims.

In the chaos outside on the surrounding streets, the police, with their name tags removed or covered, particularly singled out reporters and cameramen for assault. In the convention hall, with the galleries packed with his supporters, Mayor Daley called the signals. Television reporters Dan Rather and Mike Wallace were roughed up by the guards. Reports filtered in of the battle raging in the streets. Senator Abraham Ribicoff of Connecticut interrupted his speech to complain of "Gestapo tactics on the streets of Chicago." In front of the platform, Mayor Daley was on his feet shouting what television viewers read his lips to be saying: "Fuck you, you Jew son-of-a-bitch, you lousy mother-fucker, go home!"

The violence in the streets of Chicago came close to radicalizing a segment of the national media. Many reporters and columnists were outraged, but public opinion generally sided with the police, and in a strangely obsequious network interview the next day, Walter Cronkite turned the microphone over to Mayor Daley. As was the case when the Kent State students were killed by National Guardsmen two years later, the blame fell on the protesters and the bystanders who got in the way. Even as a majority of the American people came to believe that the war was a mistake, they felt no greater fondness toward the antiwar protesters. A person could disagree with government policy and still be patriotic, but in the eyes of a large part of the American people, those who demonstrated in the streets were not.

NIXON'S WAR

Richard Nixon was placed in the White House by an angry and bewildered electorate, and the most important decision of his presidency was one he lacked the imagination and daring to make: withdrawal from Vietnam. Had he found a way to withdraw, and had he made the commitment in 1969, he might well have gone down in history as one of the greatest of American presidents. He showed flexibility in his domestic programs. His opening to Communist China, the Strategic Arms Limitation Treaty with the Soviet Union, and his support of Israel in the 1973 Yom Kippur War were all evidences of boldness. Withdrawal would have made a proper companion to détente. As the United States established working relationships with the great Communist powers, China and the Soviet Union, the justification for the expenditure of more American lives in the rice paddies and jungles of Vietnam became increasingly questionable. Whatever the initial shock and criticism, the bulk of the war-weary American people would have come to support him. As the political sociologist Seymour Martin Lipset has phrased it, in foreign policy "the President makes opinion, he does not follow it." The national press and media would have hailed the president, and their praise might well have dampened his raging paranoia. There would have been no more antiwar moritoriums and mobilizations, no Cambodian invasion and deaths at Kent

State, no secret bombings, no conspiracy trials, no leaks, no wiretaps and surveillance, no plumbers, no break-ins, no cover-ups, and no lost presidency.

The path he chose was a different one. "I call it 'the Madman Theory,' " the president explained to his aide H. R. Haldeman. He would trade upon his known anti-Communism obsession to intimidate Hanoi with hints of nuclear attack. Within three months of his inauguration, he had widened the war with the secret bombing of Cambodia and had set himself on the path to Watergate. By the time American withdrawal came, four brutal years later, Richard Nixon's presidency was already a victim of the war. "Johnson's war" had become "Nixon's war."

As the war continued, so did the opposition. Although the FBI could produce no evidence, President Johnson had been convinced that Communist money was behind the antiwar movement. Richard Nixon was equally convinced. There was the circuslike trial of the Chicago Eight (a grab-bag collection from the street protest at the Democratic National Convention, including the radical peace activist David Dellinger, the New Left founders Tom Hayden and Rennie Davis, the Yippies Jerry Rubin and Abbie Hoffman, and the Black Panther leader Bobby Seale) and other unsuccessful conspiracy trials around the country. A growing proliferation of independent groups—doctors, lawyers, and students holding candlelight campus vigils and singing John Lennon's "Give Peace a Chance"—sought a means of showing their opposition to the war. The fall of 1969 saw huge moratorium and mobilization antiwar demonstrations followed by the weary collapse of national organizational efforts.

Sam Brown, the leader of the Moratorium, who had been youth coordinator for Senator McCarthy's presidential campaign, took the lead in organizing those who saw the war but not the American democratic system as a terrible mistake. Several score of members of Congress, as well as other national leaders, joined millions of people across the country in the nation's largest antiwar observance on the October 15 Vietnam Moratorium Day. A month later, on November 15, it was the turn of the more radical New Mobilization Committee. Over one hundred thousand demonstrators turned out in San Francisco and twice that number in the nation's capital. For thirty-eight hours, more than forty thousand people marched in single file from Arlington National Cemetery past the Lincoln Memorial and the White House to read the names of the Vietnam War dead and deposit those names one by one in wooden coffins in front of the Capitol.

Still the war went on. There was an explosion of protest on the college campuses after the 1970 invasion of Cambodia and the deaths of the Kent State and Jackson State students. The next year, an attempt by the "May Day Tribe" to disrupt traffic in the District of Columbia led to mass arrests, but after 1970 the giant street demonstrations were declining. As had occurred in the civil rights movement, exhaustion and frustration mixed with a growing backlash. Opposition to the war continued to grow, but symbolic statement in the streets had become old and weary.

THE IMPACT OF ANTIWAR PROTEST

Although it could not end the war, protest had its effect. Like Banquo's ghost at Macbeth's table, it became an uninvited player in the policy game. Antiwar protest led President Johnson into a major propaganda campaign in the fall of 1967 to convince the American people that the war was being won, which made the surprise Tet offensive seem even more of a defeat. While Johnson looked with contempt at the antiwar movement, it had a deep personal effect on him. As his young White House aide and confidant Doris Kearns reported in *Lyndon Johnson and the American Dream* (1976), the growing opposition drained his self-esteem and energy. The demonstrators who harassed him wherever he went in public made him feel himself a prisoner in the White House. Instead of the affection and public gratitude that he so much sought, the bitter denunciation from those whom his policies had tried to help made him confused and depressed. He dreamt that he was swimming in a river, but as hard as he tried, he could not reach either shore. With his decision to limit the bombing and not seek reelection, he hoped to regain his place in history by making progress in negotiating an end to the war and restoring unity at home.

Johnson's hopes for successful negotiations and restored public confidence at home were not realized. Disunity in the Democratic party, bitterness over the war, and disorder in the streets helped elect Richard Nixon president of the United States. More thoughtful than Johnson on world affairs, Nixon was not as dependent on popular approval. His character was unusual for a professional politician: solitary, distrustful, and an outsider, he was uneasy with people and shared his thoughts with few. He believed that the media and the intellectual community were hostile to him, and he had little expectation of winning support from minorities and students. His path was to outflank them. The numbers of demonstrators with which the Moratorium filled the streets in the fall of 1969 led him to shelve his secret "Duck

Hook" plan to force negotiation through the ferocity of an all-out bombing assault on North Vietnam. Again the next year, it was public outcry that led the president to call the troops out of Cambodia.

With a growing sense of beleaguerment and paranoia, the president marshalled his attack on the war, its opponents, and the press that dared to report it all. Secretly, he ordered that the Internal Revenue Service and the Justice Department's Antitrust Division move against the publishers of the *New York Times* and the *Washington Post* and the heads of NBC and CBS. Although the thrust into Cambodia in the spring of 1970 brought the greatest outpouring of protest, he was quieting the opposition through "Vietnamization," in which South Vietnamese soldiers took over more of the fighting; draft reform; the mobilization of Middle America's patriotic sentiment; and intimidation of the media. It was a masterful achievement. Before the New Mobilization could take to the streets, William Safire had helped script the best speech of Richard Nixon's presidency. Speaking "to you, the great silent majority of my fellow Americans," the president called for support for the war and against a humiliation that "only Americans," not North Vietnam, could inflict on their nation. Telegrams and letters flooded in, and popular and congressional support rallied around him. On Veterans' Day, tens of thousands of supporters carried American flags through the streets, urged on in California by Governor Ronald Reagan and led in Chicago by Mayor Daley. Under attack from Vice-President Agnew, the television networks pulled back from instant analysis of presidential speeches and diluted their coverage of the Mobilization's marchers. In the spring, longshoremen and construction workers paraded in New York's financial district in a demonstration against the antiwar protesters. The "hardhat" had become the symbol of support for the president.

THE WAR'S "OTHER AMERICA"

In reality it was more of a class than a foreign policy statement. It is common but misleading to state that working people supported a war that students and the college-educated opposed. Public opinion polls indicated that, despite significant areas of dissent, young adults and college graduates were supportive of presidential policy in Vietnam. Women, older people, and black people, and the grade-school educated were less likely to favor it. After Tet, the better educated and more affluent, who followed public affairs and foreign policy more closely, increasingly came to oppose the war, while the high-school educated provided proportionally greater support for it. By 1968, the major sectors of the population had come to believe the war was a mistake. Although they disagreed on what should be done, all income, education, and age groups strongly disapproved of the antiwar protestors. The clash between the hardhats and the antiwar demonstrators was not one of "hawks" against "doves." To support the president and the flag was to make a statement about patriotism and America, and about class, not necessarily about the Vietnam War.

Often only grade-school educated, earning between five and ten thousand dollars a year, with a culture focused on job, family, neighborhood, the work ethic, and patriotism, white working-class Americans were reacting to the pressures of social change. According to public opinion surveys, they generally felt good about the young, believed that black people should have equal opportunities, and were distressed over the war. At the same time they found their family and community values threatened by school busing; compensatory racial quotas; black people buying homes in white neighborhoods; the long hair, the lack of discipline, and the sexual behavior of the young; drugs; obscenity; the banning of prayer from the schools; taxes, and crime and violence. Black, campus, and antiwar militancy disturbed them, particularly since it was coming from people whom Middle Americans saw as being favored by the society at its own expense. Negro job and housing pressure helped stir group consciousness in ethnic communities. They had had to work for everything they had gotten, and now the blacks expected to be given it on a silver platter. It was all too much, too quickly. The rich people, who lived in the suburbs and sent their children to private schools and to college, were combining with the blacks to force change on them. Many middle Americans felt caught in the middle in a world of increasing disorder.

From the working people and the lower rungs of middle-class America came the soldiers for Vietnam, and the police. Recruited from Middle America, the police shared its values and attitudes. The average American policeman was white, had a high-school diploma, and was being paid seventy-five hundred dollars a year to risk his life to keep the streets safe. If the black ghetto saw the police as an "army of occupation," the policeman felt himself sitting on the lid of a volcano and knew that he could keep order only by aggressive patrolling. Black militants, unappreciative students, and unpatriotic antiwar protestors were a profound threat not only to order but to the political system. As the police saw it, the problem was human nature, permissiveness, the lack of respect, and outside agitators. It was the rotten apples who deliberately caused the trouble. Social reform was "coddling criminals" and "selling out to trouble makers." Kids were being brought up expecting to get whatever they yelled for; and, as FBI chief J. Edgar Hoover explained to President Johnson's National Violence Commission, Communists were in the forefront of civil rights, antiwar, and campus demonstrations. Dissent was of questionable legitimacy and akin to subversion. The sight of privileged students destroying property and dishonoring the American flag fueled police hostility and anger.

WHO FOUGHT

Life magazine's stark, gray, death-mask cover for June 27, 1969, announced, "The Faces of the American Dead in Vietnam: One Week's Toll." Inside, as in a high-school yearbook, the pages displayed, in row upon row, the names and pictures of 242 American men killed in Vietnam during the week of May 28 through June 3. Of the almost 27 million men of draft age during the war, 1.8 million served in Vietnam, and 270,000 were wounded; the names of some 58,000 who died there are engraved on the polished black granite walls of the Vietnam Veterans Memorial in Washington, D.C. Eleven million enlisted or were drafted. Sixteen million never served, exempted for physical, educational, marital and family, vocational, and hardship reasons, and other exemptions and deferments. Fifty thousand went into exile in Canada, Sweden, and elsewhere, half of them draft evaders, half deserters. An estimated quarter of a million, including many ghetto youths, did not register at all. Attempts in 1966 to limit deferments to graduate students and the top half of college classes heated up an opposition to the war that grew in intensity when general college deferments were cancelled the next year.

Draft calls were up to thirty thousand a month, and escape became a preoccupation and an art, particularly among members of middle- and upper-income families. The student newspaper at the University of Florida advised, "Use any means. Get stoned. . . . Say you're a schizoid, a queer. Refuse to sign a disclaimer that you are not a member of any subversive organization. File as a conscientious objector. It takes more time. You can't be classified and drafted during an appeal." Some, like the future political leaders David Stockman and Dan Quayle, stayed out by entering divinity school or by using family influence to enlist in the National Guard. Despite long waiting lists, more college men joined the guard than were taken by the draft. In their history of the Vietnam War draft, *Chance and Circumstance* (1978), Lawrence Baskir and William Straus, who worked for President Gerald Ford's postwar clemency board, concluded that if the National Guard had been called up, it would have ended the NFL's professional football season.

Enforcement of the draft became increasingly difficult. The Supreme Court accepted a nonreligious "deeply held conviction" for conscientious objector status (*U.S.* v. *Seeger* [1965]) though it refused to approve selective objection for men unwilling to fight specifically in Vietnam (*Gillette* v. *U.S.* [1971]). Although the draft was not, perhaps, the prime cause of the antiwar sentiment on the campuses, it did much to keep attention focused. President Nixon's answer was the 1969 draft reform law. Instead of being liable for call between the ages of nineteen and twenty-six, men were now eligible only in their nineteenth year. A draft lottery randomly placed all of the birthdays on a roster. If yours was one of the later ones drawn, you were safe; if it was one of the early ones, you prepared to go. At least you knew whether you would have to serve; and most knew that they would not. As war spending fueled inflation and threatened the prosperity of the sixties, concern about jobs and careers grew on the campuses.

The new policy of Vietnamization reduced the chances of Americans being killed. Few critics asked how the South Vietnamese army, if it could not prevail with the help of half a million American soldiers in the field, could be expected to do better without them. As the United States stepped up the bombing and accelerated the arming and training of South Vietnamese soldiers, it began withdrawing American troops. In a return to the Eisenhower and Kennedy rhetoric, the war was now "theirs to win." Although the sudden American thrust into Cambodia in 1970 and the intensive bombing of Hanoi in the spring of 1972 brought campus protests, the shootings at Kent State University, and widespread student strikes, the president's policy was helping to cool down large-scale, organized antiwar protest. With fewer American casualties and smaller draft calls, the war was more bearable, even though no more popular at home.

VETERANS

Although the antiwar movement was otherwise cooling down, a new presence had moved to its front ranks. This was the Vietnam War veteran. While most returned soldiers went back home and picked up or began their lives again, others bore witness that the war would be a lasting wound for their nation. Walter Lippmann wrote in 1967 that "a war waged without hope of a military decision degenerates into savagery." A million young men had fought in the dirty, unfathomable war of no battle lines; of free-fire zones and body counts, booby traps, and unseen enemies sheltered among the people for whose protection they and their buddies were dying; a war of massacred innocents and the loss of comrades and friends, of staying alive for 365 days and then suddenly being plucked out and flown back alone to the United States, thrust across space and psychic time to be dumped into a society that was hostile, or didn't care or want to know about the war. John Kerry, a member of Vietnam Veterans against the War, a lieutenant (j.g.) out of St. Paul's, Yale, and small boat patrol of the Mekong Delta, and a future Massachusetts senator, stood up before the television cameras at the Senate Foreign Relations Committee hearings, clean shaven and hair cut short, to tell the nation, "We wish that a merciful God could wipe away our own memories of service as easily as this Administration has wiped away their memories of us."

Most other members of the newly organized Vietnam Veterans Against the War (VVAW) expressed their feeling by continuing to wear their combat fatigues and letting their hair grow. Some angry that they had been sent into an unwinnable war, others at the kind of war it was, they bore witness against it. Early in 1971, while Lt. William Calley stood trial for the killing of more than two hundred women, children and old men at the hamlet of My Lai 4, the VVAW offered their own testimony on atrocities. During the desperate days of the American Revolution, the radical Tom Paine had written of those soul-trying times and the "summer soldiers and sunshine patriots" who would "in time of crisis, shrink from the service of their country." Calling themselves "winter soldiers," Vietnam veterans rallied in Detroit to confront the nation with the brutal things that they had personally done in Vietnam. In April, they were in Washington to return their medals and lobby Congress against the war.

Even after 1973, when the United States had given Hanoi one more ferocious bombing, shaken hands with North Vietnamese negotiators in Paris, declared the agreement to be "peace with honor," and pulled out, the war was not over for many of its veterans. Although the prisoners of war had been returned and the soldiers brought back home, America continued to have difficulty with the war. As the rest of the American people were trying to forget the war, the families of men "missing in action" and many of the veterans could not. In World War I, their problem had been called "shell shock." In World War II, the inability of the autonomic nervous system to handle the stress of combat was known as "battle fatigue." Initially the psychiatrists saw the flashbacks, the nightmares, the emotional numbness, the panic and hyperalertness, the depression, rage, and guilt, as schizophrenic. Not until 1980 did the American Psychiatric Association officially diagnose and name the condition "post traumatic stress disorder" (PTSD).

The war had been fought mainly by nineteen-year-old soldiers, their neurological and identity systems still in the process of formation. In warfare that was not comprehensible, they suffered moral pain and survivor's guilt. They had learned to act aggressively in a surreal world, had killed indiscriminately and brutally, and had seen their friends die. They had been suddenly returned to civilian life, alone, without any supportive systems to help rebuild their identity, to a world that disapproved of what they had done and didn't want to hear about it. For many, the pain and anger, the intrusive thoughts and "flashbacks," sleep disturbances, and hyperalertness produced frustration and stress, and made it difficult to return to family, school, and job.

Congress and the Veterans Administration (VA) did little to help. Not until 1979 did Congress fund an outreach program that was based on the veterans' own rap sessions. Like the Vietnam Veterans Memorial, in Washington, D.C., VA programs were primarily the result of pressure from veterans rather than of general public concern. By the 1980s, PTSD and the "flashback" had become the staple of television drama. In 1982 an outpouring of emotion accompanied the dedication of "the wall." The memorial, two polished black granite slabs set low in a hollow in the earth near the Lincoln Memorial and bearing the names of the Americans who died in the Vietnam War, was a symbolic recognition, a prayer, both for the dead and for the nation.

Even at the end of the 1980s, there were still the MIAs. Many people continued to believe that there might be Americans still alive and waiting, and Hollywood won the only victories that the nation was to have by sending its celluloid heroes Rambo and Chuck Norris back to rescue imprisoned servicemen from their "devilish" Communist captors. Somewhere in the jungles and paddy fields of Southeast Asia, amid the bodies of uncounted hundreds of thousands of Vietnamese dead, were the remains of some twenty-four hundred Americans officially listed as missing in action. That their families still sought word of them after as much as twenty years was an indication of how difficult it had been for America to realistically accept what the Vietnam War had been and how it had turned out.

THE END OF THE AMERICAN CENTURY

Almost fifty years earlier, a young intellectual named Randolph Bourne had protested against American involvement in a different war. Writing in 1917, he criticized the enthusiasm of the intellectuals for America's entry into World War I. "It has been a bitter experience," he said, "to see the unanimity with which the American intellectuals

FIG. 5. *Doonesbury* Copyright 1975 Universal Press Syndicate. Reprinted with permission. All rights reserved.

have thrown their support to the use of the war-technique." Now it struck the critics first as puzzling and then as revealing that the national security advisors McGeorge Bundy, W. W. Rostow, and Henry Kissinger, who had urged presidents Kennedy, Johnson, and Nixon onward, had come from the professorial ranks on campuses such as Harvard and Massachusetts Institute of Technology. In 1972 the prize-winning Vietnam War journalist David Halberstam ironically characterized them and others of the foreign policy elite who had supported the war "the best and the brightest," as if to echo Bourne's condemnation of "a war deliberately made by the intellectuals!"

The Vietnam War differed from World War I, in that by the end of the 1960s, the intelligentsia openly opposed the war. The leading national newspapers and columnists came to call for American withdrawal. Most of the rest of the country was wearily sick of the war, but still it went on. As Bourne had written of his war half a century before, it did not need the enthusiasm of the American people, "only their acquiescence." That acquiescence, he continued, "seems sufficient to float an indefinitely protracted war for vague or even largely uncomprehended and unaccepted purposes. Our resources in men and materials are vast enough to organize the war technique without enlisting more than a fraction of the people's conscious energy."

Starting with Senators Wayne Morse and Ernest Gruening, who had voted against the Tonkin Gulf resolution in 1964 and opposed the war all along, the number of congressional critics grew, but Congress was not willing to take the action that would have mattered and cut off the funds. According to the journalist-historian Stanley Karnow, of 113 congressional votes on various war-related issues between 1966 and 1973, only 2 went against presidential war policies. The American people, like their leaders, had come to realize that the war was not going to be won but were unwilling to accept that they had lost. How much of this was due to a sense of obligation to those Americans who had died, how much to those in South Vietnam who still lived, how much to pride, and how much was to world power relationships and the "credibility of American commitments" was beyond measurement.

In 1968, both of the antiwar candidates, Eugene McCarthy and Robert Kennedy, talked vaguely of what they would do; neither promised a quick withdrawal. Richard Nixon spoke of a "secret plan" but had none. The question seemed to be how, without winning, the United States could achieve a "peace with honor" that would free the prisoners of war, bring the troops home, and yet deny South Vietnam to Hanoi. Antiwar demonstrations had helped make people as weary of the war as they were of the marchers, but offered no apparent way to solve the problem. As angry as many people felt over the war, violence in the streets and on the campuses built no insurrectionary momentum. Protests and demonstrations did not force an end to the war. Protest built no structures. The power and the decision were still in the hands of "the system." As long as no clear solution emerged, there was no standard around which a political opposition within the system could rally. Since no one else had a reasonable plan for getting out of the war without the Communists winning, President Nixon's policy of turning the fighting over to the South Vietnamese army seemed an acceptable possible path.

By the eve of the 1972 presidential election, after four more years of fighting, bombing, negotiation, and troop withdrawals, American strength in Vietnam was down to sixty-nine thousand. Vietnamese deaths were way up, but American casualties were reduced. Shortly before the election, the American negotiator Henry Kissinger announced that "peace is at hand." The promise of Senator George McGovern, the Democratic candidate, to unilaterally stop the bombing and bring American forces home seemed somehow too extreme and not quite honorable. In the public opinion polls, Richard Nixon was seen as "the real peace candidate" who was "doing everything he can to end it." On election day, Richard Nixon was reelected with almost 61 percent of the vote.

In January 1973, after the extremely heavy Christmas bombing of North Vietnam, an agreement was signed by which prisoners were returned and American troops went home. The Vietnamese were left to fight it out among themselves. That summer, Congress made an effort to control the president's power to conduct an undeclared war. Over President Nixon's veto, Congress brought the bombing of Cambodia to a halt by refusing funds. In the fall it passed the War Powers Act, which required notification of Congress within forty-eight hours of combat involvement, and termination of the involvement within sixty days unless Congress voted to approve it. When the Communist forces rolled into Saigon in April 1975, the United States took no action. The "American Century" had ended ten thousand miles away in Vietnam.

9. The End of Optimism

As Charles Dickens began his French Revolution epic *A Tale of Two Cities:* "It was the best of times; it was the worst of times." On August 6, 1965, President Johnson signed the Voting Rights Act. Five days later, a riot in the Watts district of Los Angeles killed thirty-four people and touched off four summers of violence in the urban ghettos. Earlier that year, the president had ordered the bombing of North Vietnam and had sent American ground forces into action. Despite general prosperity and economic growth, the development of youth and consumption cultures, and a national attack on racism and poverty, everything seemed to be going wrong. The leading general histories of the 1960s (e.g., William O'Neill, *Coming Apart* [1971]; Jim Heath, *Decade of Disillusionment* [1975]; Milton Viorst, *Fire in the Streets* [1979]; William Leuchtenburg, *A Troubled Feast,* 2d ed. [1979]; and Allen Matusow, *The Unraveling of America* [1984]), have so consistently taken violence and failure as their theme that when William Chafe chose *The Unfinished Journey* as his title in 1986, the contrast seemed encouraging.

THE FAILURE OF LIBERALISM

The favorite warp on which the woof of fault is woven is the failure of liberalism. Basically, the liberals believed in improvement. Foreign policy was the containment of the Soviet Union and its Communist allies. At home, improvement meant civil rights and the War on Poverty. An expanded economy, guided by Keynesian fine tuning, would provide a sufficient dividend to help all in need, without calling on the general population for sacrifices. Keynesianism, free enterprise, pluralism, and a fostering government would bring blacks and the poor into the mainstream.

To the conservative critics Andrew Hacker (*The End of the American Era* [1971]) and Charles Murray (*Losing Ground: American Social Policy, 1950–1980* [1984]), the 1960s showed that the liberals were mistaken about the potentialities of human nature. To Theodore White (*America in Search of Itself: The Making of the Presidency, 1956–1980* [1982]), they were wrong about the benefits that might be gained from an intrusive government. For the New Left, the name of the culprit was "corporate liberalism." Who was responsible for the cold war, Vietnam, and overturning democratic regimes on behalf of corporate interests? "They are all honorable men. They are all liberals," intoned SDS president Carl Oglesby. To the acute British observer Godfrey Hodgson (*America in Our Time: From World War II to Nixon—What Happened and Why?* [1976]), the great liberal civil rights, antipoverty, educational, and health programs humanized American society and set the course of social policy. Unfortunately, he continued, both the triumphs, which increased expectations, and the failures, tore the liberal consensus to shreds. Those who had hoped for more joined those on the Left in faulting liberalism for not going far enough. Liberalism, Allen Matusow argued, failed to give the poor enough money and to reorganize political power. The necessary attempt to challenge established institutions had not been made. For William O'Neill, the fault was a failure of nerve: "Having failed to transform the human condition in a decade, they felt guilty and ashamed," he wrote.

Whether liberalism promised too much or too little, the swing away from it characterized the 1970s and the 1980s. Although it remained to be seen whether liberal social policies and the Democratic party coalitions could withstand the pounding of Ronald Reagan's and George Bush's conservatives in the 1980s and 1990s, there was a basic national shift in political perception. In the mid-1960s, a liberal consensus accepted government as the instrument with which to attack the social problems of the nation. In the mid-1980s, a conservative consensus had come to see government as the cause rather than the solution of those problems. Without himself moving, Ronald Reagan, who had been in the right wing of the Republican party in the 1960s, occupied its center in the 1980s.

BLACK SEPARATISM

Martin Luther King Jr. and the ministers of the Southern Christian Leadership Conference, the NAACP, the Urban League, and, according to the polls, an overwhelming majority of black people were integrationists, but a portion of the sixties activists had moved to the rejectionist edge. Wearied by the struggle in Mississippi and disappointed by their white liberal allies, who had not supported them at the 1964 Democratic National Convention, SNCC and CORE, the shock troops of civil rights, had turned away from biracialism.

They rejected the earlier religiously motivated leadership as "not what the times required," gave up Christ and Gandhi for Malcolm X, Fanon, and Marx, and turned away from the rural South and toward the urban ghettos of Atlanta and the North, sectarianism, the Third World, and Africa. They had been reading Frantz Fanon, the black psychiatrist from Martinique whose account of the Algerian independence war, *The Wretched of the Earth* (1963), raised the question of how to change the colonial mentality once colonialism's political rule was overthrown. The problem of black identity reached beyond civil rights.

In 1966, Stokely Carmichael replaced John Lewis as Chairman of SNCC. When he was a young boy, Carmichael's family had migrated from Trinidad, eight people initially living in a one-bedroom apartment in the Bronx. Carmichael attended New York's elite Bronx High School of Science and grew up in a world of leftist associations, taking part in demonstrations for "Fair Play for Cuba" and opposed to the House Un-American Activities Committee. He entered Howard University in 1960 and became a leader among its SNCC contingent. The next year he joined the Freedom Rides across the Deep South, walked into the white waiting room in Jackson, and spent the summer in Mississippi's Parchman Penitentiary.

Admired for his quick wit and outspokenness, he was a political intellectual, not a religious visionary like Martin Luther King Jr. As a congressional district director for the 1964 Mississippi Summer project, he got along well with white staffers and took moderate positions in SNCC's internal arguments, but he was concerned about developing black leadership and ran his programs with an all-black staff. After Mississippi, he moved into Lowndes County, a poor, rural Alabama Black-Belt county where the black people, who were a large, landless majority of the population, did not vote. Seeing little possibility in Alabama's white supremacist Democratic party, Carmichael created a party of his own in Lowndes County, selecting a black panther as its symbol. His campaign issue was not racial separation but rather breaking into the local political power system.

His election as SNCC chairman, at the age of twenty-four, drew him away from local organizing. The emergence of the slogan Black Power, combined with the image of Lowndes County's snarling black panther, helped make Carmichael the most visible black leader after Martin Luther King Jr., and the symbol of racial militancy. As he responded to the role cast upon him, his rhetoric became more heated and antiwhite. A persistent note of antisemitism alienated many Jewish civil rights supporters and further divided the movement. Against a background of urban riots and the Vietnam War, the white backlash fastened on Carmichael. He read *Malcolm X Speaks* and was thinking about Africa.

The next year, Carmichael turned up in Cuba at Fidel Castro's Latin American Solidarity Conference, where he praised Cuba and spoke of the corruption of Western values, the revolutionary struggle against capitalism in the United States, and "armed rebellion." Afterward he went off to North Vietnam by way of Moscow and Beijing. In Hanoi, Ho Chi Minh told him of visiting Harlem in the 1920s and of being attracted by Carmichael's fellow West Indian, Marcus Garvey, who had excited the black American masses with dreams about Africa. "Why don't you Africans go back to Africa?" Ho asked. "It's your home." Accepting the invitation of Shirley Graham Du Bois, the widow of the American leader who had founded both the NAACP and the Pan-African Congress and had died a Communist party member in Ghana, Carmichael flew off to visit her in Guinea and meet with President Sekou Toure and the exiled Ghanaian independence leader Kwame Nkrumah.

When Carmichael returned to the United States, he was under attack as a friend to Communism and an inciter of violence. The State Department confiscated his passport, and only the refusal of Attorney General Ramsey Clark kept an angry Lyndon Johnson from having him prosecuted for visiting Hanoi. For Carmichael, what counted now was race, and his thoughts rested on Africa. Both the remnants of SNCC and California's Black Panther party, which had taken their name from his Lowndes County symbol and now hoped to tap his organizational skills and celebrity by making him their "prime minister," found that he wasn't interested in other people's agendas or in building class coalitions on the Left.

When others in SNCC had derided Martin Luther King Jr.'s nonviolence, Carmichael had refrained. Now, in the violent spring of 1968, he told the press that the white America that had gotten rid of Marcus Garvey and Malcolm X had declared war on black people by killing King. After marrying the exiled South African folk singer Miriam Makeba, and with his passport returned, he moved to Guinea. There, he took a new, African name, calling himself Kwame Toure, after the independence leaders of Ghana and Guinea. Later, divorced from Makeba, he married a Guinean woman, Marietou. A number of his co-workers from SNCC joined the All African Revolutionary People's party, which he had founded in America. Its language was doctrinaire Marxist, and out of touch. He held that American capitalism would be overturned not by the spontaneous and anarchistic reformism of SNCC, but rather by the revolutionary consciousness of the organized masses, led by African intellectuals. America at the end of the 1980s, he argued, was more ripe for revolution than it had been in the 1960s.

SNCC's moral radicalism had come from the interaction and tension between its appeal to the national conscience through individual sacrifice, and its effort to develop grass-roots organization and leadership among the poor. This had made it the most compelling model of activism for the youthful idealism of the 1960s. As the radical edge of the civil rights movement, the young SNCC activists had developed new forms of creative disorder, nonviolent resistance, participatory democracy, and community organizing. SNCC started out religious, became secular, then revolutionary, then separatist. Black nationalism became more important than civil rights. Those who had been the inspiration of others came to look to the Black Panthers and to Africa for new vitality and guidance. In less than a decade, SNCC's intense, illuminating flame had burned out.

VIOLENCE

Although the fiery words by Black Power leaders—most notably H. Rapp Brown's speech in Cambridge, Maryland—sometimes contributed to disorder and incendiarism, all studies indicated that most explosions of violence were "home grown" and spontaneous, usually touched off by policing in the ghetto. The race riots of the 1960s were not the old, traditional white attack on blacks, with the burning of the black quarters. Black militancy and the massive growth of the ghettos would have precluded that, if anyone had had it in mind. Nor were the ghetto riots of the sixties basically aimed at white people. With expectations raised and few changes evident, inner-city residents mainly looted and set fire to white-owned businesses in a carnival of frustration and anger.

Before the rioting subsided at the end of the sixties, there had been outbreaks in many Southern cities and in almost every Northern city with a substantial black population. In their report to the National Violence Commission, Hugh Graham and Ted Gurr (*Violence in America,* rev. ed. [1979]) totaled 504 riots, involving an estimated one-third of a million participants, more than 50,000 arrests, and nearly 250 deaths, mainly of people shot by police and National Guardsmen. Burnt-out city blocks remained as memorials well into the next decade. In 1968, after the murder of Martin Luther King Jr., smoke from the burning portions of Washington, D.C., drifted over the White House and the Capitol. Two presidential study commissions, one on riots (*Report of the National Advisory Commission on Civil Disorders* [1968], chaired by Illinois governor Otto Kerner) and the other appointed after the murder of Robert Kennedy (*Report of the National Commission on the Causes and Prevention of Violence* [1969], headed by Milton Eisenhower) produced volumes of social science analysis. Both commissions reported that the conditions of segregation and poverty created a "destructive environment" in the racial ghettos. The riot commission asserted that the nation was "moving toward two societies, one black, one white—separate and unequal." White institutions created and maintained the ghetto, it stated, and "white society condones it." The violence commission reported that the United States was the leader among modern, stable, democratic nations in rates of homicide, rape, assault, robbery, and group violence and assassination. Both reports indicated that policing was as likely to produce violence as was dissent against authority. The Walker Report to the National Violence Commission (*Rights in Conflict* [1968]) pronounced the confrontation at the Democratic National Convention in Chicago a police riot. The reports produced no major policy moves, and Anthony Platt's study of riot commissions (*The Politics of Riot Commissions, 1917–1970* [1971]) concluded that they suggested no real institutional change or shifts in power.

The crucial argument was between structural and behavioral explanations of the violence. Was it the conditions or the perceptions of conditions, usually presented in "relative deprivation" analysis, that produced the explosions? The government's policy options were seen as a choice between basic social and economic reforms to remove the causes of violence and more powerful law-and-order control strategies. As the political scientist James Button (*Black Violence: Political Impact of the 1960s Riots* [1978]) summed up the conflicting perceptions, conservatives saw the collective violence as purposeless, needless, and irrational; liberals blamed it on socioeconomic conditions; and radicals saw it as a traditional weapon in the struggle for power. On the Left, violence was defended as meaningful signaling, as therapy (following the doctrines of Frantz Fanon, *The Wretched of the Earth* [1963]), as a way of forcing ruling elites to make concessions by "pushing turbulence to its outer limits" (Frances Fox Piven and Richard Cloward, *Poor People's Movements: Why They Succeed, How They Fail* [1977]), or as a way of taking power (Charles Tilly, *From Mobilization to Revolution* [1978]).

RESPONSE

The public and its leaders held to the traditional American belief in "peaceful progress," James Button maintained, even when many academics were coming to question it. Initially, sympathy for the deprived, along with a fear of disorder, led to urban aid programs such as the Model Cities Act. By 1968, congressional disillusionment, Vietnam War costs, and escalating violence produced a "law-and-order" backlash that helped elect Richard Nixon president. For the Nixon administration, the emphasis was on law and order.

It is probable that the inner cities were quieted by a combination of reduced expectations, increased policing, the realization that black neighborhoods and black people bore the costs of rioting, and sheer exhaustion. Campus demonstration and violence peaked with the 1970 invasion of Cambodia and the deaths of the students at Kent State and Jackson State. A quarter of the nation's colleges either closed or went on strike, and there were demonstrations on most other campuses. In 1970, the president of the University of Michigan and the president of Vanderbilt University told President Nixon's Commission on Campus Unrest, chaired by Governor William Scranton, that it was the Vietnam War, not the campuses, that was causing the trouble.

President Nixon, whose initial reaction to student protesters was to characterize them as "bums," pointed out that college students were only a small portion of the population. Like the ghettos, the campuses were approaching exhaustion. The young dissenters had tried nonviolence, and it had not worked. They had tried violence, and that had not worked either. The response of the political system had been to make Richard Nixon the president of the United States. Black radical leaders had been killed by their rivals or the police, or were in exile abroad. The radical student Left had failed in the streets and then self-destructed; its remaining fragments had gone underground. Malcolm X, Martin Luther King Jr., and Robert Kennedy had all been murdered. The symbolic Woodstock Nation had symbolically died at Altamont. The War on Poverty and America's economic growth and prosperity were being bled away by the Vietnam War costs and by inflation.

When the North Vietnamese armies attacked across the seventeenth parallel in the spring of 1972 and the United States responded by bombing Hanoi heavily, campus demonstrators again took to the streets, but for the last time. There was an even more severe Christmas bombing at the end of the year, but college was not in session, and there was no similar protest. Draft reform, Vietnamization, and concern about the economy and jobs cooled the action on the campuses. Henry Kissinger had announced that peace was "at hand," and Richard Nixon beat back George McGovern's challenge to the war with 61 percent of the vote, carrying every state but Massachusetts and the District of Columbia.

Whatever the outrage and anguish produced by the war, the 1968 Chicago riots, the "bust" at Columbia University, and the shootings at Kent State and Jackson State, at least a substantial portion of the American people thought that the students had gotten what was coming to them. It was America's failure to win that was responsible for much of the general disillusionment with the war in Vietnam. While the growth of both the economy and a youth generation were fundamental to the changes and the conflicts of the sixties, the civil rights movement had provided the early impetus and the "soul." Now the Vietnam War, the riots, the murders of John and Robert Kennedy and of Martin Luther King Jr., and increasing inflation shook the sense of confidence in America and its institutions.

THE END OF ALIENATION

By the mid-seventies, the political radicalism and the challenge to traditional institutions were all but gone. Daniel Yankelovich's polling studies over the period 1967–73 (*The New Morality* [1974]) strongly indicated that college students had moved closer to the general society in their attitudes toward politics and work, while the general society had moved closer to adopting the sexual and cultural values of the sixties avant-garde. "What we find today," Yankelovich wrote, "is an astonishingly swift transmission of values formerly confined to a minority of college youth and now spread throughout the generation." In parallel columns, he set forth the extent of the changes.*

Late 1960s	*Early 1970s*
The campus rebellion is in full flower.	The campus rebellion is moribund.
New life styles and radical politics appear together: granny glasses, crunchy granola, commune-living, pot-smoking, and long hair seem inseparable from radical politics, sit-ins, student strikes, protest marches, draft card burnings.	An almost total divorce takes place between radical politics and new life styles.
A central theme on campus: the search for self-fulfillment in place of a conventional career.	A central theme on campus: how to find self-fulfillment *within* a conventional career.
Growing criticism of America as a "sick society."	Lessening criticism of America as a "sick society."

*Reproduced with permission from Daniel Yankelovich, *The New Morality: Profile of American Youth in the 70's* (New York: McGraw-Hill Book Co., 1974), pp. 3–5.

THE END OF OPTIMISM **143**

The Women's Movement has virtually no impact on youth values and attitudes.

Wide and deep penetration of Women's Liberation precepts is underway.

Violence on campus is condoned and romanticized; there are many acts of violence.

Violence-free campuses; the use of violence, even to achieve worthwhile objectives, is rejected.

The value of education is severely questioned.

The value of education is strongly endorsed.

A widening "generation gap" appears in values, morals and outlook, dividing young people (especially college youth) from their parents.

The younger generation and older mainstream America move closer together in values, morals, and outlook.

A sharp split in social and moral values is found within the youth generation, between college students and the noncollege majority. The gap *within* the generation proves to be larger and more severe than the gap *between* the generations.

The gap within the generation narrows. Noncollege youth has virtually caught up with college students in adopting the new social and moral norms.

The new code of sexual morality, centering on greater acceptance of casual premarital sex, abortions, homosexuality, and extra marital relations is confined to a minority of college students.

The new sexual morality spreads both to mainstream college youth and also to mainstream working-class youth.

The challenge to the traditional work ethic is confined to the campus.

The work ethic appears strengthened on campus but is growing weaker among noncollege youth.

Harsh criticisms of major institutions, such as political parties, big business, the military, etc., are almost wholly confined to college students.

Criticisms of some major institutions are tempered on campus but are taken up by the working class youth.

The universities and the military are major targets of criticism.

Criticism of the universities and the military decreases sharply.

The campus is the main locus of youthful discontent; noncollege youth is quiescent.

Campuses are quiescent, but many signs of latent discontent and dissatisfaction appear among working-class youth.

Much youthful energy and idealism is devoted to concern with minorities.

Concern for minorities lessens.

The political center of gravity of college youth: left/liberal.	No clear-cut political center of gravity: pressures in both directions, left and right.
The New Left is a force on campus: there are growing numbers of radical students.	The New Left is a negligible factor on campus: the number of radical students declines sharply.
Concepts of law and order are anathema to college students.	College students show greater acceptance of law and order requirements.
The student mood is angry, embittered, and bewildered by public hostility.	There are few signs of anger or bitterness and little overt concern with public attitudes toward students.

The revolt of the 1960s was over. Yankelovich reported that non-college youth saw themselves as less political and "sick and tired of hearing people attack patriotism, morality, and traditional American values." A 1971 Lou Harris poll of 15- to 21-year-olds concluded that they were remarkably conservative. They were getting along with their parents and their parents' ideas, and, for the most part, they believed in hard work and thought that happiness meant having a good family life.

The counterculture also seemed just about played out, absorbed by its fratricidal twin, the great American consumer culture. Affluence and technology produced the counterculture's essential tools, and television spread its message. To an important degree, the primitive freedom of rock, drugs, and sex was dependent on transistors, tubes, speakers, and amplifiers; hallucinogens and amphetamines; and penicillin, the pill, and cash. The historian William Leuchtenburg reported that San Francisco's Fillmore West, the one-time Taj Mahal of acid rock, had been "sold to the consumer culture anaconda, Howard Johnson." The counterculture had been something of an androgynous creation, a rejection of American materialism, built on American economic prosperity and an aggressive market society that seized upon it and packaged it for sale to the young.

The reports from the seventies and the youth vote for Ronald Reagan in the eighties seemed to indicate that the sixties generation was only a temporary departure from American basics. Youth no longer appeared as a major force on the national political scene, in search of new institutional patterns and interpersonal relationships. It was no longer a generation. The Vietnam War was over, but military budgets escalated. No organization spoke for black America. Preachments about radically changing America were more likely to be heard from the Right than the Left. The poor were still poor, particularly the children. Although it may not be proper to blame the sixties and the consumer culture, three of the saddest developments in the following decades derived from both too little and too much affluence and freedom. By the eighties, teen-age pregnancy among the poor, and drugs among the young, had become national epidemics, while the dark shadow of AIDS hovered over sexual liberation.

10. Toward the Liberation of Women

THE FIRST WAVE

Although the Vietnam War and a general exhaustion were draining the energy out of the 1960s, the women's movement was gathering strength. As desegregation was forcing white society to respond to black people as individuals, so feminism was changing the lives of millions of women who were never exposed to its ideology or considered belonging to its organizations. It was not the first time that a drive for the rights for women had been stimulated by concern for the condition of black people. More than a century earlier, the women's rights movement had grown out of abolitionism. Arguments over the participation of women divided the American antislavery movement, and in 1840 the female members of the American delegation to the World Anti-Slavery Convention in London were denied the right to take part. Forced to watch silently from the galleries, Lucretia Mott and Elizabeth Cady Stanton angrily decided that they would organize their own convention on the subject of women's rights. Eight years later it took place at Seneca Falls, in upstate New York, where Stanton and her husband were living. Adopting the wording of the 1776 American Declaration of Independence, the convention declared, as a "self-evident" truth, that "all men and women are created equal," and submitted to "a candid world" a list of "repeated injuries and usurpations on the part of man toward woman." By a narrow margin, they pledged themselves to seek for women the right to vote.

The fight for suffrage was only a part of what the 1970s would call "the first wave" of American feminism. Moved by a natural-rights philosophy, the early women's movement attacked the sex distinctions of Victorian America which denied women access to education and the professions and made them "civilly dead upon marriage," unable to control their earnings and property, protect themselves against brutal husbands, or have custody of their children after divorce.

As a later historian of Victorian womanhood, Carroll Smith-Rosenberg, wrote, "Women were not found in public places." Considering the absence of standing or power with which they began, the "first wave" was remarkably bold. The goals for which Stanton and her tireless new ally Susan B. Anthony struggled were a single sexual standard and complete equality. Lucy Stone, the movement's most forceful orator, kept her own name when she married, and she and her husband wrote a pledge of equality into their marriage vows. On the radical edge, Victoria Claflin Woodhull, and her sister Tennessee, denounced the sexual double standard, by which she refused to live; and Charlotte Perkins Gilman's 1898 classic *Women and Economics* argued that economic dependence on men, based on the "sex-relation," was harmful to human progress.

By the time the women's movement secured the right to vote with the ratification of the Nineteenth Amendment to the Constitution in 1920, the goal had narrowed. Political expediency shifted the argument from the natural and equal rights of women to the more conservative grounds of the moral usefulness of the woman's vote, and the National American Woman Suffrage Association (NAWSA) had carefully distanced itself from black and immigrant women. The early twentieth century had brought both protective laws for married and working women (later called "social feminism") and better opportunities for middle-class women to obtain an education and enter the professions. Despite the excitement of the struggle for the vote, the freer life of the younger generations in the big cities and in Greenwich Village, and the appearance of the term "feminism," women's organizations were not out to change society and the relations of the sexes. Women voted basically the same way that men did, and for male candidates. The new successor of the suffragists, the League of Women Voters, settled into middle-class nonpartisanship and declined to endorse an equal rights amendment to the Constitution or the reproductive freedom represented by Margaret Sanger's mild but embattled crusade for family planning. Young women had thrown away their corsets; they drank, smoked in public, rolled their hose below the knees and considerably below their hemlines, and talked about sex and self-fulfillment as they sought to become part of the men's world rather than change its consciousness and remake it. That would come with the 1960s.

NOT WAITING FOR THE REVOLUTION

Nonetheless, the period between the first and second waves of feminism was not one of inactivity. Committed and courageous women such as Ella Baker, Septima Clark, Virginia Durr, Anne Braden, and Jeannette Rankin took stands and worked for various causes that were to become the movements of the sixties. Baker was an organizer, Clark a teacher, Durr a civil rights liberal, and Braden a progressive, and Jeannette Rankin carried her half century of peace protest into the anti–Vietnam War movement of the sixties and seventies.

Ella Baker. When Ella Baker was growing up in Norfolk, Virginia, in the days before World War I, a white boy had called her a "nigger."

She made a fist and hit him on the nose. More than fifty years later, she still struck out strongly at oppression and oppressors, but she had come to believe that organizing was more effective than violence, and she had spent her life being an unusual kind of organizer. She believed that people must make their own decisions, and it was this understanding that guided the lunch counter sit-in students into becoming a movement, and shaped the philosophy of the Student Nonviolent Coordinating Committee.

Ella Baker came to Harlem out of Shaw College, in Raleigh, North Carolina, in 1927. During the Great Depression she taught consumer education for the New Deal's WPA and organized consumer cooperatives. In the 1940s she traveled the South as a field organizer for the NAACP, was national director of its local branches, and then head of the New York City branch. When the Southern Christian Leadership Conference was organized, she became its executive director. As such, in 1960, she put together a meeting at Shaw College for the student sit-in leaders from across the South. The NAACP, CORE, and SCLC all wanted the students to be part of their own youth groups, but Miss Baker, wary of bureaucratic organizations and preacher autocracy, urged the students to treasure their own spontaneity and to think things out for themselves. The movement that they had started had a potential that was "more than a hamburger and a coke." She resigned from SCLC to work for SNCC, whose group-centered leadership she had helped bring into existence. Ella Baker knew to whom to send the young SNCC workers in communities in the Deep South; she helped them organize the Mississippi Freedom Democratic party, advised, and patiently listened. Her belief that the oppressed themselves needed to "define their own freedom" underlaid the radical efforts of the sixties.

Septima Poinsette Clark. In 1976, the year of the nation's bicentennial and of Septima Poinsette Clark's seventy-eighth birthday, she was elected to the Charleston, South Carolina, school board, from whose school system she had been fired twenty years before for NAACP activity. All of her adult life, since she began work at age eighteen in a rough, two-room schoolhouse on Johns Island off the coast of her native Charleston, she had been a teacher, and a highly gifted one. When Charleston let her go, Miles Horton brought her to the Highlander Folk School in Monteagle, Tennessee, to run an experimental "citizenship school." With skill and patience, in highly concentrated courses, she taught adults how to read, and her best students how to teach others. She believed that the way to overturn segregation was by the vote, so she taught her students to read state constitutions.

Anxious to stop a school where such subversive things were going on, the state of Tennessee raided the Highlander school and closed it down on the charge of selling alcohol without a license.

Clark's success in teaching poor black women particularly impressed Ella Baker, and so the Southern Christian Leadership Conference set Clark's program up again in a former United Church of Christ school in Dorchester, Georgia, near Savannah, as part of its Voter Education Project. The way it worked was that a busload of adult recruits would be brought in from a community such as Greenwood, Mississippi, for a week of intensive learning about how local governments operated and the procedure for getting registered. While other parts of SCLC's voter project struggled, Dorchester sent its enriched seed back to the grass roots of their communities. Clark and her teachers traveled about the South recruiting students and helping them set up hundreds of tiny citizenship schools, meeting in a shop or kitchen, teaching others "to read those election laws and to write their names in cursive." When the 1965 Voting Rights Act ended the use of literacy tests, there were no more fixed sets of questions to be learned. As Clark told interviewer Cynthia Stokes Brown, "It didn't take but twenty minutes in Selma, Alabama, to teach a woman to write her name." In Septima Clark's hometown of Charleston, there is a major expressway named after her—and a day care center.

Virginia Foster Durr. Virginia Foster Durr came from old plantation gentry, who had fought all of the South's wars, and was related to governors and congressmen. "I had been raised wanting everybody to love me and admire me like all of the Southern girls," she explained, so she found the ostracism more difficult to take than her husband did. It was particularly hard on their children, who "would sometimes say they wished I had stayed home and baked brownies as other mothers did. But what good were brownies," she said, "in a society that tolerated poverty and denied people the education to enable them to get out of poverty. . . . [and] the right to vote."

It had taken time and experience for Virginia Foster to grow out of her own prejudices. Although her family was financially pressed after her father was removed from the pulpit of Birmingham's South Highland Presbyterian Church for refusing to swear to the literal truth of the biblical story of Jonah and the whale, she was sent North for proper schooling. When she came down to dinner at Wellesley College and found a Negro girl sitting at her table, she immediately went back to her room. The housemother told her that she did not have to sit at the table, but of course, she would have to withdraw from Wellesley. Virginia thought about all of the dances, the football games, and the wonderful young men at Harvard Law, and the next day went back to the table.

Virginia's sister married a rising young lawyer name Hugo Black, and Virginia married Clifford Durr, who had been president of SAE fraternity at the University of Alabama, a Phi Beta Kappa, and a Rhodes Scholar. Cliff went to Washington to help the New Deal reorganize the banks, and then was appointed to the Federal Communications Commission. Attracted by Eleanor Roosevelt, Virginia Durr went to work for the Women's Division of the Democratic National Committee and for Southern Conference for Human Welfare, which was a broad coalition of people who were trying to do something about poverty and race in the South. She attended Senator La Follette's 1938 civil liberties committee hearings and became a leader of the movement to abolish the poll tax. This involved her with black and labor groups, radicals, and politicians. Her friend Lyndon Johnson promised to help, and did, as soon as he had the votes; but others could not stand the thought. On one occasion she brought two genteel white Methodist churchwomen from Mississippi to talk with their senator, Jim Eastland. As soon as the subject of race was mentioned, his face colored as he screamed at them, "I know what you women want—black men laying on you!"—a common obsession among Southern politicians, which Virginia Durr found not very flattering to the women, or men, of either race.

In 1948, Cliff turned down another term on the FCC, because he disapproved of the government's loyalty program, and opened a law office in Washington. While the Durrs were greatly concerned about the anti-Communist hysteria, they believed themselves safe from its touch. Virginia's anti–poll tax campaign had been open to anyone who joined in the common goal, and Cliff believed that anyone in trouble had the right to counsel. He defended a young government employee dismissed for patronizing a Marxist bookshop in Washington. The case drew publicity, and Cliff found that the radio networks and big corporations who had courted him when he was on the FCC, stayed away. The only cases he was getting were those of people without money, facing charges of disloyalty made by anonymous accusers. His admired and powerful legal friends, and the Ivy League universities, who had expressed interest in Cliff, backed away. The Durrs needed money, so Virginia, who had taken a course, taught English to the wives of foreign diplomats. The Durrs moved to Denver so Cliff could be counsel for the Farmers' Union, but the Korean War was on, and when Virginia signed Linus Pauling's petition against bombing Manchuria, the job disappeared.

Cliff was happy to be back in Alabama and always resisted the idea of leaving again. This was his world and his people, come what may. Senator Eastland subpoenaed Virginia to testify before the Internal Security Committee. The committee's informer testified that Mrs. Roosevelt would give cabinet secrets to Virginia, who would turn them over to a Communist spy ring. Virginia announced who she was and that she was going to stand mute and not have anything further to do with the committee. While her questioners raged, she stood quietly powdering her nose. When the Durrs returned to Montgomery, no one came to Cliff's Sunday school class at First Presbyterian, and the income from his law practice declined further. Virginia had taken a secretarial course and went down every day to work in the office.

Virginia claimed to have found consolation in having her "cover as a nice, proper Southern lady . . . blown by the hearing." By the time of the Montgomery bus boycott, she was friends with many of the black leaders. She had arranged for Rosa Parks to attend the Highlander Folk School, and when Mrs. Parks was arrested, Virginia and Cliff went down with the Montgomery NAACP leader E. D. Nixon to get her out of jail. These were hard times for white liberals in the South. "People don't like to remember anymore," Virginia Durr recalled, "but a lot of Southerners were forced to leave their homes." Northern friends found scholarships for the younger Durr children so they no longer would be singled out and embarrassed by their schoolteachers and called "nigger lover" and "Communist" by their classmates.

In the early sixties, the Durr house was a place where SNCC field workers on the way to Mississippi and civil rights people going to and from jail across the South would stop to spend the night. "Virginia, I understand you had some of that scum staying at your house," one "dear old lady" said to her at the time of the Selma-to-Montgomery march. "Well, I hardly think that the dean of the Yale Law School and the Sterling Professor of History at Yale are exactly scum," Virginia demurred. "They're scum to me," her neighbor replied.

Virginia and Cliff Durr had been disappointed by the way in which so many of their Washington associates and friends had not stood with them against the postwar anti-Communist hysteria. They had been disappointed a second time by the hostility of so many of their own people in Alabama over the civil rights struggle. In the longer run, the white South accepted desegregation much better than Virginia Durr expected, but she felt disappointment again that the newer generations of young people, white and black, had so greatly lost trust. Cliff and her sister's husband, Hugo Black, placed their faith in the law. Virginia Durr, herself, believed that popular participation in politics "was the answer to our problems." In the years after the 1960s, she found that the young trusted neither the law nor politics. What a tragedy it was, she lamented, that young people did not believe that the government was on their side.

Anne Braden. As neither Old Left nor New Left, Anne and Carl Braden found interracial efforts assailed by sectarianism on the left and "red-baiting" on the right. America had "let itself be divided by the notion that the test of a man is his anti-communism," Anne Braden summed up the problem, "rather than his devotion to the task at hand." As "independent socialists" engaged in labor union and interracial organizing, Anne and Carl Braden found that the battle for civil rights was inseparably wedded to the defense of civil liberties. Racial justice and the Bill of Rights were both involved in the same struggle, and both were under attack. The civil rights movement and the people who took part in it were continually faced with charges that their efforts were part of a Communist conspiracy or that their organizations were infiltrated by Communists.

Anne and Carl met as newspaper people in Louisville, Kentucky. Brought up middle class in Anniston, Alabama, with a church-awakened belief that people had a responsibility for others, Anne decided at Randolph-Macon College that her passion was journalism. After reporting for the *Anniston Star* and the *Birmingham News,* she moved to Louisville, where she and Carl worked for the *Louisville Times* and later the *Courier Journal.* Carl came from a close-knit working-class family and had been influenced by his father's Eugene Debs socialism and his mother's Roman Catholic faith. He drew Anne into his world of interracial union, church, and civil rights activity and friendships.

In 1954 Carl bought a house in a white neighborhood for a young black friend. The house was dynamited. When a police search discovered radical literature in the Bradens' home, Carl was held responsible for the bombing and spent eight months in prison until the U.S. Supreme Court decision in *Pennsylvania* v. *Nelson* (1956) overturned state sedition laws. It was not long before Carl was back in court—and prison. He and Anne had become field directors for the Southern Conference Educational Fund (SCEF), initially an operational arm of Virginia Durr's Southern Conference for Human Welfare (SCHW), which worked to integrate education, health services, and voting in the South. Called before the House Un-American Activities Committee, Carl declined Fifth Amendment protection and refused to testify. His beliefs and associations were protected by the First Amendment, he maintained, and were "none of the business" of the committee. By a five-to-four vote, the Supreme Court upheld Carl's contempt citation. Anne organized a clemency appeal that was supported by many civil rights leaders, including Martin Luther King Jr., but President Kennedy was not interested, and Carl went off to ten months in federal prison.

For a decade, from the mid-fifties to the mid-sixties, SCEF was an active force, raising funds, supporting black voter registration campaigns and interracial union organizing, publishing its monthly *Southern Patriot,* and keeping the national media informed on what was going on in the South. Anne and Carl worked well with both the Southern Christian Leadership Conference and the Student Nonviolent Coordinating Committee, and were sympathetic to SNCC's independence and growing militancy. They gave money to SNCC and funded the Southern Students Organizing Committee (SSOC) to work in white communities. As SNCC embraced black nationalism and SSOC gravitated toward SDS, the Bradens moved SCEF to Louisville, turned it more to interracial union organizing, and fought successful free-speech fights against the states of Kentucky and Louisiana. After Carl died and young black nationalists took over SCEF, Anne Braden found new ways to continue the fight for black-white cooperation, working-class organization, free speech, and opposition to the Ku Klux Klan. Seeking to place the struggle in a larger context, she explained that in times of economic and social turmoil, it served the interests of the powerful to suppress freedom behind a smokescreen of blame placed on blacks and minorities. Racism and political repression, she warned, historically go hand in hand. In 1989, the American Civil Liberties Union awarded Anne Braden its new Roger Baldwin Medal of Liberty for her lifetime contribution to civil liberties in the United States.

Jeannette Rankin. All her life, Jeannette Rankin claimed, she had believed that violence was not the solution to human problems. During her long lifetime, she had her say, publicly, about two world wars, Korea, and Vietnam. Born in 1880 on a ranch in the Montana Territory, and educated at the University of Montana, the New School of Philanthropy, and the University of Washington, she finally found her calling in the women's suffrage movement during its Washington State campaign of 1910. During the next six years, she worked for the cause in one-third of the states in the union, in time becoming a field secretary for the dominant National American Woman Suffrage Association (NAWSA).

From Montana, where she had helped win the vote for women, she became the first woman elected to the U. S. House of Representatives. She had run as a progressive Republican in 1916, promising to stand for the protection of working children, a national women's suffrage amendment, prohibition, and peace. Taking her seat just in time to vote on President Woodrow Wilson's request for a declaration of war on Germany, she was one of fifty legislators who voted "no." In words often quoted by the historians, she offered her vote with the explanation, "I want to stand by my country, but I cannot vote for war."

Defeated in the next election, she spent the next twenty years as an organizer and a lobbyist, promoting protective legislation for women, children, and consumers, and working for a variety of national peace organizations. In 1940, she rode Montana's isolationist sentiment back into Congress. "The women elected me because they remembered that I had been against our entering World War I," she said. Opposing all of President Roosevelt's preparedness and aid-to-Britain legislation, on December 8, 1941, she cast the only vote against a declaration of war against Japan. "I voted against it because it was war," she explained afterward.

During the postwar years, she became interested in Gandhi's philosophy of nonviolence and made numerous trips to India, while opposing all of her country's cold war policies. The role of women, she believed, was particularly important. Men started too many wars, she explained, and so it was important to make every woman's vote count. In 1968, at the age of eighty-eight, she appeared on the steps of the Capitol in Washington, D.C., on a cold January morning to join a protest against the "stupid and cruel" war in Vietnam. In writing about Jeannette Rankin's pacifism, the historian Joan Hoff Wilson rejected the traditional account of Rankin's vote against World War I. "She did not cry," Wilson wrote, "although some of the men did."

THE SECOND WAVE

In 1964, the conservative, Southern chairman of the Congressional Rules Committee, Howard Smith of Virginia, sought to defeat the Civil Rights Act by making it simply too ridiculous to pass. His strategy for doing this was to add "sex" to the grounds on which discrimination in employment was to be forbidden. To his surprise, the law passed. Its Title VII became the basis for equalization and affirmative action programs for women as well as for black people, and the Equal Employment Opportunity Commission (EEOC) was set up to enforce it.

The year before, in *The Feminine Mystique,* Betty Friedan had published her jeremiad against suburban, middle-class family life. Her argument that the American woman was trapped by her culture in the unsatisfying role of *house*-wife became a best-seller. Outside the domestic sphere, professional women were building supportive networks to attempt to counter on-the-job discrimination and harassment.

At least partially to win the support of Eleanor Roosevelt, who doubted his liberal convictions, President Kennedy had appointed the Commission on the Status of Women, which was copied in each of the states. Discontent over the timidity of the EEOC burst forth at the annual meeting of state commissions in 1966, and a political lobby calling itself the National Organization for Women was formed, with Betty Friedan as president.

NOW was a movement of the political center. Its main concerns were economic and social: equal treatment in education and the job market, with recognition of child-care and maternity rights; a nonpunitive approach to welfare; and the right of women to control their own reproductive lives through access to contraception and abortion.

A parallel impetus came out of the world of radical activism. As had happened with abolitionism a century before, the struggle for racial equality helped to give birth to a feminist movement. "There is something contagious about demanding freedom," Robin Morgan wrote in *Sisterhood Is Powerful* (1970). It was ironic that men were little more enlightened on the Left than on the Right. In SNCC's Deep South organizing campaigns and SDS's projects in Northern urban ghettos, "community" and "brotherhood" had left questions of "sisterhood" equality still unsolved. Mary King and Casey Hayden's memo on the aspirations of women in the movement was ridiculed by their male SNCC co-workers. At the New Left's 1967 National Conference for New Politics, the chair tried to shunt aside the women's resolution as he patted Shulamith Firestone on the head and told her, "Cool down, little girl, we have more important things to talk about than women's problems."

CASEY HAYDEN AND MARY KING

Sandra Cason, known to everybody as "Casey," and Mary Elizabeth King had been brought up in deeply religious families. Mary was a minister's daughter, and Casey had come to civil rights out of a campus Christian fellowship at the University of Texas. The Young Women's Christian Association (YWCA) sent her to the white Southern campuses to talk about academic freedom and race relations. Tom Hayden heard her speak at a National Student Association convention in Minneapolis and was captivated by the quiet clarity of her commitment and message, and her slim, blond-haired beauty. After a courtship, they were married, and he came South as SDS's liaison with the Southern struggle.

In 1962, Mary King took a spring break in her senior year for a "study tour" with her professor and a group of students to see what was going on in the South. Back at Ohio Wesleyan University, she followed Casey Hayden's advice and organized a campus race relations committee. When King graduated that spring, the YWCA asked her to come for an interview with Ella Baker and Spelman professor Howard Zinn about replacing Casey, who was going North with her husband. For the next four years, until the Student Nonviolent Co-ordinating Committee excluded its white members, the movement was King's life. She handled communications and press relations for SNCC, first in Atlanta and then from Jackson, Mississippi. Casey Hayden returned South, and both women lived within SNCC's embattled circle of commitment.

In the fall of 1964, after the Mississippi Freedom Summer, King and Hayden prepared a paper for discussion at a SNCC retreat at the Gulf Coast town of Waveland, Mississippi. Using examples, they hesitantly sought to make their co-workers aware of the assumptions of male superiority that existed within SNCC and were demonstrated by routine assignment of women to "female kinds of jobs," such as typing and housekeeping, within the movement. Anticipating ridicule and hostility, they had submitted the paper anonymously, but people soon guessed its authors. It is ironic that although Stokely Carmichael was among the few men who were sympathetic, his words have been recorded as the ultimate put-down. Mary King tells in her memoir, *Freedom Song* (1987), of a mellow night in Waveland, with a group of SNCC workers stretched out on a Gulf pier, having drunk much wine, while Carmichael launched into one of his monologues. He began by poking fun at himself and his fellow Trinidadians; eventually he got around to Hayden and King amid the pile of bodies on the pier: "What is the position of women in SNCC? The position of women in SNCC is prone!" he exclaimed, as they all roared with laughter.

The next year, in 1965, King and Hayden sent a paper titled "A Kind of a Memo" (afterward reprinted in David Dellinger's journal *Liberation*) to a number of women in SDS and the peace movement. It stirred exceptional interest. In one of the influential rallying calls of the women's movement, they sought to broaden the core civil rights value of "personhood" equality to apply to gender as well as race. Attacking what they described as "a common-law caste system," they wished to open up discussion among women. "Working in the movement often intensifies personal problems," they wrote, "especially if we start trying to apply things we're learning there to our personal lives. Perhaps we can start to talk with each other more openly than in the past and create a community of support for each."

In later years, as historians rushed to investigate women's lives and the interracial sexual relationships within the "freedom houses" of

Mississippi, Mary King and many other of the women of SNCC, black and white, came to believe that their experience and concerns were being misunderstood. Despite tensions and conflicts, in putting their lives on the line together they had been a family. Women such as Diane Nash, Ruby Doris Smith, and Fannie Lou Hamer had been leaders, and all had faced the same deadly violence as the men. In reply to the critics, Martha Norman, now herself an historian, wrote that SNCC had been "the singularly most liberating environment" of her life, and Casey Hayden recalled the unique "empowerment" she had felt in the movement. As later public interest had turned from race to gender, the struggle to change Mississippi's racially oppressive society was being forgotten, and women members rallied to SNCC's defense. It had not been their intention to "put down" the movement. "Nobody cleaned the freedom house," Casey retorted.

THE PERSONAL IS POLITICAL

Out of the civil rights movement and the New Left came groups of women sharing their experiences in a male-dominated world. The discovery that shaped the women's movement was that the personal was "political." The liberation of women was to be based on the awareness that a woman's sex was involved in all the ways that she was perceived and treated by her society. Across the country, small groups of women sitting together in living-room informality and talking about their lives came to realize that they shared common experiences in a male-dominated world. This "consciousness raising" was both revealing and exciting. From it came a heightened assault on gender-restrictive laws, such as the prohibition of abortion, and the renewal of the struggle for an equal rights amendment to the Constitution. "Consciousness raising" engendered not only a demand for equal treatment in jobs and the professions but also a radical questioning of all traditional assumptions and stereotyping about women's sexual nature and roles. This ranged from a consideration of marriage and of sex roles within the family (such as who did the housework and the child raising) to an examination of the nature of the body and the orgasm, lesbianism, rape, the relationship between sexual identity and class, and the development of women's studies and feminist criticism. Out of the shared "consciousness raising" came the emergence of a radical feminism that touched off what gave every evidence of becoming a permanent social and intellectual revolution.

In the late winter of 1969, a new women's liberation group calling itself "Redstockings" interrupted a New York State legislative committee meeting on abortion law reform and offered to give firsthand testimony. The committee, composed of a nun and fourteen men, refused the offer and moved to another room, where they could continue their work behind closed doors. The next month, Redstockings invited the press and television to an open meeting at the Washington Square Methodist Church, where women stood up and described the fear, the humiliation, and the pain of the abortions they had been forced to seek on the backstreets of America.

KATE MILLETT AND NORMAN MAILER

In 1970, Doubleday & Company published Kate Millett's angry liberationist manifesto *Sexual Politics*. In a few months, it had gone through five printings, and there she was with her face on the cover of *Time*. Growing up in St. Paul, in an Irish Catholic family whose father had wanted sons and had deserted his wife and three daughters, Millett was a Phi Beta Kappa at the University of Minnesota and took first-class honors at Oxford. Rebuffed in the New York job market and let go after a teaching stint at Barnard College, she settled down to do her doctorate in English literature at Columbia University. The result was a Ph.D. "with distinction" and the publication of her dissertation in book form, under the title *Sexual Politics*. In the late 1940s, author Kathleen Winsor avowedly read three hundred history books, wrote a sexy best-selling historical novel, *Forever Amber,* full of tight-bodiced Restoration ladies with heaving breasts and busy bedchambers, and became the sixth wife of the jazz clarinetist Artie Shaw. Millett's three-hundred book bibliography—drawn from literature, history, and the social and biological sciences—produced a bristling denunciation of the male dominance of women.

The reason was not any biological infirmity of women. From the biblical story of Adam's fall and the Greek legend of Pandora's box, the inferiority of women was a matter of gender, not sex. The psychosexual personalities of the sexes were postnatal, cultural, and learned. All of society's institutions combined to foster aggression in the male and passivity in the female. The world of men and women was one of power relationships in which "every avenue" was "entirely in male hands," and the chief institution of the patriarchy's dominance was the family.

Attacking a literary "counter revolution" that had been overtaking nineteenth-century and early twentieth-century feminist efforts, Millett singled out D. H. Lawrence, Henry Miller, and Norman Mailer as "counterrevolutionary sexual politicians." In case anyone had missed any of their graphic passages, there they were, reproduced, with comment, in *Sexual Politics*. What could the feminists have against him, Mailer asked his women's-rights friend Gloria Steinem? "You might try reading your books some day," she replied.

Never loath to be in the center of public controversy, Mailer struck back with a forty-seven-thousand-word rejoinder in *Harper's Magazine's* March 1971 issue. Labeling himself variously as "prisoner of war" and "prisoner of wedlock," and drawing upon the redoubtable experience he had gained through four marriages and having fathered six children, he attacked, excoriated, and assented, using more four-letter words and talk about the "phallus" than had ever before appeared in a family magazine. Willing to adjust to a world in which women were "writing about men and about themselves as Henry Miller had once written about woman," he drew the line at accepting the idea of a unisex world in which the womb did not make a basic difference. Barren and narrow-minded Millett misinterpreted, Mailer complained; she didn't understand the times, and missed the "dignity and tenderness," the "ecstasy," and the "sexual transcendence" of Mailer and his colleagues. Who emerged as winner of the argument? Although Mailer might have had a point about the nuances and the part that was biology, for the feminists, Kate Millett had hold of a crucial truth, which was that they lived in a world dominated by patriarchal sexual politics.

Three years later, Millett published *Flying* (1974), her lugubrious autobiographical account of bisexual struggles. Although it erased her from the media's roster of newsworthy authorities, the central perception of *Sexual Politics* remained undimmed as the women's movement gathered force. According to Susan Brownmiller, the author of *Against Our Will: Men, Women, and Rape* (1975), who had gone to Mississippi in 1964 for the Freedom Summer, after the Vietnam War protests died down the seventies were not simply a "Me Decade." For many women, it was a period of tremendous and satisfying activism, a logical extension of their earlier political work. Underlying the organizational activity and the chants of "Women's Liberation" and "Sisterhood is Powerful" was a radical examination of society's roots and a search for understanding.

FEMINIST THEORY

In the late 1960s and early 1970s, when the public's attention had otherwise turned away, exhausted, from social theory, feminism was an increasingly diverse and dynamic exception. Although much of it came out of the personal experiences and awakenings of the sixties, the French existentialist Simone de Beauvoir provided a crucial starting point. When she set out to write about her life, Jean-Paul Sartre had told her that she saw the world differently because she had not been brought up as a boy would have been. "You should look into it further," he advised. She did, and the result, in 1949, was *Le deuxième sexe,* translated to a cut-down English-language version of seven hundred crowded pages, *The Second Sex,* published by Bantam in 1953. "What peculiarly signalizes the situation of woman," she wrote in her introduction, "is that she—a free and autonomous being like all human creatures—nevertheless finds herself living in a world where men compel her to assume the status of the Other."

The core of feminism was the drive to understand, and to reverse, the condition to which de Beauvoir had given a name. Male domination of women was based not on physical strength but on control of the culture—control of consciousness. Feminism meant replacing male voices and male definitions with those of women. This went beyond achieving full participation and equality in the public and job worlds, which had belonged to men and in which "the Other" had made only a token appearance. It also meant understanding, self-possession, and women's self-determination of their biological nature and roles. For Simone de Beauvoir, to escape from being "the Other" was to escape from a falsely constructed woman's nature and completely enter the male world.

In her influential manifesto *The Dialectic of Sex: The Case for Feminist Revolution,* which she dedicated to de Beauvoir in 1970, Shulamith Firestone stated that the goal of the second wave was "not just the elimination of male *privilege* but of the sex *distinction* itself: genital differences between human beings would no longer matter culturally." The "enslavement by reproduction" from which de Beauvoir had fled was being overturned by technology. The revolution against the biological family would be won through contraception and abortion, and the diffusion of the responsibility for child rearing to the whole society.

Here again, the black struggle had anticipated the women's path. In his classic 1903 liberation cry *Souls of Black Folk,* W. E. B. Du Bois had asserted the essential "twoness" of freedom for black people. The black American "would not bleach his Negro soul in a flood of white Americanism," Du Bois had written. ". . . He simply wishes to make it possible for a man to be both a Negro and an American." Where de Beauvoir sought to escape from feminine qualities, Firestone saw them, freed from marital oppression, as constructive forces for good causes such as the preservation of the environment and the promotion of peace. The overthrow of patriarchical dominance would advance positive women's values and solidarity. As the excitement of discovery in the sixties yielded to the tasks of the seventies, "feminism" replaced "women's liberation" as the description for the movement, which grew increasingly diverse.

Women's rights meant full economic and political equality and participation in society. In battling to change the values and organization—the consciousness and structures—of that society, feminism went further. As long as the public world belonged to men, and jobs, careers, and politics were defined by male values, there could be no real equality. Women would always be "the other." This situation could only be changed by women's "empowerment," which would allow them to define their own family, job, and political values and to make their own decisions about how they were going to live their lives. Male definitions of value were particularly difficult to challenge. In the 1980s, when the returns showed that California Supreme Court chief justice Rose Bird had been defeated for reelection, largely over her opposition to the death penalty, a reporter asked her how she was taking the news. "Like a man!" she told him, and the media approvingly carried the story coast to coast. When Colorado congresswoman Patricia Schroeder shed tears upon announcing that she would not run for president, it was taken to show that she lacked the manliness necessary to operate in a public world that belonged to men.

As with blacks and other minorities, true freedom for women would come when they no longer had to give up their own uniqueness or special qualities as the price of admission to the mainstream. Feminist theorists, critics, and historians battled over how to combine a women's culture, based on a sisterhood of women's interaction and support, with the escape from the sexual distinction that underlaid the traditional maternal and family division of labor and roles. It was a painful and difficult escape to attempt. In a pathbreaking effort to combine the writing of women's history and of family history, Carl Degler decided that the discouraging title *At Odds* (1980) best described the relationship.

ON THE LIBERATION OF BLACK WOMEN

As an organized movement, feminism was not a black thing. Women's liberation was seen initially as the problem of bored, white, middle-class housewives, which paled before problems caused by racism and poverty. The frustration and anger of black men over denial of their manhood and of opportunities to get good jobs, support their families, and get ahead in the world lay at the root of all other problems. Black women activists saw their role as that of supporting their men, not trashing them the way white women were doing to white men. The solution to sexism would come with the overthrow of racial oppression.

Black male and female activists joined in anger over Daniel Moynihan's 1965 report on black poverty (*The Negro Family: The Case for National Action*), which seemed to place the blame on weaknesses in the structure of black families, rather than on a racist society.

Despite the bitter denunciation, Moynihan's strictures about the matriarchal role of women in black life were echoed in black nationalist rhetoric. Although black women had been a mainstay of the civil rights movement as they had of the black churches, leadership was mostly a male affair. The ministers of the Southern Christian Leadership Conference were used to running things, and were uncomfortable with activist women such as Septima Clark and Ella Baker, who held only subordinate roles. In the later sixties, Black Power became very much of a male consciousness movement; and Black Panthers, Black Muslims, black revolutionaries, and black poets, playwrights, and intellectuals told black women that they were part of the problem and that their role was to be subordinate.

Shirley Chisholm, the first black woman elected to Congress, contended that she had more trouble over being a woman than over being black. Michele Wallace's *Black Macho and the Myth of the Superwoman* (1979) laid it on the line, and the Boston-based Combahee River Collective expressed the growing feeling at the end of the seventies, saying, "We struggle together with Black men against racism, while we also struggle with Black men about sexism." In the flowering of black women's literature of the 1970s and 1980s, writers such as Alice Walker, Toni Morrison, Maya Angelou, and Ntozake Shange, as well as the rediscovered stories of Zora Neale Hurston, made the women's case.

ERA AND PHYLLIS SCHLAFLY'S CRUSADE

In 1972, the year that Congress sent the Equal Rights Amendment to the states for ratification, the U.S. Department of Labor reported that the median income of women employed full-time was 57.9% that of men. Of the 441 job categories listed in the U.S. Census, more than half of the working women were clustered in 20 basically lower-paid jobs in the service sector, and the growing number of female-headed households meant an increasing likelihood of poverty for the nation's children. At the same time, opportunity was expanding for educated middle-class women. The traditional elite men's and women's universities integrated their classes, and dormitories. Female enrollment expanded in professional schools, particularly in the colleges of law, where traditionally the entrance of a woman into a classroom would have been greeted with the hostile shuffling of feet by male students. Now, in the hands of the Department of Health, Education and Welfare (HEW), Title IX of the 1972 Education Act Amendments was a powerful weapon against discrimination in federally assisted educational programs; it also was used to ensure funding for women's athletics. Title VII of the 1964 Civil Rights Act, and the Equal Pay Act of the year before, were having an effect on the job world outside the campuses. In 1970, *Newsweek* brought in a freelance woman writer to do a cover story on "women in revolt" and found itself facing a discrimination complaint by its own women employees. No, it was not discrimination that women did the research and the writing positions went to the men, *Newsweek*'s editor responded uncomfortably. It was "tradition." Under pressure, *Newsweek*, AT&T, and other corporations were finding themselves greatly in need of changing their traditions.

In 1972, Congress mustered the two-thirds majority necessary to pass an equal rights amendment to the Constitution and send it to the states for ratification. "Equality of rights under the law," it read, "shall not be denied or abridged by the United States or by any state on account of sex." Congress would have the power to pass laws to enforce it, and the states had seven years in which to ratify it. As a capstone to the women's rights movement that had emerged in the late sixties, the amendment seemed primarily a symbolic statement that would bring few major changes. NOW was pushing it, and it drew support from more than four hundred organizations, including the American Bar Association, the Girl Scouts of America, the League of Women Voters, and most business and professional women's groups. It was in both the Democratic and the Republican party platforms, and organized labor had come to believe that the opening of employment opportunities to women was more important than special protective work rules. ERA was now clearly a popular, noncontroversial tribute to motherhood and women. Thirty of the necessary thirty-eight states quickly ratified it, and the rest were surely on their way.

A year later, the momentum began to slow down and eventually became reversed. Back at Berkeley, in the middle of the sixties, Mario Savio had called upon student radicals to throw their bodies against the gears of society and bring them to a halt. In 1973, a conservative, politically minded Illinois housewife was doing just that. Phyllis Stewart had grown up in St. Louis during the Great Depression, in which her father had lost his engineering job at Westinghouse and her mother had supported the family as a librarian in an art museum. Although she had a four-year scholarship to a small local Catholic college, Washington University was better, and she transferred, even though paying for it meant working full-time at night, test-firing ammunition at the St. Louis Ordnance Plant. In three years, she had graduated with Phi Beta Kappa and was off to Radcliffe for a master's degree in government. After a stint in Washington, D.C., as a researcher at the conservative American Enterprise Institute, she was back in St. Louis, where she met and, in 1949, married a conservative lawyer named Fred Schlafly, combining politics with producing a family of four boys and two girls.

Settled in Alton, Illinois, where the abolitionist Elijah Lovejoy had been lynched by a proslavery mob before the Civil War, Phyllis Schlafly had no luck in hard-fought campaigns for Congress in 1952 and 1970. Despite her growing skill and national prominence as a speaker and campaigner, she was too "uptown" for the district's farmers and working-class people, and her opponents made the most of her gender. The only kind of response that she could get to her effort to force a debate over Communist subversion was the retort that "my Harvard-educated opponent" ought to "stay home with her husband and six kids."

Foreign policy and the Communist menace were what most interested her. In 1964, she wrote a campaign tract, *A Choice, Not an Echo*, in which she denounced a conspiracy of internationalist Eastern Republicans who had deliberately picked losing candidates until a true conservative, Barry Goldwater, won the presidential nomination. Senator Goldwater lost the 1964 election to Lyndon Johnson, but 3 million copies of Phyllis Schlafly's little book were sold or handed out. The real danger, she revealed, was that Communist dupes such as Robert McNamara, Henry Kissinger, and the Council on Foreign Relations might leave a disarmed America at the mercy of the Soviet Union. When Gerald Ford became president and picked Nelson Rockefeller as his vice-president, Phyllis Schlafly knew that the Republic was in serious trouble.

She was deep into writing, in cooperation with a retired admiral, about nuclear-age weaponry and strategy when a friend asked her to take part in a debate on ERA. Although she was initially reluctant, her attention was caught by the amendment's provision for congressional enforcement. As she read it, this would mean a national redrawing of state laws on marriage, divorce, family, and employment which would turn over the federal system to "Big Brother" in Washington. Now committed, Phyllis Schlafly threw her quarter-of-a-century's experience of political organizing into the battle. Calling upon the devoted conservatives who had stood with her during her unsuccessful 1967 battle for the presidency of the National Federation of

Republican Women, she organized a network of women, reaching down into the state legislative districts, ready to enthusiastically buttonhole their representatives and fill the lobbies and galleries at the state capitols.

"Stop ERA" was hundreds of local groups, raising their own funds, running their own meetings, and connected to their leader by her telephone, her newsletters, legislative committee testimonies, rallies, and campus lectures, as well as television talk show appearances and debates with William Buckley, Betty Friedan, Donahue, and Barbara Walters. Issuing warnings about perverts, lesbians, "women's lib," the draft, and single-sex bathrooms, Schlafly turned the argument from economic and political rights to the protection of marriage and family relationships. Schlafly's energetic and powerful grass-roots campaign drew together the anti-Communist, anti-Washington conservatism of the Old Right and the family and church concern of the New Right. It mobilized the uneasiness that many women felt over the changing moral and family relationships of the sixties. Although more and more women were working outside of the home, marriage was a compact under which the man undertook to be the faithful defender and provider. If ERA meant that all things were equal, what moral force would still hold men to that compact? The ERA ratification drive stalled within three states of ratification. Utah, Nevada, Arizona, Missouri, Phyllis Schlafly's Illinois, and the South did not ratify, and a number of other states sought to reconsider. By the time it died in 1982, Phyllis Schlafly and her "Stop ERA" army, with belated help from conservative churches, had succeeded in making ratification too controversial an issue for legislators to risk supporting.

JUSTICE SANDRA DAY O'CONNOR'S CHOICE

Although its supporters vowed to come back again, ERA faded as an important national issue. Abortion took its place. With women's roles so greatly defined by their sex, reproductive freedom became a central concern to the women's movement and exploded into the nation's consciousness and politics.

In 1960, the national Food and Drug Administration had pronounced safe and effective a particular contraceptive combination of estrogen and progesterone, known as "the pill." Although the result may have relieved much individual anxiety and accelerated the sexual experiencing of the sixties, women, and particularly teenagers, kept having unwanted pregnancies. When the U.S. Supreme Court declared abortion legal in its 1973 *Roe* v. *Wade* decision, a new level of women's self-determination appeared to have been reached.

The "right of privacy," which the court found implicit within the Bill of Rights and the Fourteenth Amendment, was, Justice Blackmun wrote, "broad enough to encompass a woman's decision whether or not to terminate her pregnancy." During the first three months, the state basically could not interfere; after that its "interest" grew. In the second trimester, the state could impose restrictions to protect the mother's health, and in the final period it could act to protect both mother and unborn child.

The question of abortion became an emotionally enflamed dividing line in American society. For the pros, it was "freedom of choice" and "the right of a woman to control her own body"; for the antis, it was "murder." For vast numbers of women and men in the middle, it was a difficult moral and political decision that cut across practically all other religious, racial, gender, class, and political lines. Although battles raged over the public funding of abortion and the picketing of clinics and women's health centers, *Roe* v. *Wade* seemed firmly written into the law of the land.

When the Republican revival of the 1980s enabled Ronald Reagan to begin filling the federal judiciary with social conservatives, the possibility of a reversal became increasingly likely, and the intensity of conflict increased. In 1981, President Reagan appointed Sandra Day O'Connor as the first woman justice of the U.S. Supreme Court. Sandra Day grew up on a 166,000-acre ranch in the semiarid Gila River Basin country of southeastern Arizona. An honors graduate from Stanford University, she was one of a small number of women in Stanford's Law School, where she served on the *Law Review* along with John O'Connor. In 1952, Sandra Day graduated with high honors, third in her class, two places behind future chief justice William Rehnquist. None of the prominent California law firms would hire her. Her only job offer was for the position of legal secretary—which she turned down. It is possible that this experience may have contributed to her early enthusiasm for ERA and her concern about day care, family planning, and job and salary discrimination against women.

Married to John O'Connor, affluent, and settled in Phoenix, she raised a family, practiced law part-time, and immersed herself in civic affairs and Republican party politics. She served for six years in the Arizona Senate, rising to be Republican majority leader. As a trial judge in Arizona's Maricopa County, she saw the underside of life as she sat on cases involving burglary, drugs, rape, and murder. Newly appointed to the Arizona Court of Appeals, from which Ronald Reagan tapped her for the United States Supreme Court, she was a supporter of the death penalty, but had not written opinions on post-sixties controversies such as busing, school prayer, and abortion. As a child, she had disliked the long bus rides from the ranch to school, and as a judge she found the exclusionary rule on improperly obtained evidence too broadly applied. Apart from women's issues, the tumults of the sixties seem to have passed her by. Her political and legal thinking was mainstream Republican conservatism, shaped by experience in the Arizona legislature and courts and favored the "compelling interest" of the state rather than a jurisprudence of "fundamental rights." The federal courts should practice restraint and defer to the decisions and intent of the legislatures and state judicial processes.

In her interview with President Reagan, she told him that abortion was "personally abhorrent." The National Right to Life Committee and fundamentalist spokesmen pointed out that her record in the Arizona Senate had been less clear, and they denounced her appointment. As President Reagan filled more vacancies on the Court, it began tipping to the conservative side. By the end of the 1980s, with four justices willing to overturn *Roe* v. *Wade,* the deciding vote was in the hands of Justice O'Connor. The 1989 *Webster* v. *Reproductive Health Services* decision indicated what was ahead for the 1990s. By a five-to-four margin, the Court gave state legislatures greater freedom in regulating abortion, but Justice O'Connor was not yet willing to give them the right to prohibit it. Did such laws place an "undue burden" on women, she asked of each case? The way the antiabortion forces read the situation, with a sufficiently carefully drafted law, she might well go further.

As "prochoice" supporters responded angrily to the *Webster* decision, it was clear that the 1990s would see the abortion issue bitterly fought out in state campaigns and legislatures—and in the streets—across the nation. Feminism's "second wave" had done much to change national consciousness and begin opening up the job market and the public world for women. With the issue of abortion, it had come up not only against a reaction to the 1960s, but also against a fundamental question of the biological nature of women, and how morality and tradition interpreted it.

11. Legacies and Continuities

RACE

Although the streets of the nation had become politically quiet after the American withdrawal from Vietnam, the experience of the sixties had a marked impact on the consciousness and on the structures of American society. The civil rights movement and the Vietnam War were the two great shocks of the decade. If the war was socially and morally disruptive, the civil rights struggle was a profoundly constructive experience. The desegregation of public life had moved beyond the possibility of reversal. When the black people of Montgomery began their boycott in 1955, they were asking only for more courteous treatment on the buses. The excitement of the struggle in Montgomery, Greensboro, Albany, Birmingham, and Jackson; in the bus terminals, lunch counters, and voter registration lines; and in the streets and jails of countless towns and cities across the South exploded the aspirations of black America. A decade later, nothing short of full equality would do.

The opening of opportunity ("Opportunity is the motivator!" was the message of King's young associate the Rev. Jesse Jackson) and the growth of the black vote changed the nature of race relations, from the jailhouse to the statehouse. The civil rights movement forced race relations into the American consciousness. It was like a picture projected onto a national television set that could not be tuned out or turned off, and it changed the consciousness of white as well as of black people. "The lunch counters in Greensboro had joined the buses of Montgomery, Gandhi's salt marshes, and Thoreau's Walden," the historian Harvard Sitkoff wrote in *The Struggle for Black Equality* (1981), "as focal points in the quest for justice through nonviolent civil disobedience." These were the symbols of the acceptance of that struggle as a part of the national legend of "America as progress." The civil rights movement reached through white guilt, conscience, and fear of disorder, to change the structure of race relations and of America's institutions. From that change in structure, further changes in consciousness took place with remarkable rapidity, but not for all.

Race is a category of uncertain meaning. Mainly, it is defined by the way people react to it. How important it is depends on the cultural values and the social arrangements based upon it. The term "racism," like "sexism" in the male-female relationship, means prejudice. For women's experience, the concept of "gender" has come to indicate the values and arrangements applied to sex. No similar culturally neutral term has developed for race, but in the decades that followed the civil rights revolution of the 1960s, it was the circumstances of socioeconomic class that shaped the lives of many African Americans. There was opportunity and upward movement for the black middle classes, but although a major, multi-million-dollar National Research Council study, "A Common Destiny: Blacks and American Society" (1989), denied that a "culture of poverty" existed, a disadvantaged black underclass was still being left behind in a world of female-headed, single-parent households, teenage pregnancies, illiteracy, unemployment, drug abuse, crime, and persistent poverty. If the leading cause of death for the white teenager from the suburbs was the automobile, for the young black ghetto male it was homicide.

ON THE CAMPUSES

On the campuses, where the students of the sixties had asked for relevance and a hand in shaping their education, their participation produced few new ideas and no shift of power, even with the appointment of students to academic committees. Undergraduates remained anonymous in large classes taught by graduate assistants, and students surrendered to the technotronic society, pursuing degrees in business, science and engineering, computer studies, law, and medicine rather than in the liberal arts and the humanities. Concerned universities started rebuilding their general education requirements, and though the number of courses in non-Western studies grew, Black Studies programs languished. In the 1960s, the SDS leader Todd Gitlin had helped mount the attack on the alienating nature of American society and the dehumanizing impersonality of its universities. A quarter of a century later, speaking to a national convention of historians, Professor Todd Gitlin wryly described giving examinations to his massed hundreds of unprotesting sociology students crowded into chairs in the only available room large enough to hold them—Berkeley gymnasium.

During the prosperous years of the 1960s, students generally expected to graduate into a world of promising job opportunities that lay waiting for them outside the campus gates. This confidence declined substantially during the inflation of the 1970s. One of the results was a growing seriousness about grades. Another was the pressure to get into the professional schools. In the 1970s, the most sought-after degrees were those in law and medicine. At the end of the 1970s, one of the leading students of American education, David Riesman, wrote that "one consequence of the understandable hunger for a secure place in an uncertain world has been a disastrous brain-drain of talented young people into the law." A similar pattern in medicine, he lamented, was that medical schools were overtraining general practitioners when they should be preparing them for the "different work of public health or preventive medicine." In the 1980s and the early 1990s, the rush was into the schools of accounting and business administration.

The most visible sixties contribution to higher education was the respectability of Marxist critical analysis in the social sciences and literature, within a general emphasis on race, gender, class, and ethnicity. With the rise of the monetarists, economics tended to be the most conservative discipline. Political scientists, immersed in policy, process, and quantification, were the least interested in grand theory. Anthropologists focused on the material conditions that shaped culture, and historians shifted their explorations from elite culture and politics to the social experience of women, blacks, the poor, Hispanics, Native Americans, ethnics, and the others who had forced their way into the national awareness in the sixties. In college English departments, the young scholars who were not working through the French postmodernist texts were exploring the previously little-known writing of women and minorities. For the most part, with the surprising exception of a late-blooming radical school of "critical legal theory" that established its contested foothold at Harvard and other prestigious law schools, Marxist analysis was not heavily ideological.

This shift in focus did not receive unquestioning approval. If the colleges of business administration ignored it, the conservative philosophers at the University of Chicago were willing to do battle with it. As the Nobel Prize–winning economist Milton Friedman had rejected the Keynesian guidance of the economy, so the Chicago-trained jurist Robert Bork, whose nomination to the Supreme Court was rejected by the U.S. Senate, bitterly criticized what he claimed was the Court's departure from the "original intent" of the Constitution. Chicago's "law and economics" program prepared future conservative jurists, and the Chicago humanist Allan Bloom wrote a 1987 bestseller, *The Closing of the American Mind,* in which he denounced everything about the 1960s as a sell-out of true elite values.

If the University of Chicago's guardians of the absolute looked upon the 1960s with disdain, a quarter of a century later many other Americans searched for its meaning with pain, nostalgia, and—for the young—a regret that they had missed it. While many people saw the decade as the beginning of a moral disorder, "the sixties" had once again become fashionable in the late 1980s and the early 1990s. The growing literature on the Vietnam experience numbered hundreds of novels and memoirs, and political scientists competed to explain how the mistaken decisions had been made. As the graduate students, young teachers, and activists of the 1960s established themselves on university faculties, they taught popular courses on the war. Their experiences, combined with memorializations of fallen leaders and memories of the causes and the excitement of the sixties, flooded the market with autobiographies, memoirs, and histories.

After World War II, popular access to higher education had increased greatly. The struggles and movements of the sixties were reflected in the recruitment of black students, the rising tide of Asian-Americans, the influx of more than a third of a million foreign students, and a beginning trickle from the Hispanic-American communities. Professional paths were gradually welcoming women, who also made up a large portion of the older people who were returning to college to improve their job skills or to change or open up their lives.

The role of the university as foster parent for its students was gone. Off campus and, to a large degree, on, students were now free to live their personal lives—which meant primarily late hours and their sex lives—as they wished. The death of *in loco parentis* was part of the cultural change that was taking place.

Preachers denounced "the new morality," and the political scientist Andrew Hacker lamented that "the end of the American era" was caused by the mediocre majority that no longer knew its place.

THE CROWDING OF CHANGES AND EVENTS

The anthropologist Maxine Margolis (*Mothers and Such* [1984]) offered a cultural materialist's warning against putting too much emphasis on ideas and politics. After all, Simone de Beauvoir's *The Second Sex* had been widely read in the United States for more than a decade before Betty Friedan wrote *The Feminine Mystique,* with little resulting action. By the latter sixties, the increasing flood of women into the job market, facing low-paying, dead-end work combined with all the traditional home responsibilities, created the discontent "that led to the rebirth of feminism and the popularity of books that decried the contemporary version of women's 'proper place'."

By the end of the sixties, a major shift had taken place in American family dynamics. As the Baby Boom birthrate declined and inflation grew, the traditional picture of the husband at work and the wife at home with the children no longer described the American family. By the 1990s, more than half of American mothers with children less than one year old were working outside the home. The two-paycheck family was becoming both a necessity and the prevailing pattern.

The demographic argument offered a worthwhile reminder of the importance of social trends. Combined with the massing of the unique events of the decade, they produced the particular configurations that are known as "the sixties." The growing flood of women into the job market, changing sexual attitudes, the pill, pot, rock, the youth culture, and the feminist revolt, King, Kennedy, Johnson, Mississippi, Berkeley, the Vietnam War, liberalism, Black Power, the Baby Boom, the "deauthorization" of tradition and authority, and more, all interacted.

Events have their own power. The crowding of the campuses made the explosion at Berkeley possible, but would there have been a Berkeley without a Mississippi and the civil rights contagion? While the social base is an important part of the explanation of what took place, its usefulness in prediction is more limited. The growth of the college population and the depersonalization of the classroom continued in the seventies, yet there were no more explosions, and hardly even any complaints. The homosexual population of New York's Greenwich Village was nothing new, but when the gays made their stand and battled the police in the streets around the Stonewall Inn during the late June days of 1969, they changed the patterns of their life in America.

It was the combination of social trends, events, self-awareness, and possibilities that made the sixties a watershed for the emergence of new group consciousnesses. Almost two decades after he had returned from the Mississippi Freedom Summer to find himself a movement leader at Berkeley, Mario Savio wrote, "I believe that the rising of Black People, which brought on the '60s,' marked the historic end of the viability of social oppression in America. Thereafter one oppressed group after another—American Indians, Latinos, Women, Homosexuals, etc., collectively threw off the yoke." A revolutionary breaking of categories was under way.

Although the sixties helped bring rising consciousness and organization to groups that historically had lacked representation and power in society—from "black is beautiful" to "welfare rights," "brown power," "women's liberation," and "gay liberation"—by the end of the decade the widespread sense of reshaping America and its values was gone. The 1960s had been uniquely a young people's decade. An active minority of young people had taken a lead in the civil rights and antiwar movements, and had terrorized college presidents and enraged regents. Young people fought in Vietnam and against the police in the streets of Chicago, canvassed for Eugene McCarthy and voted for Richard Nixon, made the headlines, experimented with drugs and communal living arrangements, produced their own music, changed the nation's sexual morality, and set the styles for its culture. Now, along with millions of others, they were absorbed into the make-a-living world and were taking their place in the institutional structures of society. In a Yankelovich poll in the mid-1980s, 64 percent reported that they had become more conservative in their political views.

With public passion all but exhausted, the popular mood became less political and more materialistic and self-centered, as had happened after the Civil War and each of the two great world wars of the twentieth century. The novelist Tom Wolfe, recorder of American vanities, named the 1970s the "Me Decade" and found the central characteristic of the 1980s to be a "hunger for money." Commitment was no longer in style. Presidents Nixon, Ford, Carter, and Bush offered no broad new social constructions; and Ronald Reagan, the most conservative president since his hero Calvin Coolidge, set his administration to diminishing the government's social role and responsibilities. For the most part, the social movements of the sixties had become interest groups seeking attention and power within society rather than trying to transform it.

RONALD REAGAN AND THE COMING OF THE REPUBLICAN EIGHTIES

With its presidential candidates—George McGovern, Jimmy Carter, Walter Mondale, and Michael Dukakis—appearing more dour than electrifying, the national Democratic coalition fell apart in the 1970s and 1980s. That this occurred was the product of the changing conditions of the 1970s as well as a reaction to the 1960s. While state elections depend principally on local issues, personality, and incumbency, presidential politics is shaped by class, culture, the state of the economy, concern about morality, national pride, and confidence in government. In the 1970s, the Democrats no longer appeared to be the party of the common man, and the Republicans had broadened their image to reach beyond the business community, the affluent, and older-stock Americans, as the representative of a broadened middle America.

The greatest political shift had been in the South, which moved into the presidential Republican column. It had begun before the sixties. Civil rights and the growing black role in the Democratic party played a part, but the Republican combination of militant anti-Communism and low-tax, antiunion, probusiness values appealed to the conservative individualism of both the white middle and working class. In 1948, Strom Thurmond, the Democratic governor of South Carolina, had carried the Deep South as a protest against his party's more racially liberal presidential candidate, Harry Truman. Forty years later, Senator Thurmond, now a Republican, was the dean of his new party's growing array of Southern senators, governors, and congressmen.

A law-and-order and family-values backlash replaced civil rights as the great morality drama of the post-sixties' decades. Permissiveness was blamed for crime in the streets, and for the counterculture and the spoiled, unpatriotic kids who had rioted on college campuses. In the eyes of many traditionally Democratic, white, working-class, ethnic voters, the party that had come to represent the mainstream aspirations of America during the years of the Depression, World War II, and postwar prosperity was abandoning them for black, brown, and sexually perverse minorities.

The cost of the Vietnam War, together with the slowing down of productivity in America's aging industrial sector, touched off a decade of inflation in the 1970s. The devastating 1973 Arab oil embargo quadrupled the price of oil, and the Iran-Iraq war more than doubled it again in 1979. By the end of the decade, the cost of living was more than twice what it had been in 1970, interest rates were approaching 20 percent, and unemployment was up to 8 percent. Foreign relations was just as upsetting. First there had been the unsuccessful war in Southeast Asia, then the oil embargo and the long lines at the pumps waiting to buy gasoline; now the United States watched helplessly while fifty-three Americans were held captive by the radical students at the U.S. Embassy in Iran and were paraded bound and blindfolded before the television cameras. Many Americans were confused and angry. The government that spent their tax money on welfare, bused their children away from neighborhood schools, and gave job preferences to minorities could not maintain order in the streets, keep the economy healthy, and command respect for the flag overseas.

The heart of Great Society liberalism had been the attempt to use government to solve society's problems. Now the conservative reaction blamed government for the problems, and promised to restore stability and order, economic growth, traditional family values, and America's self-confidence and world prestige by building up defense, reducing social spending, deregulating business, and cutting taxes.

Traditional Republican conservatives found themselves with new allies. The self-styled "neoconservatives," who published in Irving Kristol's *Public Interest* and Norman Podhoretz's *Commentary,* were former liberal intellectuals who had been distressed by campus disorder and the New Left's attack on standards. The New Religious Right, led by the evangelist Pat Robertson and Jerry Falwell and his "Moral Majority," sought to return prayer to the public schools and battled against abortion and the other evils of what they described as the false religion of "secular humanism." A New Right, led by Richard Viguerie, Terry Dolan's National Conservative Political Action Committee, the American Enterprise Institute, and the Heritage Foundation combined the social issues of the religious conservatives with computerized fund-raising, conservative political action committees, think tanks, and negative campaigning. Uninterested in compromise and fearful of betrayal, the New Right kept uneasy watch on Republican moderates and pragmatists and worried that "the prags" might get through to Ronald Reagan.

The wisdom of the national pollsters is that rank-and-file Democrats and Republicans share much the same mix of opinions and are less polarized than are party elites and interest-group activists. In part reacting to the changes and tumults of the 1960s, the social engineering of national government, and the Vietnam War, the country had become more conservative. How this was to be translated into national policy depended on the elites whom the voters raised to power.

Not the least of the new Republicans, and representative of millions of other former Democrats, was Ronald Reagan, who at the age of sixty-nine became president of the United States. In 1981, Ronald Reagan entered the White House as the spokesman for the conservative shift in consciousness and resolved to build it into the institutional structures of the nation. Reagan had graduated from Illinois's Eureka College in the fourth year of the Great Depression of the 1930s. His father worked for the WPA, and Reagan was an enthusiastic New Deal Democrat. He particularly admired and copied the confident style of Franklin Roosevelt. As a Republican, he quoted Roosevelt, used FDR's anthem, "Happy Days Are Here Again," and resolutely claimed that it was the Democratic party, not Ronald Reagan, that had strayed. As union president of Hollywood's Screen Actors Guild, Reagan became involved in the ideological politics of the McCarthy era and was disillusioned by the intrigues of the pro-Soviet Left.

He voted for Dwight Eisenhower, and toured the country as media spokesman for General Electric and corporate America, warning GE plant workers and local chambers of commerce against the dangers of Washington's interfering with free enterprise. In 1960 he was a Nixon Democrat, and two years later he switched to the Republican party. Conservatives watching his 1964 nationally televised "A Time for Choosing" campaign speech for Barry Goldwater knew that they had a new champion. From the moment he was elected governor of California in 1966, his sights were set upon the White House. Already a master of symbolic politics, he began his administration by firing the president of the University of California, Clark Kerr.

GOVERNMENT SERVICE

George Bush was to be the last of the World War II presidents. The youth of the 1960s entered their forties in the 1980s, and by the 1990s they were moving into the nation's institutional leadership. The media insisted on calling them the Baby Boomers, but they were much too mixed to form a generation. They included the 2 million who had gone to fight in Vietnam and perhaps as many who had at one time or another demonstrated against the war. Despite the Vietnam protests, wartime military service continued to be an advantage in American politics. Although most of the veterans who served in Congress were of World War II vintage, the Vietnam veterans were beginning to appear. Two former POWs and navy fliers, the Republicans Jeremiah Denton, from Alabama, and John McCain, who replaced Arizona's Barry Goldwater, were elected to the Senate. So were the Nebraska Democrat Bob Kerrey, who had lost part of his leg and gotten the Congressional Medal of Honor in Vietnam; Iowa's Tom Harkin; the former navy lieutenant and VVAW member John Kerry from Massachusetts, who had commanded patrol boats in the Mekong Delta; and Virginia's ex-marine governor Chuck Robb. Joining them in the upper chamber were the returned Peace Corps volunteers Christopher Dodd from Connecticut, Paul Tsongas from Massachusetts, and West Virginia's Jay Rockefeller. Ohio's John Glenn was the first American to orbit the earth, and New Mexico's Harrison Schmitt had walked on the moon. Although all of them were primarily men of the center, their experiential frames of reference came from the complex, crowded events of the sixties.

COLIN LUTHER POWELL was the first chairman of the Joint Chiefs of Staff to have known only the Vietnam War, and was its first black member. His parents, Luther and Maud Powell, had migrated from Jamaica to the New York City borough of Queens, not far from the Bronx apartment where Stokely Carmichael's Trinidadian family would settle. Luther Powell was a shipping clerk and Maud Powell a seamstress. The path upward for their son, Colin, was education and the army. He graduated from the City College of New York two years before Carmichael started at Howard University, and he entered the army as a second lieutenant with an ROTC commission. He married in 1962 and went off to his first tour of duty in Vietnam as an advisor to South Vietnamese troops, while his wife went home to her parents in Birmingham for the birth of their son. Returning with a Purple Heart to Ft. Benning at Christmastime in 1963, he was refused service in a Columbus, Georgia, restaurant. His family's accounts of black life in Birmingham and the events of the summer's civil rights struggle made him "disheartened and angry." He admired Martin Luther King Jr., but in 1968 he went back to Vietnam as a combat infantry officer.

His path to the top in the modern U.S. Army was two tours in Vietnam and more education. He earned a master's degree in business administration and won a coveted White House fellowship, which placed him in the new governmental nerve center, the Office of Management and Budget. After ever larger troop commands and Pentagon assignments, he returned from Germany to the National Security Council and moved up to the position of Ronald Reagan's national security advisor. In 1989, George Bush chose Colin Powell to be chairman of the Joint Chiefs of Staff. In that post, Powell directed the planning that at the end of the year overthrew the Panamanian strongman General Noriega.

LIVES AND COMMITMENTS

The decade had left its mark not only on America's laws and politics but also on lives and commitments, and on the way in which people related to society and the political system. Although the age had come to look in a different direction, an augmented ethic of voluntarism and service remained. For the most part, it was to be found among college-educated, middle-class men and women in journalism, law, teaching, medicine, and the health care and social service professions. Its politics led through the feminist, environmental, antinuclear, consumer, and community service movements, whose causes continued to attract young high-school and college students. At its edges, on the Right and the Left, it challenged both the liberal consensus and the corporate world's deeply ingrained tradition of ignoring the social impact of its business decisions.

Many of the veteran activists of the sixties continued to work among minorities and the poor, particularly in the inner-city ghettos of America, and in the barrios and *favelas* overseas. The former Peace Corps volunteers who mounted a vigil in the Capitol on the twenty-fifth anniversary of John Kennedy's death were some of the 130,000 returned men and women who had served in ninety-two countries. In addition to the three former Peace Corps volunteers who went into the Senate, more than half a dozen served in the House of Representatives, and others brought their knowledge and concern into the foreign service, the development agencies, and the universities.

Many of the social activists of the sixties turned to education and the helping professions. Studies indicate that perhaps almost half of the Mississippi Freedom Summer volunteers went into teaching, law, and medicine. Of those who became college professors, joined by a number of former SNCC staffers in African-American Studies programs, most were to be found in history and sociology, sharpening their criticism of American nationalism and the racial and class structures. Others went to the inner cities as teachers, lawyers, doctors, planners, counselors, and social workers in the network of agencies and organizations fostered by the Economic Opportunity and Older Americans Acts of the 1960s and the early 1970s. They ran housing and job-training programs, legal aid clinics, and mental health and counseling services, and served on NAACP and ACLU boards. Among the Mississippi Freedom Summer volunteers, only Massachusetts congressman Barney Frank sought major political office. Intellectually radicalized, for the most part they remained distrustful of careerism and political leadership roles. They became authors, documentary film makers, magazine and newspaper writers, and feminists, measuring their lives more by social usefulness than by career achievement. Many of the early leaders of Students for a Democratic Society also found their way to the universities, where, like Todd Gitlin and Richard Flacks, they sought to understand and write books about the movement of which they had been a part. Joyce Ladner came out of the Student Nonviolent Coordinating Committee and Mississippi to interpret race relations as professor of sociology at Howard University. Bernice Johnson Reagon entered the movement in Albany, Georgia, and carried forward its "freedom song" inspiration with her highly praised "Sweet Honey in the Rock" singers, and as director of the Smithsonian Institution's Black American Culture program.

The civil rights staffers of the Southern Christian Leadership Conference and the Student Nonviolent Coordinating Committee emerged more oriented toward traditional politics and power. Martin Luther King Jr.'s young SCLC aides Jesse Jackson and Andrew Young claimed national roles. C. T. Vivian and other ministers struggled to keep the organization going and sought a new focus in organized efforts to counter the Ku Klux Klan. Through his presidential campaigns in the 1980s, Jackson fought his way into leadership of the Democratic party's crucial black constituency. After serving as ambassador to the United Nations during President Carter's administration, Andrew Young was twice elected mayor of Atlanta, a city where many of the civil rights activists of the 1960s had gathered. Marion Barry, who had come out of Nashville's intensely committed moral community to be SNCC's first chairman, gathered his 1960s co-workers around him to help make him mayor of Washington, D.C., and build an old-style political machine soiled by corruption and cocaine. John Lewis, who succeeded Barry as chairman of SNCC, defeated his fellow staffer and Georgia legislator Julian Bond for Andrew Young's old congressional seat in Atlanta. In smaller communities across the South, former SNCC field secretaries and directors such as Albany (Georgia) City Commissioner Charles Sherrod, Lowndes County (Alabama) Commissioner Robert Mants, and Whitehall (Alabama) Mayor Johnny Jackson, became part of the black political presence. Hollis Watkins, the twelfth child of a Mississippi sharecropper, was one of those who had refused Lyndon Johnson's "compromise" at the 1964 Democratic National Convention in Atlantic City. In the 1980s, he ran the successful campaigns of Mississippi's first black congressman since Reconstruction, Robert Espy. In 1988, no one questioned his delegate credentials at the Democratic National Convention in Atlanta.

CITIZEN ACTION

American intellectual historians have periodically taken a renewed interest in the observations of the nineteenth-century French visitor Alexis de Tocqueville. In the 1980s they looked with particular interest at his report on the striving for community and on American voluntarism. "Americans of all ages, all stations of life, and all types of disposition are forever forming associations," he wrote. "In every case at the head of any new undertaking, where in France you would find the government or in England some territorial magnate, in the United States you are sure to find an association."

Across American society, an expanded, multilevel citizen activism had taken root. Church organizations, neighborhood associations, and locally supported social services were the traditional volunteer paths. State and federal government agencies and volunteer centers coordinated national programs that had survived from the 1960s. In a networking of local and national organizations, environmentalist societies rallied against what they saw as "the Reagan antienvironmental revolution." Consumer groups attacked corporate policy and the laxness of governmental concern. Peace and antinuclear groups challenged the cold war and defense policies, and grass-roots organizers sought to unite local-issue groups into political alliances that would be the power base of a new progressive movement. On the Right, organizers and demonstrators used the tactics of the civil rights movement to attempt to reverse the social changes of the sixties.

Predominantly white, middle class, and status quo, neighborhood organizations have historically been concerned with protecting property values against commercial, class, or racial-mix intrusion. By the 1980s, the acronym NIMBY ("Not in My Backyard") had come to sum up their resistance to accepting public housing and other governmental social programs. The Right-to-Life movement was different. Acting out of deep religious convictions, for which they were willing to face arrest and imprisonment, the antiabortion protestors led by Operation Rescue's Randall Terry incorporated the street tactics and moral commitment of the sixties in a movement that promised to be a continuing part of the activist landscape.

The United Way was neither territorial nor political. Replacing the old Community Chest, its consolidated fund-raising supported an estimated 137,000 local social service organizations, from boys' clubs and girls' clubs, blood banks, and adoption agencies to spouse abuse shelters. Mixtures of federal, state, and local funding supported crisis centers, rape and crime victim advocacy, juvenile guardian *ad litem* representatives, housing repair, and food distribution. Relying completely on their own fund-raising, the Habitat for Humanity's volunteers, including ex-president Jimmy Carter, poured the concrete and pounded in the nails to build homes for the poor, in a fast-spreading, nondenominational, practical witnessing of the spirit.

On a national level, the federal government's ACTION administered the surviving volunteer programs from the New Frontier and the Great Society. In the later 1970s, it was headed by Sam Brown, a former youth organizer for Eugene McCarthy, with the ex-SNCC staffers Mary King as deputy director and John Lewis in charge of domestic programs. It combined the Peace Corps, VISTA, and various senior citizen programs such as RSVP, Senior Companions, and Foster Grandparents.

In 1962, the nature writer Rachel Carson had described a world in which people woke up to discover that pesticides had killed all the wildlife and the birds. Her book *Silent Spring* dramatically focused public attention on environmental threats that expanded to include toxic waste and nuclear pollution. Although the environmental movement embraced a great many different problems and concerns, it basically adopted environmental science Professor Barry Commoner's "first law of ecology": "Everything is connected to everything else."

Beginning with the Wilderness Act in 1964, Congress passed laws dealing with clean air and clean water, endangered species, land and water conservation, and scenic rivers. The 5 million members of Hardline preservationist organizations such as the Wilderness Society, the National Wildlife Federation, and the Sierra Club, and protectionists such as the Audubon Society, were joined by recreationists and the League of Women Voters in research, lobbying, litigation, and public demonstration, and found newly formed allies in Common Cause, Friends of the Earth, Environmental Action, Ralph Nader's various public interest groups, and uncounted local organizations.

The modern consumer and environmentalist movements did not initially rise out of public concern or presidential agendas. Rather, they came out of Congress, and they helped ignite a public-interest sector that has brought major changes in business-government-citizen power relationships. Consumerism appeared first, Democratic senators from the North began to hold hearings on marketplace concerns. For Connecticut's Abraham Ribicoff and New York's Robert Kennedy, the issue was automobile safety. For Michigan's Philip Hart it was deceptive labeling. For Washington's Warren Magnuson, it was inflammable bedding and clothing. As a result of these hearings, between 1966 and 1968 Congress charged the government with regulating highway safety and air pollution, hazardous substances, fire-resistant fabrics, gas pipeline and coal mine safety, honesty in packaging and labeling, loan and credit charge information, stricter meat inspection, and dangerous pesticides. In 1970, three new agencies, the Occupational Safety and Health Administration (OSHA), the Consumer Product Safety Commission (CPSC), and the Environmental Protection Agency (EPA), institutionalized the government's expanded regulatory responsibilities.

Lyndon Johnson had seen the consumer and environmental acts as extensions of his Great Society program which did not significantly increase his budget. Richard Nixon saw the consumer laws as strengthening his blue-collar support and the stronger clean air and water law revisions as a necessary counter to the environmental politics of his likely presidential opponent, Maine senator Edward Muskie. Neither president realized the shifts of power that were involved. Much of the regulation of pollution and job safety and health would now pass from the states into the hands of the national government. The new environmental laws were much more extensive than those that had existed before, and they too meant significant changes in the existing power relationships. They mandated state plans and environmental impact statements, set strict standards and timetables, and provided for citizen lawsuits in federal courts to force compliance. As the business and public policy historian David Vogel sets forth in *Fluctuating Fortunes: The Political Power of Business in America* (1989), "During the 1970s, the public interest movement replaced organized labor as the central countervailing force to the power and values of American business." With the federal courts willing to give standing to public interest and class-action suits and accept oversight responsibilities, the new laws had opened up the economic system and the culture to organized citizen activism.

Public opinion polls showed that protecting the environment had emerged as a major political issue. Summertime air pollution in the big cities and an oil leak from the rigs in California's Santa Barbara channel helped to produce a sense of crisis. The fight for environmental values particularly appealed to the better-educated and more affluent, to community groups, and to young people. A major long-run strength of the movement was, as David Vogel pointed out, that it was "able to articulate an alternative view of how the quality of life in America ought to be judged." Beginning with the 1970 Earth Day observances on college campuses, student interest remained high, and the environmental movement, unlike the campus activism of the 1960s, provided an opportunity to stay involved after graduation. In reaction to the antienvironmental drive of the Reagan administration, with its high-profile leadership by Interior Secretary James Watt and EPA administrator Anne Burford, angry recruits poured into the proenvironmental organizations. Fund-raising was facilitated by the electronic revolution that made possible the computerized, targeted-mailing technology that also fueled the angry mobilization of the New Right.

Across the country, Ralph Nader's Public Interest Research Groups (PIRGs) drew college students into the environmental and consumer movements. In 1965, Nader, a graduate of Princeton and of Harvard Law School, published *Unsafe at Any Speed,* a study that argued that the automobile industry's lack of concern for safety was responsible for thousands of highway deaths. General Motors' Corvair was his prime example. When it came out at a congressional hearing that GM was searching his private life in the hope of discrediting him, Nader sued for invasion of privacy. The $425,000 that General Motors eventually paid to settle the suit went into further investigations of misbehavior by business and government. Nader's pressure helped create both the 1966 National Traffic and Motor Vehicle Safety Act and the Consumer Product Safety Act. His groups of young lawyers, known as Nader's Raiders, produced critical studies of the performance of federal regulatory agencies. On college speaking tours, Nader urged students to organize campus-based public interest research groups. Operating on more than one hundred campuses in twenty-five states and Canada, often despite opposition from student Young Republican clubs, PIRGs researched, lobbied and litigated about toxic waste and acid rain, brown-lung protection, bottle bills, recycling, "lemon laws," renters' rights, utility rates, property assessments, redlining, and consumer pricing abuses; and battled the powerful Educational Testing Service (ETS), demanding that it reform its examination systems.

While severely critical of business and government, both environmentalism and public interest were basically within-the-system movements. On the oceans, however, Greenpeace sailors joined portions of the antinuclear and peace movements who moved toward the edge in their willingness to undertake direct action to confront a peril that many of their members believed threatened human survival, and Earth First confronted lumbermen in the forests of the Pacific Northwest. Concern over damage to the environment had produced the antinuclear movement. In 1974, Ralph Nader organized a Critical Mass Conference and combined with the Sierra Club, the Friends of the Earth, the Union of Concerned Scientists, and the National Resources Defense Council to oppose the production of nuclear power. While the main efforts of a growing alliance of environmental, scientific, church, women's, student, labor, and local groups were focused on research, education, and lobbying, particularly after the reactor accident at Pennsylvania's Three Mile Island in 1979, the direct action wing, led by the Clamshell Alliance in New England and the Abalone Alliance on the West Coast, prepared for civil disobedience to halt the opening of new nuclear power plants.

A wide array of local and national church, environmental, antinuclear, foreign policy, and peace groups formed interacting networks. The national Catholic peace movement Pax Cristi USA, along with representatives from the Baptists, the Disciples, and other mainline churches, joined with the traditional Quaker, Brethren, and Mennonite peace churches in organized protest over nuclear weapons and foreign policy. Opposition to the American role in Central America in the 1980s sent volunteers to Nicaragua and created refugee aid organizations such as the Committee in Solidarity with the People of El Salvador (CISPES), which broke the law in order to help refugees settle in the United States. Women Strike for Peace, SANE/FREEZE, the War Resisters League, and other protest organizations from the 1960s and earlier decades, took part in the coalitions. Activists went to jail for symbolically pouring blood on missile nose cones and Trident torpedo tubes, and for invading launch sites and submarine bases. Like environmentalism, the peace movement, particularly with its antinuclear focus, involved high-school and college students in a movement world that carried over into their adult lives.

It was the hope of some citizen activist leaders that this spirit of social concern and its voluntaristic structure could be organized into a new, populist political movement. Its success would depend on organizing statewide, regional, and national alliances of grass-roots and issue-oriented groups that distrusted the policies and the interconnections of big business and big government. From participation in local, voluntary community organization would come the necessary skills and citizenship dedication. Harry Boyte, its leading chronicler and theorist, optimistically called citizen activism "the backyard revolution." The patron saint and model for community organizing was Saul Alinsky, who had begun his work in the immigrant wards of Chicago during the Great Depression of the 1930s. Reaching out to senior citizens, unions, neighborhoods, tenants, women's groups, ethnic organizations, environmentalists, consumers, and the poor, the new activists copied Alinsky's pattern of developing local leadership and building on concrete neighborhood issues. Organizing around rent control, utility rates, garbage collection and municipal services, toxic waste disposal, taxes, redlining, and expressway planning, they sought to build cooperation with other community groups into state and regional coalitions.

There was a dizzying proliferation of names and initials. Succeeding the sixties-bred National Welfare Rights Organization, the Association of Community Organizations for Reform Now (ACORN) a lower-income neighborhood organization that began in Little Rock, Arkansas, spread into some two dozen states. San Antonio's Communities Organized for Public Service (COPS) reached out to help fellow Hispanics in California confront the developers and the utilities and get their share of municipal spending, while the Southwest Voter Registration Education Program worked on developing the electoral clout. With Alinsky training, Cesar Chavez fought to bring unionism to Mexican-American farm workers in California and enlisted church, civil rights, AFL-CIO, and celebrity support in boycotts of the resisting grape and lettuce growers. Tom Hayden's Campaign for Economic Democracy (CED), which helped to lead a revolt of middle-class renters against developers and condominium converters in Los Angeles' Pacific Coast suburb of Santa Monica, hoisted him into the state legislature and spread to other cities as Campaign California. Chicago's Citizen Action Program (CAP) got help from the International Machinists Union in fighting an expressway plan, utility pollution, and bank redlining. The CAP coalition, started by Alinsky before his death in 1972, came to include Campaign California, the Illinois Public Action Council's more than one-hundred organizations, Massachusetts Fair Share's one hundred thousand dues-paying members, and similar organizations in twenty-one other states, claiming close to 2 million members.

Generally ignored by the national media, citizen action depended on professional organizing and door-to-door canvassing, networking and coalition building, and sometimes on help from businesses and foundations. Funds from the Midas Muffler Corporation, the Rockefeller Foundation, and a new conduit for mainstream church social action called the Inter-religious Foundation for Community Organization (IFCO) enabled Saul Alinsky to set up a training institute in

Chicago which served as a model for others, including Heather Tobis Booth's Midwest Academy in Chicago.

Heather Tobis had gone to Mississippi in the summer of 1964 to work in the Freedom Schools and voter registration. Returning to the University of Chicago, she was active in the antiwar movement, feminism, daycare, and local issues, and married Paul Booth, an early leader in SDS and now a union organizer. When she lost her job because of union activity, she sued. In 1973, with the back pay, plus interest, that she won, she organized the Midwest Academy. By the end of the 1980s the academy had sent out some sixteen thousand community organizers to work with African Americans, Hispanics, blue-collar workers, farmers, the poor, the elderly, and middle-class whites. Steve Max, who had come to SDS from the Old Left, took charge of training.

The academy's short courses, in Chicago and around the country, taught citizen activists how to organize, raise funds, research and network local "gut issues," lobby, and set up public hearings, petition drives, demonstrations, and "accountability sessions" with elected officials. The long-range goal was "empowerment" and social change. Through their role in winning concrete benefits, people would gain a sense of their ability to deal with the problems that affected their lives. The result would be to change the balance of power. The values were those of the sixties, and this time the necessary structures were going to be built to make the victories last. The Citizen Labor/Energy Coalition (CLEC), which Heather Booth and International Machinists Union president William Winpisinger had first put together in Chicago, confronted the utility industry and the oil and gas producers across the country on energy rates and industry structure. Booth became the national codirector of Citizen Action, and the Midwest Academy became its training arm.

Concerned with policy decisions, the citizen action movement was increasingly involved in electoral politics, supporting its own members as well as those friendly to its concerns. The more radical wing of citizen action had never identified itself with "liberalism," and more centrist political candidates found the label to be a handicap in the Reagan-Bush reaction of the 1980s. Those who hoped for the emergence of a new third force in American society liked to describe themselves as "progressives."

Those who saw their future within the Democratic party preferred the names "populism," or "democratic populism." They reached out to the economic anxieties of their working- and middle-class constituents, and to senior citizens, attacking the Republicans for their favoritism to big business and the wealthy. As a "populist Democrat" supported by a minority, labor, and citizen activist coalition, Jim Hightower became Texas's highly visible commissioner of agriculture, and Tom Harkin was elected senator from Iowa with a "progressive populism" campaign. Moving into national politics in the 1980s, Citizen Action played an important part in the victories of Harkin; Paul Simon of Illinois; Brock Adams of Washington; and the congressional Populist Caucus leader Lane Evans of Illinois. From the caucus, Albert Gore of Tennessee, Barbara Mikulski of Maryland, Tom Daschle of South Dakota, and Quentin Burdick and Kent Conrad of North Dakota also moved up to the Senate. Among the score of caucus members in the House was Jim Weaver of Oregon, whose great-grandfather had been a general in the Civil War and in 1892 was the presidential candidate of the first Populist party.

By the end of the 1980s, more than a thousand community leaders, political activists, grass-roots organizers, elected officials, and national candidates were taking part in the Midwest Academy's annual conferences. Health care and child care, utility bills, and toxic waste were prime citizen action issues. Despite the conservatism of the 1980s, the older traditions of populist and New Deal politics were combined with Saul Alinsky's grass-roots and ethnic organizing, SNCC's experience in the Deep South and SDS's ERAP efforts in the Northern ghettos, to perpetuate the radical spirit of the 1960s.

The disenchantment with government that meant votes for Ronald Reagan's presidency also raised opposition to his interventionist policy in Central America. The message of Vietnam, reinforced by the Russian debacle in Afghanistan, showed the limitations and perils of power. Although Vietnam, the Watergate scandal, and the Iran-Contra affair weakened popular confidence in military interventionism, Richard Nixon could not let go. In 1985, ten years after the fall of Saigon, he denounced those who had opposed the Vietnam War: "Vietnam was a crucially important victory in the Soviet Union's war for control of the strategically critical Third World," he wrote in *No More Vietnams*. "It was an important victory not so much because it gave the Soviets dominance over Vietnam but because it left the United States so crippled psychologically that it was not able to defend its interests in the developing world, the battleground in the ongoing East-West conflict that is best characterized as Third World war." Also thinking back about what the sixties had meant, a former Mississippi Freedom Summer volunteer valued the decade differently, concluding that "the antiwar movement of the 1960's is the main reason why there are not 10,000 US troops in El Salvador right now."

In 1990, when President George Bush committed massive American forces to confront the Iraqi invasion of Kuwait, outgrowths of Vietnam and sixties peace groups were soon standing on street corners with their protest signs and marching against going to war. The "lessons" of Vietnam were argued by opponents and supporters. The military leadership's reading of the lesson was the need for "overwhelming force," and the President promised that "this time" the United States was going to win. When he eventually requested authorization for the use of force, among the members of Congress voting on the resolution were twenty-six who had supported Lyndon Johnson's Gulf of Tonkin resolution twenty-seven years before. Although it passed, this time twelve of them voted with the majority and fourteen against.

Quietly confident over the strength of American democracy and the American economy, the political leaders and the social scientists of the 1950s could not have predicted the interaction of events which made the 1960s. They did not glimpse the underlying currents and gathering forces that were to break through to the surface. The decade of the 1960s turned out to be no "end to ideology." In a massing unique to the American experience, practically every classic social conflict or question erupted into the streets of the nation as a challenge to social stasis and stability: the individual vs. society, self-expression vs. authority, social justice vs. order, integration vs. separation, change vs. stability, reform vs. revolution, nonviolence vs. violence, spiritual values vs. materialism, and rationality vs. the irrational; war, peace, and the obligation to one's country; poverty, generational conflict, fathers and sons, black and white, empowerment, Chicanos, Native-Americans, male and female, lesbian and gay rights, sexual liberation, and the sensory exploration of the world of drugs. Never before had so many simultaneous challenges been loaded onto the circuits of American life.

At the end of the 1980s, Tom Hayden turned up at a reunion of SNCC staffers and reminisced about the sixties. Now the chair of the higher education appropriations subcommittee of the California legislature and a within-the-system pragmatist, he reflected that change comes in unexpected ways. The radicals of the sixties, he said, had really believed that they could change the world, and they gave their whole lives to the movement. It had been a rare apocalyptic moment, and it was in the nature of such efforts that they could not become enduring organizations. "You can't turn a volcano into a skyscraper," he reflected. Nevertheless, even after the subsidence of the passions of the sixties had emptied the campuses and the streets of protesters, much from the decade remained.

Bibliographical Essay

The conflict and confusion of the 1960s has continued to be reflected in the writings of its critics and historians. Attempts to sum up began in the journals of opinion at the end of the decade. David Halberstam wrote in *McCall's* (January 1970), "Well, good-by to all that, to the Sixties, to all that hope and expectation. It started so well, a belief that it was all going to work, that all the pieces would come together for a golden era of American social and cultural progress, victory over the darker side of our nature, victory over injustice. It ended in pain, disillusionment, bitterness, our eyes expert in watching televised funerals." Richard Rovere commented in the *New York Times Magazine* (December 14, 1969) that "steadily declining civility and mounting instability" had made it a "slum of a decade."

As it published a collection of essays written by noted American historians for its 1970 Independence Day issue, *Newsweek* found the nation in "a recession of the spirit." Richard Hofstadter called the sixties an "Age of Rubbish" marked by polarization and a decline in the sense of vocation. For Andrew Hacker, the dominant self-centeredness meant a decline in the American spirit. Eugene Genovese and Staughton Lynd agreed in blaming capitalist priorities and a corporate warfare economy. For Daniel Boorstin, the problem was "hypochondria": the national ills were "imaginary and non-historical." Americans were too present-minded in their belief in "ruthless absolutes and simple-minded utopias." Society needed to give up "the voguish reverence for youth and for the 'culturally deprived'" and to stop looking to the superior wisdom of "the vulgar community." Although Arthur M. Schlesinger, Jr., felt that America was "experiencing an extreme crisis of confidence," by comparison with the views of others, his rejection of an "inexorable decline" seemed optimistic. The increasing velocity of social change meant the loss of familiar guideposts and social stability. Such acceleration creates anxiety and problems, whatever the system of ownership and ideology, he explained. The political scientist Hans J. Morgenthau reflected in the *New York Review of Books* (September 24, 1970) that the distribution of power in America had survived the sixties as it had all previous reform movements. What did change in America were "the relations of government to different social groups as well as the conditions of the groups themselves."

Not surprisingly, the guardians of the high culture found the sixties noisy, self-centered, and undisciplined. Writing in the *New York Times Book Review* (December 21, 1969), Alfred Kazin noted the "absence of masterpieces" in a period more noted for "social turmoil than for its belief in high art," despite the resourcefulness of the novelists in their "stratagems and devices." The poet Louis Simpson (*New York Times Book Review,* December 28, 1969) was happier with the poetry of the sixties than Kazin was with the novels. "Long Live Blake! Down With Donne!" properly described a decade that had extended its awareness in coming "a long way from the timid and silent fifties," he wrote. In summing up the "sensibility" of a decade that had rejected the end of ideology, Daniel Bell (*Commentary,* June 1971) described its distinctive mode of modernism as "a concern with violence and cruelty; a preoccupation with the sexually perverse; a desire to make noise; an anti-cognitive and intellectual mood; an effort once and for all to erase the boundary between 'art' and 'life;' and a fusion of art and politics." Those who disapproved of the ideology and angst of the sixties might have taken comfort from the political sociologist Philip Rahv (*Time,* August 15, 1977), who commented coolly on the decade, "Nothing can last in America more than ten years."

With the passage of time, a crucial element of the sixties found more favor with its historians. Christopher Lasch (*New York Review of Books,* February 2, 1984) warned against trivializing the counterculture and the radicalism of the sixties by losing sight of their "moral urgency." The Berkeley historian Leon Litwack, in a *California Monthly* interview on the twentieth anniversary of the Free Speech Movement (December 1984), explained, "What is happening now, in the Reagan era, is that people are trying to reinterpret the sixties as a period of excess: We over-reached ourselves; the war on poverty was misguided altruism; the civil rights movement demanded too much too fast; the movement descended into apocalyptic fantasy; the counter culture died from an overdose; the antiwar movement made us soft and flabby; I don't agree. I think few generations cared more deeply about this country. It was a generation that opted for the highest kind of loyalty. It defined loyalty to one's country as disloyalty to its pretenses, a willingness to unmask its leaders, a calling to subject its institutions to critical examination. That, to me, is real patriotism."

At least for the next quarter century, the studies of the sixties were written by people whose lives, in one way or another, had been emotionally touched by the decade. In an experience akin to that of the Great Depression and World War II, and unlike the 1950s, 1970s, and 1980s, everyone had been a participant as private lives had merged into the public life of the nation. The first histories of the decade were

William L. O'Neill's sprightly and broad-ranging *Coming Apart: An Informal History of America in the 1960's* (Chicago: Quadrangle, 1971), and David Burner, Robert Marcus, and Thomas West, *A Giant's Strength: America in the Sixties* (New York: Holt, Rinehart & Winston, 1971), which briefly offered the criticism of liberalism that has been the principal theme of the histories of the sixties. In *America in Our Time* (Garden City, N.Y.: Doubleday, 1976), Godfrey Hodgson set forth the structure of liberal American society. Through a series of insightful though not uncontroversial case studies, Allen Matusow's *The Unraveling of America: A History of Liberalism in the 1960s* (New York: Harper & Row, 1984), published as part of the New American Nation series, argued the failure of liberalism. The sixties newsman Milton Viorst offered a forceful account of the "clear-cut moral cogency" of the issues that underlaid the social disorder in his *Fire in the Streets* (New York: Simon & Schuster, 1979). William Leuchtenburg's *A Troubled Feast: American Society since 1945,* rev. ed. (Boston: Little, Brown, 1979) is a fast-moving but authoritative weave of the experience of postwar America. William Chafe's excellent interpretive book *Unfinished Journey: America since World War II,* 2d ed. (New York: Oxford University Press, 1991) examines the roles of race, class, and gender in American public life. Although impressed with the social gains of the sixties, Chafe describes the loss of the postwar sense of "abundance and optimism" and the will to seek social equality. Sohnya Sayres et al., eds., *The Sixties without Apology* (Minneapolis: University of Minnesota Press, 1984) is a radical, double-barreled-shotgun commentary on just about everything in the sixties. Ronald Berman, *America in the Sixties: An Intellectual History* (New York: Free Press, 1968), is a conservative rebuttal to the decade.

The 1960s were so overwhelming that the preceding years seemed almost forgotten by the historians. However, at the end of the 1980s, William L. O'Neill, *American High: The Years of Confidence, 1945–1960* (New York: Free Press, 1987), and John Diggins, *The Proud Decades: America in War and Peace, 1941–1960* (New York: Norton, 1988), offered well-written popular histories by serious academics. In *A History of Our Time,* 3d ed. (New York: Oxford University Press, 1991), editors William Chafe and Harvard Sitkoff provide a useful set of readings on postwar America. James Haskins and Kathleen Benson, *The 60s Reader* (New York: Viking Kestrel, 1988), is a good beginning point for young, and older, adults.

THE CIVIL RIGHTS MOVEMENT

The basic histories of the black experience in America are John Hope Franklin, *From Slavery to Freedom: A History of Negro Americans,*

5th ed. (New York: Knopf, 1980), and August Meier and Elliott Rudwick, *From Plantation to Ghetto,* 3d ed. (New York: Hill & Wang, 1976). The classic studies of race and Southern politics are Gunnar Myrdal, *An American Dilemma: The Negro Problem and Modern Democracy,* 2 vols. (New York: Harper & Row, 1944); V. O. Key, *Southern Politics in State and Nation* (New York: Knopf, 1949); and C. Vann Woodward, *The Strange Career of Jim Crow,* 3d ed. (New York: Oxford University Press, 1974). Neil McMillen, *Dark Journey: Black Mississippians in the Age of Jim Crow* (Urbana: University of Illinois Press, 1989), is the best history of a single state. The resistance to civil rights is described in Numan V. Bartley, *The Rise of Massive Resistance: Race and Politics in the South during the 1950's* (Baton Rouge: Louisiana State University Press, 1969), and Neil R. McMillen, *The Citizens' Councils: Organized Resistance to the Second Reconstruction, 1954–64* (Urbana: University of Illinois Press, 1971). David Chalmers, *Hooded Americanism: The History of the Ku Klux Klan,* 2d rev. ed. (Durham: Duke University Press, 1987), tells the history of more than one hundred years of vigilante violence.

Aldon D. Morris explains the role of indigenous black institutions, organizations, leaders, and networks, and particularly the black churches, in *The Origins of the Civil Rights Movement: Black Communities Organizing for Change* (New York: Free Press, 1984). Doug McAdam approaches the same story from the viewpoint of sociological "political process" model analysis in *Political Process and the Development of Black Insurgency, 1930–1970* (Chicago: University of Chicago Press, 1983). Both of these works are examples of the new political sociology analysis of "resource mobilization." A good example of the community base of the civil rights movement is *The Montgomery Bus Boycott and the Women Who Started It: The Memoir of Jo Ann Gibson Robinson,* ed. David Garrow (Knoxville: University of Tennessee Press, 1987). An outstanding oral history source for the civil rights movement of the 1960s is the interviews conducted by Howell Raines, *My Soul Is Rested: Movement Days in the Deep South Remembered* (New York: Putnam, 1977). The struggle can be experienced through a brilliant, even-handed, two-part, fourteen-hour Public Broadcasting System series "Eyes on the Prize," produced by Henry Hampton and Blackside, Inc., Boston, Massachusetts, and inexpensively available on videocassette. Part 1, first shown in 1986, covers the movement through the 1965 voting rights campaign in Selma. Part 2, first shown in 1990, carries the story into the 1980s. A companion volume of pictures and text, by Juan Williams, has been published under the same title, *Eyes on the Prize* (New York: Viking Penguin, 1987); and a collection of interviews conducted for the series, Henry Hampton and Steve Fayer, eds., with Sarah Flynn, *Voices of Freedom* (New York: Bantam Books, 1989), has also been published. Robert Weisbrot, *Freedom Bound: A History of America's Civil Rights*

Movement (New York: Norton, 1990), is a balanced, informative, analytical account. The themes underlying Weisbrot's history of the progress of civil rights in America are the limitations of the black-liberal coalition, the failure to translate political into economic progress, and the Reagan administration's abdication of federal concern for racial equality and the lives of millions of white and black people living at or below the poverty line. The attitudinal studies conducted for *Newsweek* by the pollsters William Brink and Louis Harris have been published as *The Negro Revolution in America* (New York: Simon & Schuster, 1964) and *Black and White* (New York: Simon & Schuster, 1967).

The best beginning point for the study of Martin Luther King Jr. is his *Why We Can't Wait* (New York: Harper & Row, 1964), which contains his "Letter from Birmingham Jail." David L. Lewis's basic *King: A Biography*, 2d ed. (Urbana: University of Illinois Press, 1978), is complemented by Stephen B. Oates's stylish account of the life of the civil rights leader, *Let the Trumpet Sound: The Life of Martin Luther King, Jr.* (New York: Harper & Row, 1982). David Garrow's *Protest at Selma: Martin Luther King, Jr., and the Voting Rights Act of 1965* (New Haven: Yale University Press, 1978) shows King's strategy of confrontation. For *The FBI and Martin Luther King, Jr.* (New York: Norton, 1981), Garrow used the Freedom of Information Act to gather the sources for an analysis of J. Edgar Hoover's vendetta against King. Adam Fairclough's *To Redeem the Soul of America: The Southern Christian Leadership Conference and Martin Luther King, Jr.* (Athens: University of Georgia Press, 1987) integrates King into the history of the organization he led. David Colburn's study of the civil rights struggle in St. Augustine, *Racial Change and Community Crisis: St. Augustine, Florida, 1877–1982* (New York: Columbia University Press, 1985) underlines King's political sophistication.

David Garrow's Pulitzer Prize–winning *Bearing the Cross: Martin Luther King, Jr., and the Southern Christian Leadership Conference, 1955–1968* (New York: Morrow, 1986) is based on exhaustive research (which Garrow generously shares with other historians), including a massive collection of FBI documents and phone tap records obtained through the Freedom of Information Act. It is an impressively researched account of the centrality of King's Christian faith to his life in the civil rights movement. Although King's story appeared to have been fully told, Taylor Branch widens and deepens the scope and anchors King in the world of the black churches in the monumental first of his two volumes, *Parting the Waters: America in the King Years, 1954–63* (New York: Simon & Schuster, 1988), which received the Pulitzer Prize the year after David Garrow's book did.

For other organizations, Congress of Racial Equality founder James

Farmer's *Lay Bare the Heart: An Autobiography of the Civil Rights Movement* (New York: Arbor House, 1985) does just that. August Meier and Elliott Rudwick have written a comprehensive history, *CORE: A Study in the Civil Rights Movement, 1942–1968* (New York: Oxford University Press, 1973). Clayborne Carson did the same for the Student Nonviolent Coordinating Committee in his sensitive and definitive prizewinning organizational history *In Struggle: SNCC and the Black Awakening of the 1960s* (Cambridge: Harvard University Press, 1981).

James Silver, *Mississippi: The Closed Society* (New York: Harcourt Brace, 1964), and Anne Moody, *Coming of Age in Mississippi* (New York: Dial, 1970), tell what life was like, in Mississippi, for a white college professor and a black teenager, respectively. The best contemporary accounts from inside the Mississippi Freedom Summer are Sally Belfrage, *Freedom Summer* (New York: Viking, 1965); William McCord, *Mississippi: The Long, Hot Summer* (New York: Norton, 1965); Howard Zinn, *SNCC: The New Abolitionists* (Boston: Beacon, 1965); Len Holt, *The Summer That Didn't End* (New York: Morrow, 1965); and Elizabeth Sutherland, ed., *Letters from Mississippi* (New York: McGraw-Hill, 1965). In *We Are Not Afraid: The Story of Goodman, Schwerner, and Chaney and the Civil Rights Campaign for Mississippi* (New York: Macmillan, 1988), Seth Cagin and Philip Dray provide a dramatic narrative of violence, death, and courage, which illustrates how difficult it was to bring racial reform and justice to Mississippi. Don Whitehead's earlier *Attack on Terror: The FBI against the Ku Klux Klan in Mississippi* (New York: Funk & Wagnalls, 1970) was the prime source for the television reenactment of the murder of the three civil rights workers. Michal Belknap, *Federal Law and Southern Order: Racial Violence and Constitutional Conflict in the Post-Brown South* (Athens: University of Georgia Press, 1987), believes that the national government had the authority and should have intervened earlier and more forcefully to protect civil rights in the South. Eventual state moves in that direction, he maintains, were prompted by the fear of anarchy. Kenneth O'Reilly, *Racial Matters: The FBI's Secret File on Black America, 1960–1972* (New York: Free Press, 1989), shows that at least one sector of the government was not hesitant to do what it wanted to do; but it was not for civil rights.

Mary Aickin Rothschild, *A Case of Black and White: Northern Volunteers and the Southern Freedom Summers, 1964–1965* (Westport: Greenwood, 1982), is the best account of the experience of the summer volunteers. James Forman, who was SNCC's able executive secretary during its activist years, in *The Making of Black Revolutionaries* (New York: Macmillan, 1972), and Cleveland Sellers, in *The River of No Return: The Autobiography of a Black Militant and the Life and Death of SNCC* (New York: Morrow, 1973) give insider accounts of the bitter struggles within the movement. From the time Mary King graduated from Ohio Wesleyan University in 1962 until SNCC's white staffers were expelled, SNCC was her life, and it was not easy for her to build a new and useful life afterward, as she relates in *Freedom Song: A Personal Story of the 1960s Civil Rights Movement* (New York: Morrow, 1987). Polly Greenberg, *The Devil Has Slippery Shoes: A Biased Biography of the Child Development Group of Mississippi* (New York: Macmillan, 1969), shows the battle against Washington that the head start nursery schools of Mississippi had to fight for survival. John Dittmer, at Depauw College, is currently at work on what the evidence indicates will be an excellent general history of the civil rights struggle in Mississippi. James Loewen and Charles Salis, eds., *Mississippi: Conflict and Change,* rev. ed. (New York: Pantheon, 1982), is an outstanding public-school text.

Among the many stories that await a fuller telling are the lives of five important civil rights radicals: Miles Horton, whose Highlander Folk School trained generations of white and black labor and civil rights activists; James Dombrowski, of the Highlander Folk School, the Southern Conference for Human Welfare, and the Southern Conference Educational Fund, who won a Supreme Court case against the state of Louisiana that extended the free speech protection of the First Amendment; radical theorists and activists Bayard Rustin and James Forman; and Rev. C. T. Vivian, who carried on the Christian idealism of Martin Luther King Jr. and the SCLC after King's death.

THE COURTS, THE PRESIDENTS, POLITICS, CIVIL RIGHTS, AND POVERTY

Alfred Kelley and Winfred Harbison's *The American Constitution: Its Origins and Development* (New York: Norton) has become the classic and remains the essential textbook on constitutional history, though readers should compare the fifth edition (1976) with the more conservative and ideological interpretations of the seventh edition (1991) of Herman Belz, who has assumed responsibility for the book since the deaths of Harbison and Kelley. Richard Kluger, in *Simple Justice: The History of Brown* v. *Board of Education: Black America's Struggle for Equality* (New York: Knopf, 1976), tells the story of the legal battle against school segregation so well that he has helped launch a genre of histories of landmark cases. Bernard Schwartz, *Super Chief: Earl Warren and His Supreme Court—A Judicial Biography* (New York: New York University Press, 1983), is an informative and insightful source on the chief justice; and R. H. Sayler, et al., eds., *The Warren Court: A Critical Analysis* (New York: Chelsea House, 1969); Alpheus T. Mason, *The Supreme Court from Taft to Burger,* 3d ed. (Baton Rouge: Louisiana State University Press, 1979); and Norman Dorsen, ed., *The Evolving Constitution: Essays on the Bill of Rights and the U.S. Supreme Court* (Middletown, Conn.: Wesleyan University Press, 1987), offer guidance for the Warren and Burger Courts.

J. W. Peltason, *Fifty-eight Lonely Men: Southern Federal Judges and School Desegregation,* rev. ed. (New York: Harcourt Brace, 1971), reports the difficult task of supervising desegregation. Robert F. Kennedy Jr., *Judge Frank M. Johnson: A Biography* (New York: Putnam, 1978), and Tinsley E. Yarbrough, *Judge Frank Johnson and Human Rights in Alabama* (University, Ala.: University of Alabama Press, 1981), tell the story of the forceful federal district judge who confronted his law-school classmate Governor George Wallace in Alabama. Jack Bass, *Unlikely Heroes: The Dramatic Story of the Southern Judges of the Fifth Circuit Who Translated the Supreme Court's Brown Decision into a Revolution for Equality* (New York: Simon & Schuster, 1981), shows the creative role of four great jurists who served on the U.S. Fifth Circuit Court of Appeals. William Kunstler, *Deep in My Heart* (New York: Morrow, 1966); Charles Morgan, *One Man, One Voice* (New York: Holt, Rinehart & Winston, 1979); and Arthur Kinoy, *Rights on Trial: The Odyssey of a People's Lawyer* (Cambridge: Harvard University Press, 1983), are the stories of three civil rights lawyers, one from the South and two from elsewhere.

The opening up of voting rights, public transportation, and public education are studied in Steven F. Lawson, *Black Ballots: Voting Rights in the South, 1944–1969* (New York: Columbia University Press, 1976) and *In Pursuit of Power: Southern Blacks and Electoral Politics, 1965– 1982* (New York: Columbia University Press, 1985); Catherine Barnes, *Journey from Jim Crow: The Desegregation of Southern Transit* (New York: Columbia University Press, 1983); and Hugh Davis Graham, *The Uncertain Triumph: Federal Education Policy in the Kennedy and Johnson Years* (Chapel Hill: University of North Carolina Press, 1984). Diana Ravitch, *The Troubled Crusade: American Education, 1945–1980* (New York: Basic Books, 1983), is an outstanding account of the ways in which education stands in the center of social conflict and change in America. Betsy Levin and Willis Hawley, eds., *The Courts, Social Science, and School Desegregation* (New Brunswick: Rutgers University Press, 1977), is a useful collection of papers on social science research. The changes that the sixties brought in Southern politics are analyzed in Numan Bartley and Hugh Graham, *Southern Politics and the Second Reconstruction* (Baltimore: Johns Hopkins University Press, 1975), and Jack Bass and Walter DeVries, *The Transformation of Southern Politics: Social Change and Political Consequences since 1945* (New York: Basic Books, 1977). Earl Black and Merle Black, *Politics and Society in the South*

(Cambridge: Harvard University Press, 1987), studies the growth of the Republican party in the contemporary South. Jack Bloom, *Class, Race, and the Civil Rights Movement* (Bloomington: Indiana University Press, 1987), is representative of the current emphasis on the class basis of race relations and exploitation.

Elizabeth Jacoway and David Colburn, eds., *Southern Businessmen and Desegregation* (Baton Rouge: Louisiana State University Press, 1982), recounts what happened in fourteen Southern cities; and William Chafe, *Civilities and Civil Rights: Greensboro, North Carolina, and the Black Struggle for Freedom* (New York: Columbia University Press, 1980), shows how the white leadership politely maintained control. Individual studies by Alan Anderson and George Pickering, *Confronting the Color Line: The Broken Promise of the Civil Rights Movement in Chicago* (Athens: University of Georgia Press, 1986), and Richard Pride and J. David Woodard, *The Burden of Busing: The Politics of Desegregation in Nashville, Tennessee* (Knoxville: University of Tennessee Press, 1985), show how difficult desegregation has been. J. Harvie Wilkinson III, *From Brown to Bakke: The Supreme Court and School Integration, 1954–1978* (New York: Oxford University Press, 1979) and Raymond Wolters, *The Burden of Brown: Thirty Years of School Desegregation* (Knoxville: University of Tennessee Press, 1984), contend that the Supreme Court went much too far. The best continuous source on what was happening in the South in the areas of race relations, civil rights, health, education, and poverty during the 1960s is *New South*, the monthly magazine of the Southern Regional Council. The South's oldest interracial organization, since its founding in 1944 the SRC has engaged in regional research and programs while encouraging local interracial contact and cooperation. Its magazine continues publication under the title *Southern Changes*.

For the role of the presidency, Jim F. Heath, *Decade of Disillusionment: The Kennedy-Johnson Years* (Bloomington: Indiana University Press, 1975), recounts the political developments of the decade. Henry S. Parmet, *JFK: The Presidency of John F. Kennedy* (New York: Dial, 1983), provides the best-balanced account of John Kennedy in the White House. Arthur M. Schlesinger Jr., *Robert Kennedy and His Times* (New York: Ballantine, 1978), and Harris Wofford, *Of Kennedys and Kings: Making Sense of the Sixties* (New York: Farrar, Straus & Giroux, 1979) offer insiders' views of the men at the center and the way in which decisions were made. Carl M. Brauer, *John F. Kennedy and the Second Reconstruction* (New York: Columbia University Press, 1977), shows the president's growing involvement in the civil rights struggle. Victor Navasky, *Kennedy Justice* (New York: Atheneum, 1971), is more critical. The crucial legislative struggle over the 1964 Civil Rights Act is best covered in Charles Whalen and Barbara Whalen, *The Longest Debate: A Legislative History of the 1964 Civil Rights Act* (New York: New American Library, 1985). Richard Goodwin wrote eloquent speeches for John Kennedy and Lyndon Johnson, and took part in both Eugene McCarthy's and Robert Kennedy's 1968 presidential campaigns. He reminisces about the excitement, and about the "paranoid" behavior of Johnson in the White House, in *Remembering America: A Voice from the Sixties* (Boston: Little, Brown, 1988).

The leading Southern historians T. Harry Williams ("Huey, Lyndon, and Southern Radicalism," *Journal of American History*, September 1973), and Joe B. Frantz ("The Metamorphosis of Lyndon B. Johnson," *Journal of Southern History*, February 1979) credit Johnson with deep concern for the poor. Richard Goodwin's future wife, Doris Kearns, was a young White House fellow from Harvard when Lyndon Johnson picked her as confidant and then postpresidential aide to help him write his autobiography. Critics have never been sure how much of his inner self he actually revealed to her, but they have nevertheless been influenced by her *Lyndon Johnson and the American Dream* (New York: Harper & Row, 1976). Paul Conkin, *Big Daddy from the Pedernales: Lyndon Johnson* (Boston: Twayne, 1986), is a balanced, single-volume biography. *Exploring the Johnson Years* (Austin: University of Texas Press, 1981) and *The Johnson Years* (Lawrence: University Press of Kansas, 1987), edited by the University of Texas historian Robert Divine, offer the best survey of the Johnson administration. Carl Brauer has studied the origins of the War on Poverty in "Kennedy, Johnson, and the War on Poverty," *Journal of American History* (June 1982). Sar Levitan and Robert Taggard describe Johnson's social programs in *The Promise of Greatness* (Cambridge: Harvard University Press, 1976). The economist Robert Haveman analyzes the rise of social welfare and transfer payment spending and the development of public policy analysis in *Poverty Policy and Poverty Research: The Great Society and the Social Sciences* (Madison: University of Wisconsin Press, 1987). John Schwartz offers a positive assessment of Great Society programs in *America's Hidden Success: Twenty Years of Public Policy* (New York: Norton, 1983). Charles Murray, the author of *Losing Ground: American Social Policy, 1950–1980* (New York: Basic Books, 1984) is the leading 1980s critic of antipoverty programs. Negative findings also come from Allen Matusow, *The Unraveling of America: A History of Liberalism in the 1960s* (New York: Harper & Row, 1984). Theodore White, *America in Search of Itself: The Making of the President, 1956–1980* (New York: Harper & Row, 1982), found the programs all too costly and intrusive. Three accounts written by historians of poverty and welfare, James T. Patterson, *America's Struggle against Poverty,*

1900–1980 (Cambridge: Harvard University Press, 1981); Walter Trattner, *From Poor Law to Welfare State: A History of Social Welfare in America,* 3d ed. (New York: Free Press, 1984); and Michael Katz, *In the Shadow of the Poorhouse: A Social History of Welfare in America* (New York: Basic Books, 1986), are cautiously hopeful. Marshall Kaplan and Peggy Cucity, eds., *The Great Society and Its Legacy: Twenty Years of U.S. Social Policy* (Durham: Duke University Press, 1986), presents an assessment by leading experts. The extensive Oral History interviews in the Lyndon Baines Johnson Library, in Austin, Texas, are available on microfiche from University Publications of America, Bethesda, Maryland, and include the White House Central Files for the War on Poverty. Hugh Davis Graham, *The Civil Rights Era: Origins and Development of National Policy, 1960–1972* (New York: Oxford University Press, 1990), is the first broad look at the governmental role during the sixties.

CAMPUS PROTEST

Calvin B. T. Lee, *The Campus Scene, 1900–1970* (New York: McKay, 1970), and Helen Lefkowitz Horowitz, *Campus Life: Undergraduate Cultures from the End of the Eighteenth Century to the Present* (New York: Knopf, 1987), provide good general accounts of student life. In *Uses of the University* (Cambridge: Harvard University Press, 1963), Clark Kerr, then president of the University of California, described the conflicting roles of the modern university which touched off the campus unrest. In *The Young Rebels: Notes on Committed Youth* (New York: Harcourt, Brace & World, 1968), Kenneth Keniston contrasts the youth of the sixties with those of the fifties, described in his *The Uncommitted: Alienated Youth in American Society* (New York: Harcourt, Brace & World, 1965). A special number of the *Journal of Social Issues* (July 1967), and early SDSer Richard Flacks, *Youth and Social Change* (Chicago: Markham, 1971), profile the leaders of the campus protest. The sociologist Lewis Feuer's Freudian analysis, *The Conflict of Generations: The Character and Significance of Student Movements* (New York: Basic Books, 1969), presents a massive history of student movements around the world, including those of the sixties in the United States, on which Seymour Martin Lipset focuses in *Rebellion in the University* (Chicago: University of Chicago Press, 1971). Seymour Martin Lipset and Sheldon Wolin, eds., *The Berkeley Student Revolt: Facts and Interpretations* (Garden City, N.Y.: Anchor, 1965), is a collection of the accounts and analyses of the campus controversy that touched it all off. W. J. Rorabaugh, *Berkeley at War: The 1960s* (New York: Oxford University Press, 1989) puts it all together. Other campus conflicts are described in Cushing Strout and David Grossvogel, *Divided We Stand: Reflections on the Crisis at Cornell* (Garden City: Anchor, 1970); William H. Orrick Jr., *Shut It Down! A College in Crisis: San Francisco State College, October 1968–April 1969* (Washington, D.C.: U.S. Government Printing Office, 1969); Lawrence Eichel et al., *The Harvard Strike* (Boston: Houghton Mifflin, 1970); Jerry L. Avorn et al., *Up against the Ivy Wall: A History of the Columbia Crisis* (New York: Atheneum, 1968); Archibald Cox, *Crisis at Columbia* (New York: Vintage, 1968); and Roger Kahn, *The Battle for Morningside Heights* (New York: Morrow, 1970). Although national attention has focused on a few leading institutions such as Berkeley, Columbia, and Harvard, most of the nation's campuses were touched by university reform, the civil rights struggle, the New Left, and antiwar protest. Along with contemporary accounts in local journals, retrospective articles are appearing in alumni magazines and other local sources. In the interests of maintaining an available record, the author of this volume would be appreciative of receiving copies of such published materials.

THE NEW LEFT

The journals *Liberation, Studies on the Left,* and *New Left Notes* present the thinking of radical dissent. Judith Clavir Albert and Stewart Albert, eds., *The Sixties Papers: Documents of a Rebellious Decade* (New York: Praeger, 1984), is an accessible source for radical manifestos and speeches. C. Wright Mills can be approached through *The Power Elite* (New York: Oxford University Press, 1956) and *The Sociological Imagination* (New York: Oxford University Press, 1969). The standard history of Students for a Democratic Society is Kirkpatrick Sale, *SDS* (New York: Random House, 1973). The contemporary analysts Paul Jacobs and Saul Landau, *The New Radicals* (New York: Random House, 1966), and Jack Newfield, in *A Prophetic Minority* (New York: New American Library, 1966), offered sympathetic and often insightful analysis. John P. Diggins, *The American Left in the Twentieth Century* (New York: Harcourt Brace Jovanovich, 1973); James Weinstein, *Ambiguous Legacy: The Left in American Politics, 1900–1975* (New York: New Viewpoints, 1975); Milton Cantor, *The Divided Left: American Radicalism, 1900–1975* (New York: Hill & Wang, 1978); Lawrence Lader, *Power on the Left: American Radical Movements since 1946* (New York: Norton, 1979); and Irwin Unger, *The Movement: A History of the American New Left* (New York: Dodd, Mead, 1974), measure the place of the sixties in the history of the American Left.

In the 1980s, there was a revival of interest in the radicalism and the culture of the sixties. The New Left activists were telling their stories and reassessing what had happened—often still from the perspective of the Left—and they were frequently joined by younger historians. Maurice Isserman, *If I Had a Hammer: The Death of the Old Left and the Birth of the New Left* (New York: Basic Books, 1987), explores the continuities. A late-sixties SDSer, James Miller, in *Democracy is in the Streets: From Port Huron to the Siege of Chicago* (New York: Simon & Schuster, 1987), values the idealism of the early years and the potential of "participatory democracy," as does Wini Breines, *Community and Organization in the New Left, 1962–1968: The Great Refusal* (New York: Praeger, 1982), who dissents from the Left critics and liberal academics in arguing that the antiorganizational ethic and the spontaneous community are the only real hope for changing political consciousness. Todd Gitlin, combining his roles as university professor and former activist in *The Whole World Is Watching: Mass Media in the Making & Unmaking of the New Left* (Berkeley: University of California Press, 1980), explores the impact of the media on the history of SDS. In a general history built around his own experiences, *The Sixties: Years of Hope, Days of Rage* (New York: Bantam Books, 1987), Gitlin conveys much of the intensity and excitement of the period and offers insightful comment. Coming to the sixties from the Old Left, Gitlin's fellow SDSer Richard Flacks, now California sociology professor, seeks a path for the Left intellectuals in *Making History: The Radical Tradition in American Life* (New York: Columbia University Press, 1988). Interest in the New Left has remained high among the intellectuals. With the publication of memoirs and histories at the end of the 1980s, a reviewers' debate took place in the journals of opinion: Hendrik Hertzberg, "Part of the Solution, Part of the Problem," *New York Times Book Review* (June 21, 1987); Paul Berman, "Don't Follow Leaders," *New Republic* (August 10, 1987); Winifred Breines, "Whose New Left?" *Journal of American History* (September 1988); Alan Brinkley, "Dreams of the Sixties," *New York Review of Books* (October 22, 1987); Scott McConnell, "Resurrecting the New Left," *Commentary* (October 1987); James Miller, "Tears and Riots, Love and Regrets," *New York Times Book Review* (November 8, 1987); Sean Wilenz, *Nation* (November 14, 1987); and Jon Wiener, "The New Left as History," *Radical History Review* (Fall 1988).

Tom Hayden remains the central philosopher, icon, media celebrity, and whipping boy of the New Left. His narrative *Reunion: A Memoir* (New York: Random House, 1988) will be read as autobiography and record, and attacked both for what he glosses over and for what critics of both the Right and the Left want to see in him. The sociologist Harold Jacobs, who had been a Red Family member with Hayden in Berkeley, offers a psychodynamic analysis of him in "Tom Hayden:

The Waning of a Politics of Vision," *Tikkun* (May/June 1989), and faults him further for abandoning radicalism. In *Destructive Generation: Second Thoughts about the Sixties* (New York: Summit Books, 1989), Peter Collier and David Horowitz savage him for everything. Because *Destructive Generation* has something important to say, it is unfortunate that it is presented with such malice and lack of discrimination. Collier and Horowitz, who were editors of *Ramparts* during the sixties, have traversed the American political scene to end up supporting Ronald Reagan in the 1980s. They present a picture of the New Left activists, supporters, and friendly editorial columnists as unable to tell the difference between heroes, hoods, and homicidal maniacs, deeply involved in dishonesty and psychological and sexual games, and the willing tools of totalitarian regimes of the Left. Because the language and the attack are so condemnatory and dismissive, and the defense of the status quo so total, the issues they raise are lost in the polemical heat.

The twentieth anniversary of a high point of 1960s turmoil brought forth many volumes in 1988. In 1969, Stephen Spender, *The Year of the Young Rebels* (New York: Random House), had profiled the 1968 uprisings at Columbia University and the Sorbonne, and in West Berlin and Prague. Now, David Caute, *The Year of the Barricades: A Journey through 1968* (New York: Harper & Row, 1988), and Ronald Fraser et al., *Nineteen Sixty-Eight: A Student Generation* (New York: Pantheon Books, 1988), also included what was going on around the world. Caute attempts the broadest coverage, but offers it in fragments and without interpretation. Fraser et al. go deeper, using interviews with student activists in six industrial countries. For the American story, Irwin Unger and Debi Unger, in *Turning Point: 1968* (New York: Scribners, 1988), provide a broad and lively account of what they see as the climax of a process by which social reform was isolated from the political mainstream.

THE COUNTERCULTURE

Useful accounts of the disconnectedness of the fifties which foreshadowed the dissenting culture of the sixties are Lawrence Lipton, *The Holy Barbarians* (New York: Messner, 1959), and Bruce Cook, *The Beat Generation* (New York: Scribners, 1971). Theodore Roszak, *The Making of a Counter Culture* (Garden City, N.Y.: Doubleday, 1969), gave a name to the cultural dissent of the 1960s and praised its rejection of rationality and technology. Milton Yinger, *Countercultures: The Promise and the Peril of a World Turned Upside Down* (New York: Free Press, 1982), presents a general sociological analysis of the phenomena. The literary critics Richard Poirier, in *The Performing Self* (New York: Oxford, 1971) and Morris Dickstein, in *Gates of Eden: American Culture in the Sixties* (New York: Penguin, 1977), relate the high culture to the popular and dissenting cultures. The role of music of the sixties is discussed in R. Serge Denisoff and Richard A. Petersen, eds., *The Sounds of Social Change* (Chicago: Rand McNally, 1972), and in two new books by social scientists: John Orman, *The Politics of Rock Music* (Chicago: Nelson-Hall, 1985), and Herbert London, *Closing the Circle: A Cultural History of the Rock Revolution* (Chicago: Nelson-Hall, 1985). Nicholas Schaffner, *The Beatles Forever* (Harrisburg: Stackpole, 1977), covers the Beatles best. Susan Sontag, *Against Interpretation* (New York: Farrar, Straus & Giroux, 1966), is the high-culture manifesto that asserted the dominance of the "new sensibility," best illustrated by the selections in Gerald Howard, ed., *The Sixties: The Art, Politics, and Media of Our Most Explosive Decade* (New York: Washington Square Press, 1982). From its appearance in 1967, *Rolling Stone* magazine has been a leading spokesman of American rock music and popular culture.

The "new journalism" of the sixties can be sampled in Tom Wolfe, *The Purple Decades: A Reader* (New York: Farrar, Straus & Giroux, 1982). The new literary sensibility is exemplified in Norman Mailer, *Advertisements for Myself* (New York: Putnam, 1959), *The Presidential Papers* (New York: Putnam, 1963), *Armies of the Night: History as a Novel, the Novel as History* (New York: New American Library, 1968), and *Miami and the Siege of Chicago: An Informal History of the Republican and Democratic Conventions of 1968* (New York: New American Library, 1968), as well as his sexual polemics in *The Prisoner of Sex* (Boston: Little, Brown, 1971).

Richard King, *The Party of Eros: Radical Social Thought and the Realm of Freedom* (Chapel Hill: University of North Carolina Press, 1972), is an excellent study of the Freudians Paul Goodman, Herbert Marcuse, and Norman O. Brown, and what King calls their "new transcendentalism." Marcuse's most influential contribution to the sixties was *One-Dimensional Man: Studies in the Ideology of Advanced Industrial Society* (Boston: Beacon, 1964). A good introduction to Paul Goodman is his "The New Reformation," *New York Times Magazine* (September 14, 1969).

The San Francisco scene is chronicled in Charles Perry, *The Haight-Ashbury: A History* (New York: Random House, 1984). The basic analytical study of communes is Rosabeth M. Kanter, *Commitment and Community: Communes and Utopias in Sociological Perspective* (Cambridge: Harvard University Press, 1972). Sixties communes can be sampled in the historian Laurence Vesey's *Communal Experience: Anarchist and Mystical Counter-Cultures in America* (New York: Harper & Row, 1973), and in the communalist Richard Fairfield's *Communes USA: A Personal Tour* (Baltimore: Penguin, 1972). Jonathan Eisen, ed., *Altamont: Death of Innocence in the Woodstock Nation* (New York: Avon, 1970) is an early collective account of what went wrong in the counterculture. Charles Reich's best-seller *The Greening of America* (New York: Bantam, 1970), was the decade's most optimistic statement about the lasting effects of the cultural transformation of the sixties, and Andrew Hacker, *The End of the American Era* (New York: Atheneum, 1971), was the most pessimistic. The general histories of the sixties, William L. O'Neill, *Coming Apart: An Informal History of America in the Sixties* (Chicago: Quadrangle, 1971); Godfrey Hodgson, *America in Our Time* (Garden City, N.Y.: Doubleday, 1976), William Leuchtenburg, *A Troubled Feast: American Society since 1945* (Boston: Little, Brown, 1979); and Allen Matusow, *The Unraveling of America: A History of Liberalism in the 1960s* (New York: Harper & Row, 1984), have excellent chapters on the decade's culture, and Todd Gitlin conveys the excitement of the sixties in *The Sixties: Years of Hope, Days of Rage* (New York: Bantam Books, 1987).

VIETNAM

The Vietnam War and those who were involved in it are not going "gently into that good night." The flood of histories, policy studies, memoirs, novels, movies, and television stories about the war flows unabated. Generally accepted as the two best single-volume accounts are the academic historian George Herring's *America's Longest War: The United States and Vietnam, 1950–1975,* 2d ed. (Philadelphia: Temple University Press, 1986), and the newsman-historian Stanley Karnow's *Vietnam: A History* (New York: Viking, 1983) which is the basis of Public Television's 1983 prize-winning documentary series "Vietnam: A Television History."

The war experience is well represented in personal accounts by a young marine officer, Philip Caputo, *A Rumor of War* (New York: Holt, Rinehart & Winston, 1978), and a correspondent, Michael Herr, *Dispatches* (New York: Knopf, 1977). The Vietnam War particularly saw the emergence of the journalist as participant-observer and historian, exemplified by Bernard Fall's *A Street Without Joy* (Harrisburg, Pa.: Stackpole, 1972); David Halberstam's *The Making of a Quagmire* (New York: Random House, 1965) and *The Best and the Brightest* (New York: Random House, 1972); Seymour Hersh's *My Lai 4: A Report on the Massacre and its Aftermath* (New York: Random House, 1970); and Neil Sheehan's Pulitzer Prize–winning *A Bright Shining Lie: John Paul Vann and America in Vietnam* (New York: Random House, 1988). Sandra

Taylor considers the participant-observer phenomenon in "Reporting History: Journalists and the Vietnam War," *Reviews in American History* (September 1985). Daniel Hallin, *The "Uncensored War": The Media and Vietnam* (New York: Oxford University Press, 1986) is an absolutely vital study on how the press and television covered the war. Kathleen Turner offers an able presentation in *Lyndon Johnson's Dual War: Vietnam and the Press* (Chicago: University of Chicago Press, 1985). The published proceedings of two 1980s conferences on the Vietnam War, Peter Braestrup, ed., *Vietnam as History: Ten Years after the Paris Peace Accords* (Washington, D.C.: University Press of America, 1984), and Harrison Salisbury, ed., *Vietnam Reconsidered: Lessons from a War* (New York: Harper & Row, 1984), provide commentary from leading authorities on various sides of various issues, including how well the media performed. A principal forum for discussion of the role of the media is the *Columbia Journalism Review*. Richard Clurman, *Beyond Malice: The Media's Years of Reckoning* (New Brunswick, N.J.: Rutgers University Press, 1988), testifies as to how little journalists, generals, and diplomats liked each other. U.S. Army military historian William M. Hammond's article "The Press in Vietnam as Agent of Defeat: A Critical Examination," *Reviews in American History* (June 1989), based on his *The United States Army in Vietnam: Public Affairs, the Military and the Media, 1962–1968* (Washington, D.C.: U.S. Government Printing Office, 1989), concludes that the media followed, rather than formed, public opinion, which was turned against the war by rising casualties and the absence of a strategy for winning.

In *The Irony of Vietnam: The System Worked* (Washington: Brookings, 1979), Leslie Gelb (who directed the Pentagon Papers project during the Vietnam War) and Richard Betts reject the "quagmire" argument that the Vietnam War was the ill-considered action of an improperly informed president. They maintain that President Johnson was kept properly informed about Vietnam but feared that decisive action would lead to a domestic backlash. Larry Berman, in *Planning a Tragedy: The Americanization of the War in Vietnam* (New York: Norton, 1982), which is generally considered the best account of White House policy making, agrees. He pictures President Johnson in 1965 steering his policy to avoid either being tagged by the conservatives with the "loss" of Vietnam, or losing the support of congressional liberals for his Great Society programs. For an extended history of the Johnson policy, see Larry Berman, *Lyndon Johnson's War: The Road to Stalemate in Vietnam* (New York: Norton, 1989).

Melvin Small's *Johnson, Nixon, and the Doves* (New Brunswick, N.J.: Rutgers University Press, 1988) is an excellent study. President Johnson's decision not to run for reelection is told in Herbert Schandler,

The Unmaking of a President: Lyndon Johnson and Vietnam (Princeton, N.J.: Princeton University Press, 1977), and Townsend Hoopes, *The Limits of Intervention: An Inside Account of How the Johnson Policy of Escalation in Vietnam Was Reversed,* 2d ed. (New York: Norton, 1987). Documentary material drawn from Lyndon Johnson's White House files is presented in *Vietnam, the Media, and Public Support for the War,* available on microfilm from University Publications of America, Bethesda, Maryland. A cautious reading of Henry Kissinger, *White House Years* (Boston: Little, Brown, 1979), is necessary for understanding President Nixon's policy; and Stanley Kutler, *The Wars of Watergate: The Last Crisis of Richard Nixon* (New York: Knopf, 1990), gives an unexcelled picture of the tension inside the Nixon White House.

For how the American people felt about the war, see Louis Harris, *The Anguish of Change* (New York: Norton, 1973), John E. Mueller, *War, Presidents, and Public Opinion* (New York: Wiley, 1973); and William Lunch and Peter Sperlich, "American Public Opinion and the War in Vietnam," *Western Political Quarterly* (March 1979). In *An American Ordeal: The Antiwar Movement of the Vietnam Era* (Syracuse, N.Y.: Syracuse University Press, 1990), the peace historians Charles DeBenedetti and Charles Chatfield conclude: "Organized opposition to the war came mainly from middle-class, college-educated whites, materially comfortable and motivated by largely moral considerations. Politically liberal and sympathetic to social justice causes, antiwar activists were also tolerant of changes in popular culture, sexual mores, and race relations. In contrast, the great majority of Americans favoring disengagement from Vietnam. . . . according to public opinion analysts . . . were in the lower economic class, often women and blacks, with grade-school educations and low-prestige jobs. Politically inarticulate and generally isolationists, these disaffected citizens opposed the war as a waste of men and money. . . . Suspicious of most authority, they seemed ambivalent in the face of cultural change, but they made no secret of their dislike for active protestors and street demonstrators."

George Herring, "American Strategy in Vietnam: The Postwar Debate," *Military Affairs* (April 1982), and Fox Butterfield, "The New Vietnam Scholarship," *New York Times Magazine* (February 12, 1983), offer the best analyses of the rising revisionist arguments over why the war was lost. The political scientist Guenter Lewy was the first academician allowed access to classified U.S. Army, Air Force, and Marine Corps records. His *America in Vietnam* (New York: Oxford University Press, 1978) made everyone angry: the military because he told them that airpower and traditional doctrine could not have won in Vietnam, and the opponents of the war because he justified what became the American war against the civilian population of South Vietnam. "The Vietnam experience," he writes, "was more complex than ideologues on either side could allow."

The U.S. Army War College, in Carlisle, Pennsylvania, is full of bright young colonels with two tours of duty in Vietnam and four rows of ribbons on their chests, on their way to the rank of general. Colonel of Infantry Harry G. Summers Jr., an instructor at the War College, fought in Korea as well and wears six rows of medals. In 1981, the War College published his *On Strategy: The Vietnam War in Context,* which was widely regarded by military people as an authoritative analysis, from the viewpoint of army doctrine, of the war and what went wrong. According to Summers, because the policy makers and the military professionals failed to focus on North Vietnam as the true source of the war, the United States exhausted its forces and popular support at home in the political task of counterinsurgency and nation building in the South instead of undertaking the proper military task of defeating external aggression. In an April 1975 visit to Hanoi, Summers told a North Vietnamese colonel, "You know you never defeated us on the battlefield." "That may be so," the North Vietnamese officer replied, "but it is also irrelevant." The United States must never again go to war without a clear strategic understanding of how the army should be used, Summers argues, or without the full support of the American people expressed through a declaration of war.

The details of the organizations and the ebb and flow of the anti–Vietnam War movement are presented in Thomas Powers, *Vietnam: The War at Home* (New York: Grossman, 1973), and Nancy Zaroulis and Gerald Sullivan, *Who Spoke Up? American Protest against the War in Vietnam, 1963–1975* (Garden City, N.Y.: Doubleday, 1984), which contend that the movement was responsible for forcing the American withdrawal. Charles DeBenedetti, *The Peace Reform in American History* (Bloomington: Indiana University Press, 1980), presents a history of the American peace movement, and Milton Katz, *Ban the Bomb* (Westport, Conn.: Greenwood Press, 1986), presents a history of SANE, the Committee for a Sane Nuclear Policy. DeBenedetti's posthumous *An American Ordeal: The Antiwar Movement of the Vietnam Era* (Syracuse, N.Y.: Syracuse University Press, 1990), prepared for publication by his fellow peace historian Charles Chatfield, maintains that "the American people consistently resented the antiwar movement but increasingly agreed with its arguments and conclusions." The movement lacked unity and was "more assembled than it was organized," DeBenedetti and Chatfield conclude, and in its internal history its liberals won out over its radical wing. Although the withdrawal of public support for the war was not in direct proportion to the strength of the antiwar movement, the movement did reach government policy makers through its impact on articulate elites, and it led both Johnson and Nixon into trouble. President Johnson responded to antiwar opposition by expanded promises of success and Nixon by illegal covert action against his critics. By 1971, the American public had come to see "domestic disunity" as more troublesome than the war. The various social movements of the sixties, including the antiwar protest, are to be found in the journals of opinion, particularly the *New York Times Magazine,* the *New York Review of Books,* the *New Republic,* the *Nation,* and *Ramparts. Liberation,* edited by David Dellinger, is the best primary source.

Peter C. Rollins, "The Vietnam War: Perceptions through Literature, Film, and Television," *American Quarterly* (Summer 1984), is a highly useful bibliographical survey of the fast-growing field of the study of the impact of the Vietnam War on American society. The malfunctioning of the draft is described in Lawrence Baskir and William Straus, *Change and Circumstance: The Draft, the War, and the Vietnam Generation* (New York: Knopf, 1978). Peter Goldman and Tony Fuller turned their *Newsweek* assignment on the veterans of C Company, Second Battalion, Twenty-eighth Regiment, of the Army's First Division into *Charlie Company: What Vietnam Did to Us* (New York: Ballantine, 1983). In *The Wages of War: When America's Soldiers Came Home—From Valley Forge to Vietnam* (New York: Simon & Schuster, 1989), Richard Severo and Lewis Milford maintain that the nation has never treated its veterans well.

VIOLENCE

Violence during the sixties can be studied in the general reports of the national riot and violence commissions: *Report of the National Advisory Commission on Civil Disorders* (New York: Bantam, 1968), known as the Kerner Commission report; and *Report of the National Commission on the Causes and Prevention of Violence* (New York: Bantam, 1969), known as the Eisenhower Commission report. Among the task force reports prepared for the Eisenhower Commission, Hugh Davis Graham and Ted Gurr, eds., *Violence in America: Historical and Comparative Perspectives,* 3d ed. (Beverly Hills: Sage, 1979); Jerome Skolnick, *The Politics of Protest* (New York: Ballantine, 1969); and the report on the Chicago riots, Daniel Walker, director, *Rights in Conflict* (New York: Dutton, 1968), are particularly informative. Hugh Graham's essay

"Violence, Social Theory, and the Historians: The Debate over Consensus and Culture in America," which will appear in a forthcoming new edition of Graham and Gurr, should be read.

Henry Bienen, *Violence and Social Change* (Chicago: University of Chicago Press, 1968), is a good review of the literature of the sixties. Black nationalism and black anger are set forth in *The Autobiography of Malcolm X* (New York: Grove Press, 1965), written with Alex Haley; Stokely Carmichael and Charles V. Hamilton, *Black Power: The Politics of Liberation in America* (New York: Vintage, 1967); and William H. Grier and Price M. Cobbs, *Black Rage* (New York: Basic Books, 1968). Robert Conot, *Rivers of Blood, Years of Darkness* (New York: Bantam, 1967), is a forceful account of the Watts riot. Anthony Platt draws together useful critiques of urban riots and their investigations in *The Politics of Riot Commissions, 1917–1970* (New York: Macmillan, 1971). James Button provides a similarly helpful summary of the theories about the riots and how the government responded, in *Black Violence: Political Impact of the 1960s Riots* (Princeton: Princeton University Press, 1978). James A. Michener details the context and the events of the Kent State shootings in *Kent State: What Happened and Why* (New York: Fawcett, 1971); and Governor William Scranton's commission puts campus dissent in broader perspective in *The Report of the President's Commission on Campus Unrest* (Washington, D.C.: U.S. Government Printing Office, 1970). Irwin Unger and Debi Unger, in *Turning Point: 1968* (New York: Charles Scribner's Sons, 1988), gather together all the currents that flowed through that violent year.

WOMEN, YOUTH, AND MIDDLE AMERICA

Three highly useful collections of documents, essays, and bibliographies on the history of the women's experience in America are Mary Beth Norton, ed., *Major Problems in American Women's History* (Lexington, Mass.: D. C. Heath, 1989); Linda Kerber and Jane De Hart, eds., *Women's America: Refocusing the Past*, 3d ed. (New York: Oxford University Press, 1991), which contains an excellent essay by De Hart, "The New Feminism and the Dynamics of Social Change"; and Gloria Hull, Patricia Bell Scott, and Barbara Smith, eds., *All the Women Are White, All the Blacks Are Men, But Some of Us Are Brave: Black Women's Studies* (New York: Feminist Press, 1982). Black lesbian and feminist viewpoints are expressed in Barbara Smith, ed., *Home Girls: A Black Feminist Anthology* (New York: Kitchen Table—Women of Color Press, 1983). In the early years of "the second wave," of feminism, collections of manifestos and articles such as Robin Morgan, ed., *Sisterhood Is Powerful: An Anthology of Writings from the Women's Liberation Movement*

(New York: Random House, 1970); Leslie Tanner, ed., *Voices from Women's Liberation* (New York: New American Library, 1970); and Anne Koedt, Ellen Levine, and Anita Rapone, eds., *Radical Feminism,* (New York: Quadrangle, 1973), were an important part of the movement. Jo Freeman, *The Politics of Women's Liberation: A Case Study of an Emerging Social Movement and Its Relation to the Social Policy Process* (New York: McKay, 1975), is a good insider's account. As a middle-of-the-road, glossy, mass-marketed, feminist monthly magazine, *Ms.* (1972–) has not pleased more radical feminists, who have disliked its commercialism, its moderation, and former editor Gloria Steinem's politics.

The classic account of "the first wave" of the women's movement is Eleanor Flexner, *Century of Struggle: The Woman's Rights Movement in the United States,* rev. ed. (Cambridge: Harvard University Press, 1975).Nancy Cott explains the early twentieth-century emergence of "feminism" as a matter of "identity and consciousness" in *The Grounding of Modern Feminism* (New Haven, Conn.: Yale University Press, 1987). The English translation of Simone de Beauvoir's *The Second Sex* was published in New York by Bantam in 1952. Betty Friedan, *The Feminine Mystique* (New York: Norton, 1963), helped raise the consciousness of middle-class women in the 1960s. Sara Evans, *Personal Politics: The Roots of Women's Liberation in the Civil Rights Movement and the New Left* (New York: Knopf, 1980), shows a parallel development on the Left, where women contrasted "the movement's egalitarian ideals with the replication of sex roles within it." In recounting how women's experience in organizing and collective action during the sixties provided a basis for the emergence of the women's movement, Evans provides an influential, seminal case study for the theory that movements need such "social space" for development. Shulamith Firestone, *The Dialectics of Sex: The Case for Feminist Revolution* (New York: Bantam, 1971), is a key statement of radical ideology. Michele Wallace, *Black Macho and the Myth of the Superwoman* (New York: Dial, 1979) calls upon black women to assert their identity in a world of white racism and black male chauvinism. An excellent history of black women's experience is Paula Giddings, *When and Where I Enter: The Impact of Black Women on Race and Sex in America* (New York: Morrow, 1984). Jacqueline Jones, *Labor for Love, Labor for Sorrow: Black Women, Work, and the Family from Slavery to the Present* (New York: Basic Books, 1985), tells the working class story.

Gerda Lerner, *The Majority Finds Its Past: Placing Women in History* (New York: Oxford University Press, 1979), is a proper beginning for a look at the tasks of the historian; and Joan Wallach Scott offers an introduction to the uses of deconstructionism for women's history in

"Gender: A Useful Category of Historical Analysis," *American Historical Review* (December 1986) and *Gender in History* (New York: Columbia University Press, 1988). Among the many new journals dealing with the women's experience, *Feminist Studies* (1972–) and *Signs* (1975–) are particularly useful on theoretical and historical levels.

All of the major accounts of the civil rights struggle in the South— Clayborne Carson, *In Struggle: SNCC and the Black Awakening of the 1960s* (Cambridge: Harvard University Press, 1981); David Garrow, *Bearing the Cross: Martin Luther King, Jr., and the Southern Christian Leadership Conference, 1955–1968* (New York: Morrow, 1986); Taylor Branch, *Parting the Waters: America in the King Years, 1954–63* (New York: Simon & Schuster, 1988); and especially Mary Elizabeth King, *Freedom Song: A Personal Story of the 1960s Civil Rights Movement* (New York: Morrow, 1987)—pay tribute to Ella Baker, who is the subject of a moving 1981 television documentary, "Fundi: The Story of Ella Baker," available from Fundi Productions, Inc., New York, New York, produced by Mississippi Freedom Summer volunteer Joanne Grant. Cynthia Stokes Brown, *Ready from Within: Septima Clark and the Civil Rights Movement* (Navarro, Calif.: Wild Tree Press, 1986), is based on interviews with Septima Clark. Virginia Durr tells her own story in *Outside the Magic Circle: The Autobiography of Virginia Foster Durr*, ed. Hollinger Bernard (University, Ala.: University of Alabama Press, 1985). Anne Braden's life is partially found in her account of the early days with Carl in Louisville, *The Wall Between* (New York: Monthly Review Press, 1958), and in Irwin Klibaner, "The Travail of Southern Radicals: The Southern Conference Educational Fund, 1946–1976," *Journal of Southern History* (May 1983), and *Conscience of a Troubled South: The Southern Conference Educational Fund, 1946–1966* (Brooklyn, N.Y.: Carlson Publishing Co., 1989). Joan Hoff Wilson recounts the public life of Jeannette Rankin in "Jeannette Rankin and American Foreign Policy," *Montana: The Magazine of Western History* (Winter-Spring 1980).

Other women whose activity spanned the trough between the two waves include the birth-control crusader Margaret Sanger (1883– 1966), whose life's crusade is set forth in David Kennedy, *Birth Control in America: The Career of Margaret Sanger* (New Haven, Conn.: Yale University Press, 1970), and viewed with disappointment in Linda Gordon, *Woman's Body, Woman's Right: Birth Control in America* (New York: Penguin, 1976). Suffrage militant Alice Paul (1885–1977) and her National Woman's party, isolated from other women's concerns, kept up a demand for an equal rights amendment. The battles of Jessie Daniel Ames (1883–1972) and the Association of Southern Women for the Prevention of Lynching are described by Jacquelyn

Dowd Hall, *Revolt Against Chivalry: Jessie Daniel Ames and the Women's Campaign against Lynching* (New York: Columbia University Press, 1979). John Salmond, *Miss Lucy of the CIO: The Life and Times of Lucy Randolph Mason, 1882–1959* (Athens: University of Georgia Press, 1988), tells how, at the age of fifty-five, Lucy Randolph Mason capped a long career of working for women's and children's causes by setting out to work for civil liberties and interracial industrial unionism in the South. Despite threats and violence, Lillian Smith (1897–1966) writing from her camp on Old Screamer Mountain, near Clayton, Georgia, sought to open up the heart of the South in her daring novel *Strange Fruit* (New York: Reynal & Hitchcock, 1944) and her other writings, including *Killers of the Dream* (New York: Norton, 1949) and her integrationist journal *South Today* (1937–45).

James Barber and Barbara Kellerman, eds., *Women Leaders in American Politics* (Englewood Cliffs, N.J.: Prentice-Hall, 1986), is a broadly useful contemporary collection. Barbara Sinclair, *The Women's Movement: Political, Socioeconomic, and Psychological Issues*, 2d ed. (New York: Harper & Row, 1979) does a good job of trying to record everything. Gilbert Steiner, *Constitutional Inequality: The Political Fortunes of the Equal Rights Amendment* (Washington, D.C.: Brookings, 1985); Mary Frances Berry, *Why ERA Failed* (Bloomington: Indiana University Press, 1986); and Joan Hoff Wilson, ed., *Rights of Passage: the Past and Future of ERA* (Bloomington: Indiana University Press, 1986), recount the history and the context of the attempts to add an equal rights amendment to the Constitution. Phyllis Schlafly, *The Power of the Positive Woman* (New York: Arlington House, 1977), and Carol Felsenthal, *The Sweetheart of the Silent Majority: The Biography of Phyllis Schlafly* (Garden City, N.Y.: Doubleday, 1981), help complete the story.

William H. Chafe, *Women and Equality: Changing Patterns in American Culture*, rev. ed. (New York: Oxford University Press, 1991), and Maxine Margolis, *Mothers and Such: Views of American Women and Why They Changed* (Berkeley: University of California Press, 1984), offer structural approaches to the emergence of feminism among the working women of America. Joan Hoff Wilson, "The Unfinished Revolution: Changing Legal Status of Women," *Signs* (Autumn 1987), is a useful summary. Carl Degler, *At Odds: Women and the Family in America from the Revolution to the Present* (New York: Oxford University Press, 1980) combines women's history and the history of the family.

Daniel Yankelovich, *The New Morality: A Profile of American Youth in the 70's* (New York: Macmillan, 1974) presents his survey data and analysis of changing youth values from the late sixties into the early seventies. That portion of the American population that was not young, black, poor, or dissenting in the sixties can be studied in the

Newsweek articles (October 6, 1969) republished as Richard Lemon, *The Troubled America* (New York: Simon & Schuster, 1969); Richard Scammon and Ben Wattenberg, *The Real Majority* (New York: Coward-McCann, 1970); Louise Kapp Howe, ed., *White Majority: Between Poverty and Affluence* (New York: Random House, 1970); Murray Friedman, ed., *Overcoming Middle Class Rage* (Philadelphia: Westminster Press, 1971); Sar A. Levitan, ed., *Blue-Collar Workers* (New York: McGraw-Hill, 1971); and Robert Coles, *The Middle Americans: Proud and Uncertain* (Boston: Little, Brown, 1971).

In *Post-Conservative America: People, Politics, and Ideology in a Time of Crisis* (New York: Random House, 1982), Kevin Phillips, who coined the terms "New Right" and "Sun Belt," records the political revolution he had predicted in *The Emerging Republican Majority* (New Rochelle, N.Y.: Arlington House, 1969). A good introduction to the American Right is Paul Gottfried and Thomas Fleming, *The Conservative Movement* (Boston: Twayne, 1988). Among the contributors to the rise of Republican party strength, *Commentary* editor Norman Podhoretz, in *Breaking Ranks* (New York: Harper & Row, 1979), provides an account of the journey from the liberal Left to the neoconservative Right. In *What I Saw at the Revolution: A Political Life in the Reagan Era* (New York: Random House, 1990), Peggy Noonan tells how a New Jersey night-school college student from a Kennedy-loving Irish Catholic family got off the bus on the way to an antiwar rally and became a writer of memorable speeches for the Reagan White House and George Bush's 1988 presidential campaign. Richard Viguerie's *The New Right: We're Ready to Lead,* with an introduction by Jerry Falwell (Falls Church, Va.: Viguerie Co., 1981) explains his own success as being built on four elements—single-issue groups, multiissue conservative groups, coalition politics, and direct-mail campaigns that reach out to the people whom Rev. Falwell describes as profamily, promorality, prolife, and pro-American.

CITIZEN ACTION

Alexis de Tocqueville's observations on the American habit of voluntary association can be found in J. P. Mayer's edition of the George Lawrence translation of de Tocqueville's *Democracy in America* (1835; Garden City, N.Y.: Doubleday, 1969), vol. 2, pt. 2, ch. 5. David Chalmers, "Committed, Proud, and Distrustful: The Mississippi Volunteers 20 Years Later," *USA Today* (September 1984), and Doug McAdam, *Freedom Summer* (New York: Oxford University Press, 1988), tell how the Mississippi experience influenced the lives of the summer volunteers. A study of a group of West Coast sixties radical students by

Jack Whalen and Richard Flacks, *Beyond the Barricades: The Sixties Generation Grows Up* (Philadelphia: Temple University Press, 1989), concludes that "the legacy of the sixties movement lives on most fully in the moral outlooks, political orientations, and life-styles of those in the generation who became part of the 'intelligentsia.' "

Saul Alinsky set forth his approach in *Rules for Radicals: A Pragmatic Primer for Realistic Radicals* (New York: Vintage, 1971), and his story is told by P. David Finks, *The Radical Vision of Saul Alinsky* (New York: Paulist Press, 1984), and Sanford Horwitt, *Let Them Call Me Rebel: Saul Alinsky, His Life and Legacy* (New York: Knopf, 1989). David Vogel, *Fluctuating Fortunes: The Political Power of Business in America* (New York: Basic Books, 1989), is an informative analysis of the national politics of consumer and environmental policy. Kelley Griffin explains the Public Interest Research Group (PIRG) movement in *Ralph Nader Presents: More Action for a Change* (New York: Norton, 1987), and Jerome Price does the same for the antinuclear movement in *The Antinuclear Movement* (Boston: Twayne, 1982). Mark Kann, *Middle Class Radicalism in Santa Monica* (Philadelphia: Temple University Press, 1986), is a history of community activism in California. John Herbers, "Grass-Roots Groups Go National," *New York Times Magazine* (September 9, 1983), is one of the few national press notices of citizen action.

The grass roots theorist and historian Harry Boyte describes the citizen action movement in *The Backyard Revolution: Understanding the New Citizen Movement* (Philadelphia: Temple University Press, 1980), and Robert Fisher puts it into a historical context in *Let the People Decide: Neighborhood Organizing in America* (Boston: Twayne, 1984). In *Free Space: The Sources of Democratic Change in America* (New York: Harper & Row, 1986), Boyte and Sara Evans trace through American history the democratic participation theory Evans presented in *Personal Politics: The Roots of Women's Liberation in the Civil Rights Movement and the New Left* (New York: Knopf, 1980). In *Citizen Action and the New American Populism* (Philadelphia: Temple University Press, 1986), Boyte joins with the Midwest Academy's founder-director Heather Booth and its curriculum director Steve Max to think about the larger possibilities of the movement. *Citizen Action News* (225 W. Ohio Street, Suite 250, Chicago, Illinois 60610) is the journal of the movement.

Index

About the Author

During the 1960s, David Chalmers was a Fulbright professor at the Universities of Sri Lanka, Tokyo, and the Philippines, and lectured in Vietnam and Korea. He took part in the civil rights movement in Gainesville, Florida, and went to jail with Martin Luther King Jr. in St. Augustine. He wrote a history of the Ku Klux Klan, *Hooded Americanism*, and worked for the Group Protest and Demonstration Task Force of the National Violence Commission which President Johnson appointed after the murder of Robert Kennedy in 1968. Initially a supporter of American involvement in Vietnam, he crossed over into opposition in 1967 and worked for state and national anti-war candidates, speaking from the same platforms as Eugene McCarthy in 1968 and George McGovern in 1972. He has been the University of Florida's Teacher-Scholar of the Year, its Distinguished Alumni Professor, and now holds the rank of Distinguished Service Professor of History.

Composed by Capitol Communication Systems, Inc.,
in Baskerville text and Helvetica Medium display.
Printed on 50-lb. Cream White Sebago
and bound in Holliston Roxite linen cloth
by R. R. Donnelley & Sons Company.